Politics or Principle?

SARAH A. BINDER
and
STEVEN S. SMITH

Politics or Principle?

Filibustering in the United States Senate

BROOKINGS INSTITUTION PRESS
Washington, D.C.

Library of Congress Cataloging-in-Publication data
Binder, Sarah A.
Politics or principle? : filibustering in the United States Senate / Sarah A. Binder and Steven S. Smith.
p. cm.
Includes bibliographical references and index.
ISBN 0-8157-0952-8 (alk. paper). — ISBN 0-8157-0951-X (pbk. : alk. paper)
1. United States. Congress. Senate--Freedom of debate.
2. Filibusters (Political science)--United States. I. Smith, Steven S., 1953- . II. Title.
JK1161.B56 1997
328.73'071—dc20 96-25372
CIP

9 8 7 6 5 4 3 2 1

The paper used in this publication meets the minimum requirements of the American National Standard for Information Sciences Permanence of Paper for Printed Library Materials, ANSI Z39-48-1984.

Typeset in Bembo

Composition by Harlowe Typography, Inc.
Cottage City, Maryland

Printed by R. R. Donnelley and Sons Co.
Harrisonburg, Virginia

THE BROOKINGS INSTITUTION

The Brookings Institution is an independent organization devoted to nonpartisan research, education, and publication in economics, government, foreign policy, and the social sciences generally. Its principal purposes are to aid in the development of sound public policies and to promote public understanding of issues of national importance.

The Institution was founded on December 8, 1927, to merge the activities of the Institute for Government Research, founded in 1916, the Institute of Economics, founded in 1922, and the Robert Brookings Graduate School of Economics and Government, founded in 1924.

The Board of Trustees is responsible for the general administration of the Institution, while the immediate direction of the policies, program, and staff is vested in the President, assisted by an advisory committee of the officers and staff. The by-laws of the Institution state: "It is the function of the Trustees to make possible the conduct of scientific research, and publication, under the most favorable conditions, and to safeguard the independence of the research staff in the pursuit of their studies and in the publication of the results of such studies. It is not a part of their function to determine, control, or influence the conduct of particular investigations or the conclusions reached."

The President bears final responsibility for the decision to publish a manuscript as a Brookings book. In reaching his judgment on the competence, accuracy, and objectivity of each study, the President is advised by the director of the appropriate research program and weighs the views of a panel of expert outside readers who report to him in confidence on the quality of the work. Publication of a work signifies that it is deemed a competent treatment worthy of public consideration but does not imply endorsement of conclusions or recommendations.

The Institution maintains its position of neutrality on issues of public policy in order to safeguard the intellectual freedom of the staff. Hence interpretations or conclusions in Brookings publications should be understood to be solely those of the authors and should not be attributed to the Institution, to its trustees, officers, or other staff members, or to the organizations that support its research.

The new Senate chamber, 1859

To Forrest and Noa

—S.A.B.

To Barbara, Tyler, and Shannon

—S.S.S.

Foreword

PERHAPS NO FEATURE of legislative procedure has received more attention and less scrutiny than the Senate filibuster. Far from being subjected to critical assessment, the filibuster has reached almost mythical proportions in the history of American politics. Conventional wisdom holds that the right of unrestricted debate in the Senate helps to moderate extreme legislation, blocks passage of measures opposed by a popular majority, and is inseparable from the origins and traditions of the Senate.

As the policymaking environment of the Senate has changed in recent decades, the potential harm caused by the filibuster has intensified. Old Senate rules coupled with modern Senate conditions create an overwhelming incentive for senators to exploit their procedural prerogatives. And this tendency has increased in the past quarter century. In the entire nineteenth century, there were 23 manifest filibusters; by contrast, in 1970–94 there were 191.

In *Politics or Principle?* Sarah Binder (Brookings Governmental Studies program) and Steven S. Smith (Department of Political Science, University of Minnesota) show that key propositions of the conventional wisdom about the filibuster are inaccurate. Most important, political interests—not philosophical commitments to minority rights and free speech—underpin the evolution of rules governing Senate debate. Binder and Smith argue that in an era of unprecedented filibustering and related obstructionism, old ways of doing business are impairing the Senate's capacity to meet its modern responsibilities. They maintain that substantial reform of Senate rules is long overdue.

Finding little theoretical or empirical support for conventional defenses of the filibuster, Binder and Smith suggest reforms intended to provide a better balance between debate and action. The authors do not advocate tampering with the Senate's tolerance for extended debate: long debate has served the Senate well, often making bills from the House more palatable to both a Senate majority and the president. They argue, however, that after lengthy (even exhaustive) debate, a chamber majority should eventually be allowed to cast a final vote on legislation and nominations. The authors suggest progressively lowering the number of votes required to invoke cloture, granting instead a longer period for floor debate; limiting the number of motions that can be filibustered for any one bill; and tightening limits on debate in the last month or so of each session of Congress. The authors also evaluate other proposals that have occasionally been suggested for the Senate, such as bringing back round-the-clock filibusters. They conclude that such proposals are unlikely to succeed because individual senators simply have too much leverage under current rules. Showing instead that senators' views about the filibuster are shaped by more short-term strategic policy and political considerations, Binder and Smith argue that senators never lose sight of the consequences of institutional reform for their own political and often partisan agendas. They conclude that the current rules will change only when more than a two-thirds majority of senators see that reform is in their political and legislative interest.

The authors are grateful to Stanley Bach, Ross Baker, Richard Beth, David Brady, Gerald Gamm, Forrest Maltzman, Thomas Mann, Mathew McCubbins, and Donald Ritchie for their advice and helpful comments. They also wish to thank Eric Lawrence and Patrick MacDonald for their superb research assistance. The assistance of Matthew Cook with the Senate Historian's Photographic Collection is also greatly appreciated. Venka MacIntyre and Deborah Styles edited the manuscript, Tara Adams Ragone verified its factual content, Carlotta Ribar proofread the pages, and Julia Petrakis prepared the index.

The views expressed in this book are those of the authors and should not be ascribed to the trustees, officers, or other staff members of the Brookings Institution.

MICHAEL H. ARMACOST
President

October 1996
Washington, D.C.

Contents

Photographs

Tables

Figures

Politics or Principle?

Henry Clay and the Compromise of 1850

1

The Politics and Principle of the Filibuster

PERHAPS NO FEATURE of legislative procedure has received more attention—and less scrutiny—than the Senate filibuster. Certainly no other congressional rule has been the focus of a Hollywood film starring Jimmy Stewart. Yet for all its fame, the filibuster has escaped careful critical assessment, at least since the first and last book on the subject appeared in 1940.[1] Instead, the filibuster has reached almost mythic proportions in the history of American politics. According to conventional wisdom, the right of unrestricted debate in the Senate helps moderate extreme legislation, blocks passage of measures opposed by a popular majority, and is inseparable from the origins and traditions of the Senate. Such claims are, in fact, mostly myth: there is scarce theoretical or empirical support for much of the received wisdom about the Senate filibuster.

Not everyone has fallen for the myth of the filibuster. Indeed, many members and observers of the Senate have pointed out that the right of extended debate is a liability to the power and effectiveness of the Senate. Recently, Senator Tom Harkin (Democrat of Iowa) suggested to his colleagues that old chamber rules were strangling the power of the Senate: "There comes a time when tradition has to meet the realities of the modern age. The minority's rights must be protected. The majority should not be able to run roughshod over them, but neither should a vexatious minority be able to thwart the will of the majority and not even permit legislation to come up for a meaningful vote."[2] No reform could be more important for the Senate or the nation, Harkin would argue in 1995, "than slaying the dinosaur called the filibuster."[3] The senator from Iowa is not the first to call for fundamental reform of the Senate. Almost as soon as the first organized filibuster occurred in 1837, no less a Senate giant than Henry Clay (Whig of Kentucky) called for strict limits on senators' right of extended debate. As early as 1841 and as recently as 1995, senators frustrated with the power of Senate minorities to block the majority urged their colleagues to create a workable system of majority rule.

Reformers, however, have enjoyed only incremental success in their efforts to limit the freedom of debate in the Senate. To be sure, entirely unrestricted debate has been prohibited since the adoption of Senate Rule 22 in 1917, which permitted a supermajority of the Senate to invoke cloture, or cut off debate, on pending legislation. Today, however, a minority of the Senate can still exploit the right of extended debate to prevent a majority from casting a vote on legislative measures or on executive and judicial nominations favored by a chamber majority. Even the threat of a filibuster by a single senator is often powerful enough to thwart a time-constrained majority from pursuing portions of its legislative agenda or to force changes in pending legislation. As the policymaking environment of the Senate has changed in recent decades, the potential harm of the filibuster has only intensified. Old Senate rules coupled with modern Senate conditions create an overwhelming incentive for senators to exploit their procedural prerogatives. For example, in 1995 Senator Jesse Helms (Republican of North Carolina) held ambassadorial nominations and a major weapons treaty hostage for action on an unrelated bill to restructure the State Department, and in 1994 Senate Republicans filibustered any measure that they thought would help Democratic incumbents in the coming election.[4] No party has a monopoly on the tools of obstruction, of course. Democrats, too, have shown themselves willing to exploit Senate rules. In 1996, for example, Democrats blocked consideration of a constitutional amendment to impose congressional term limits. Neither is the filibuster exclusively used by the minority party: in 1996 a Republican majority blocked consideration of a bipartisan bill to reform campaign finance laws.

Why is filibuster reform so difficult? In the view of some observers, senators—past and present—have failed to place significant restrictions on the freedom of debate because Senate majorities have always wanted it that way. The lack of debate limits, they argue, reflects the framers' original intent for the Senate, is an integral part of Senate tradition, and, most

From Freebooters to Filibusters

The time it takes to recount the history of the word *filibuster* might itself be enough to constitute a filibuster. Although the term only came into vogue in the Senate in the mid- to late nineteenth century, the word filibuster has much earlier roots. It appears to have originated with the English *free* and *booty* and the Dutch *vrij* and *buit*. Combined into *vrijbuiter*, the word became a Dutch term for looters and robbers—those who lived on others' booty and spoils. *Vrijbuiter* was later transformed by the English into *flibutor* and then anglicized into *freebooter*, a word used as early as 1726 for pirates or plunderers. The French then borrowed *flibutor* and translated it into *flibustier*, before lending it to the Spanish—who turned it into *filibustero*, describing pirates and adventurers who plundered the Spanish West Indies in the seventeenth century. The word *filibusteros* was adopted by Americans in the mid-nineteenth century and applied to men who marauded across Central America and the West Indies. By the 1850s, William Walker, who tried to foment insurrection in Nicaragua, was well-known as an American *fillibuster*—his exploits documented in a popular book, *Filibusters and Financiers*. Within decades, the word filibuster was ripe for application in the U.S. Senate—where senators were learning rebellious techniques for holding up legislation they opposed. Though heralded as a great Senate tradition today, the filibuster certainly has no such noble linguistic roots.

Sources: Craig M. Carver, "Word Histories: Filibuster," *Atlantic Monthly*, vol. 272, no. 5 (November 1993), p. 164; "Filibuster," *The Encyclopedia of the United States Congress*, Donald C. Bacon and others, eds., vol. 2 (Simon and Schuster, 1985), pp. 833–35.

important, follows directly from senators' principled, shared interests in protecting free speech and minority rights. Such conventional portrayals also suggest that the filibuster causes little harm: no measures favored by a popular majority, it is said, have ever been killed by a filibuster. Moreover, supermajority requirements are held to be essential to ensuring moderate, bipartisan compromise in the Senate, in comparison with the distinctly partisan outcomes likely in the House. Finally, the rise of partisan filibustering in recent years is said to be an aberration in an otherwise noble tradition of extended debate; senators have historically reserved the filibuster for only the most momentous issues of the day. If these and other notions about the Senate filibuster are true, there is little reason to ask why Senate reformers have been unable to secure more radical procedural change: Senate rules, it would seem, are maintained because they protect the interests of the Senate, its members, and the broader American polity.

As this book demonstrates, however, little of this conventional wisdom about the filibuster is true. Empirical regularities about the politics of the filibuster suggest quite the opposite. Senate rules protecting extended debate have lasted not because of senators' collective interests in protecting minority rights and free speech, but because the rules serve as a foundation of senators' personal political power. Senators' positions on procedural reform follow predictably from their political interests. Indeed, senators have been quite willing to write debate limits into law on select issues such as trade and budget matters when they believe such restrictions will serve their policy views. By offering a richer theoretical and empirical account of the origins and development of extended debate in the Senate, we hope to show that the choice of institutional arrangements in the Senate—as much as the choice of policy—is a decidedly strategic matter.

The political and largely contingent nature of senators' support for extended debate contradicts the constitutional and historical arguments often offered in defense of the filibuster. In an era of unprecedented filibustering and related obstructionism, these old ways of doing business are impairing the Senate's capacity to meet its current responsibilities. Balanced reform that would be sufficient to empower a chamber majority—of partisan or bipartisan stripes—yet consistent with the Senate's unique size, tradition, and duties is long overdue.

The Framers and Minority Rights in the Senate

In the classic anecdote about the origins of the Senate, Thomas Jefferson—in France during the Constitutional Convention—asked George Washington about the purpose of the new Senate.[5] "Why," asked Washington, "did you pour that coffee into your saucer?" "To cool it," Jefferson replied. "Even so," responded Washington, "we pour legislation into the senatorial saucer to cool it." That the Senate was intended to be the more deliberative and reasoning of the two chambers is well known. In designing the Senate, the framers chose institutional features with an eye to restraining any ill-considered or rash legislation passed by the popularly elected House. With its smaller size, longer terms, older members, staggered elections by state legislative elite, and exclusive power to advise and consent on treaties and nominations, the Senate was expected to act "with more coolness, with more system and with more wisdom, than the popular branch."[6]

Interestingly, delegates to the convention did not write into the Constitution any procedural protections for Senate minorities. As detailed in chapter 2, apparently the framers did not discuss or anticipate whether Senate minorities would be empowered to halt the actions of a determined Senate majority. Nor should one expect the framers to have endorsed such a view, since they had seen full well in the experience of the Continental Congress what harm supermajority requirements could bring. In urging ratification of the Constitution in the Federalist Papers, both James Madison and Alexander Hamilton made clear that the experiment with supermajorities under the Articles of Confederation had been a dismal one and that they did not intend to repeat it under the new Constitution. Commenting on the effects of supermajority requirements in legislative settings, Madison argued, "In all cases where justice or the general good might require new laws to be passed, or active measures to be pursued, the fundamental principle of free government would be reversed."[7]

Had the framers taken stock of the Senate's performance after its first few decades, they would no doubt have liked what they saw. Although the Senate in 1806 had dropped its previous question motion—its only potential means of permitting a majority to cut off debate and vote on pending measures—the early Senate appears to have had little trouble with obstructionist senators. On occasion senators would talk against time in an effort to delay action on measures they opposed, but the practice of exploiting the rules (or the lack thereof) to block Senate action failed to take root in the original Senate.[8] With the small workload, the lack of sustained partisan acrimony, and limited contact with an outside public in the early years, Senators had little incentive to exploit the rules for political gain. It was widely assumed in these first decades that measures would be brought to a vote for final consideration and that a simple majority would be sufficient for ending debate on even the most controversial legislative business.

By the end of the nineteenth century, however, such assumptions were forgotten. Had the framers been able to assess the state of the Senate after its first century in operation, they would have been surprised, if not dumbfounded, by what they saw. Senators showed little restraint in choosing which bills to filibuster. In 1890, for example, filibusterers targeted an important civil rights measure and a decidedly parochial appropriations provision affecting the purchase price of armor plate. Taking advantage of the constitutionally mandated adjournment of Congress on March 4 of the odd-numbered years, senators perfected the art of exploiting the rules at the end of the session to block action on measures they opposed or to force adoption of provisions they favored. The time constraint imposed by the forced end of the session left chamber leaders quite often hostage to the demands of a filibustering minority.

By the early twentieth century, unrestrained filibustering had wreaked havoc on the Senate as the framers intended it to function. As explained in chapter 3, during the course of the nineteenth century the set of incentives and constraints senators faced when devising a legislative strategy changed radically. Partisan minorities, as well as individual senators, discovered that taking advantage of chamber rules to delay action—through extended debate or numerous amendments and procedural motions, quorum gamesmanship, slow committee or conference deliberation, and other obstructive means—yielded favorable political dividends. At times, the parliamentary situation so favored minority coalitions, partisan or otherwise, at the expense of manifest majorities that many members and observers of the Senate called for strict limits on the right of debate. As one historian argued in 1893: "In our day, with a larger House and Senate, with greater interests at stake, with this immense volume of business pressing for attention, it is right and necessary that the majority should cut down some of the privileges the minority have so long enjoyed. . . . The time for dilatory motions, for refusals to answer roll calls, for time-consuming debate, has gone by."[9] But filibuster reform proved impossible—proposals reaching the floor were simply filibustered—until public and presidential pressures in 1917 bullied the Senate into accepting a cloture rule (Rule 22) that allowed two-thirds of the Senate to cut off debate.

The Modern Senate Filibuster

If filibustering seemed to have reached unbearable levels at the end of the nineteenth century, today's levels are surely beyond belief. Although the number of senators required to invoke cloture and cut off debate has periodically gone down (table 1-1), attempted filibusters have gone up exponentially. "Today," observed former senator Charles Mathias in 1994, "filibusters are far less visible but far more frequent. The filibuster has become an epidemic, used whenever a coalition can find 41 votes to oppose legislation. The distinction between voting against legislation and blocking

Table 1-1. *Major Rule Changes and Procedural Rulings Affecting the Senate Filibuster*

Year	*Procedural change*
1806	Previous question motion omitted from Senate rules.
1870	Senate sustains a decision of the chair that a senator may read papers in debate that are irrelevant to the subject matter.
1884	Senate amends Rule 8 to make motions to proceed to any matter before 2 o'clock nondebatable.
1897	Chair rules that quorum calls cannot be ordered unless business has intervened.
1908	Rulings of the chair establish several precedents: —Chair can count senators to determine whether a quorum is present to do business. —Debate cannot be considered intervening business, meaning that more than debate must take place between quorum calls. —Senators can be prevented under the rules from speaking on the same subject more than twice in one day.
1917	Rule 22 adopted: two-thirds of the Senate present and voting required to invoke cloture.
1935	Ruling of the chair establishes that senators yielding twice for a quorum call while the same question is before the Senate lose control of the floor.
1948	Chair expresses opinion that cloture cannot be applied to procedural motions to take up legislation.
1949	Senate, overturning ruling of the vice president, votes to prohibit application of cloture to procedural motions.
1949	Rule 22 amended: —Cloture raised to two-thirds of entire Senate membership. —Cloture may be applied to procedural motions, except motions to consider changes in Senate rules.
1959	Rule 22 amended: —Cloture lowered to two-thirds of senators present and voting. —Cloture may be applied to motions to consider changes in Senate rules.
1975	Rule 22 amended: —Cloture lowered to three-fifths of the Senate membership (sixty votes). —Two-thirds of senators present and voting for motions to consider changes in Senate rules.
1979	Rule 22 amended to cap post-cloture debate at 100 hours.
1986	Rule 22 amended to reduce post-cloture debate to 30 hours.

Sources: U.S. Senate, Committee on Rules and Administration, Senate Cloture Rule, S. Rept. 99-95, 99 Cong., 1 sess. (GPO, 1985); Franklin L. Burdette, *Filibustering in the Senate* (Princeton University Press, 1940); Walter J. Oleszek, *Congressional Procedures and the Policy Process*, 4th ed. (Congressional Quarterly Press, 1996), p. 326.

a vote, between opposing and obstructing, has nearly disappeared."[10] Even Russell Long (Democrat of Louisiana), who fought cloture reform from the late 1940s into the 1970s, later admitted that "there is today more power in the hands of a single person, more leverage to impede the process, than there used to be."[11] A close inspection of the changes in the use of Senate Rule 22 clearly shows that the number of filibusters has increased in recent decades and that the dynamics favoring obstructionism in the late nineteenth century have only intensified in this century.

The Mechanics of Rule 22

Short of negotiating an agreement to limit debate and set a time for a final vote by gaining the consent of every senator (a "unanimous consent agreement," in Senate terms), the Senate's only option for restricting debate is to invoke cloture under Rule 22.[12] Cloture motions can be applied at a number of steps in the legislative process: on the motion to proceed to a bill after the morning hour; on amendments, bills, or conference reports; and on any of the three motions used to request and go to conference with the House.[13] In the absence of cloture, a determined minority can filibuster legislation at any of these stages in the legislative game.

Under Rule 22, any senator can file a cloture motion in favor of cutting off debate, provided sixteen senators have signed the motion. Two days after a cloture motion is presented to the presiding officer, it is ripe for a vote (if a quorum is present) one hour after the Senate convenes. As soon as the cloture motion is filed with the presiding officer, some important restrictions take effect: only amendments deemed germane (or related) to the underlying bill can be filed, and they must be filed before 1 P.M. on the first day after a cloture motion is filed. Second-degree amendments—or "perfecting" amendments to other amendments—can only be filed up until one hour before the vote on cloture. If cloture is invoked, only germane amendments can be offered; in other words, the imposition of cloture provides Senate leaders with a valuable means of narrowing the terrain of debate and reducing uncertainty about the final scope of the bill. In exchange for giving up the right to filibuster the bill, senators are assured that they will not be surprised by any unrelated amendments (that they might otherwise want to filibuster) after cloture is invoked.

Two elements of the cloture rule have been changed periodically since Rule 22 was adopted: the number of senators required to invoke cloture and the number of hours of debate permitted after cloture is invoked. Originally, two-thirds of the Senate present and voting was required to invoke cloture (table 1-1). The threshold was raised in 1949 to require the vote of two-thirds of the entire Senate membership and was lowered twice—first in 1959 to a two-thirds vote of senators present and voting, and then in 1975 to three-fifths (or sixty votes) of the entire Senate (see chapter 6). On motions to alter Senate rules, however, a higher threshold has been retained: two-thirds of the Senate's members must be present

Table 1-2. *Success Rates of Cloture Votes, by Period, 1917–94*
Percent unless otherwise specified

Size of coalition voting for cloture	*1917–49*	*1949–59*	*1959–75*	*1975–94*
Supermajority (cloture invoked)	21	0	26	41
More than a majority, less than a supermajority (cloture failed)	16	67	44	46
Less than a majority (cloture failed)	63	33	30	13
Number of cloture votes	19	3	81	284

Source: Senate Roll-Call Votes, Inter-University Consortium for Political and Social Research (File #00004).

and voting to restrict debate. Because Rule 22 never specified the time allotted for debate after cloture was invoked, senators exploited that loophole in the late 1970s to create what became known as the "post-cloture" filibuster.[14] The Senate limited post-cloture debate to 100 hours in 1979 and then tightened the limit to 30 hours in 1986. In the wake of the latter change, each senator is restricted to one hour of debate on a first-come, first-serve basis.

With the reduction in the threshold for cloture, the number of cloture votes and their rate of success have gone up (table 1-2). Between 1917 and 1949, the preponderance of votes on cloture failed, and in nearly two-thirds of these votes, supporters of cloture failed even to garner a Senate majority. In contrast, between 1959 and 1975, when the cloture threshold returned to two-thirds of those present and voting, cloture supporters failed to obtain the support of a chamber majority only 30 percent of the time, but cloture was invoked only a quarter of the time a motion was filed. When cloture was reduced to a three-fifths threshold in 1975, the number of cloture votes exploded, and their rate of success nearly doubled (reaching 41 percent between 1975 and 1994). Most striking, supporters of cloture who had secured the support of at least a majority of the chamber essentially broke even: nearly half the time they won (41 percent), and nearly half the time they lost (46 percent). Supermajority requirements of Rule 22 have clearly prevented sizable majorities from proceeding to a vote on a host of legislative matters (see chapters 4 and 5).

Trends in Senate Obstructionism

Accompanying the change in attempted and successful cloture rates is the rather explosive increase in the number of manifest filibusters since the late 1960s. A simple count of the number of filibusters shows great variation in the tendency of senators to filibuster over time (figure 1-1).[15] Periods of robust filibustering occurred between the 1890s and the 1930s

Figure 1-1. *Senate Filibusters, 1789–1992*

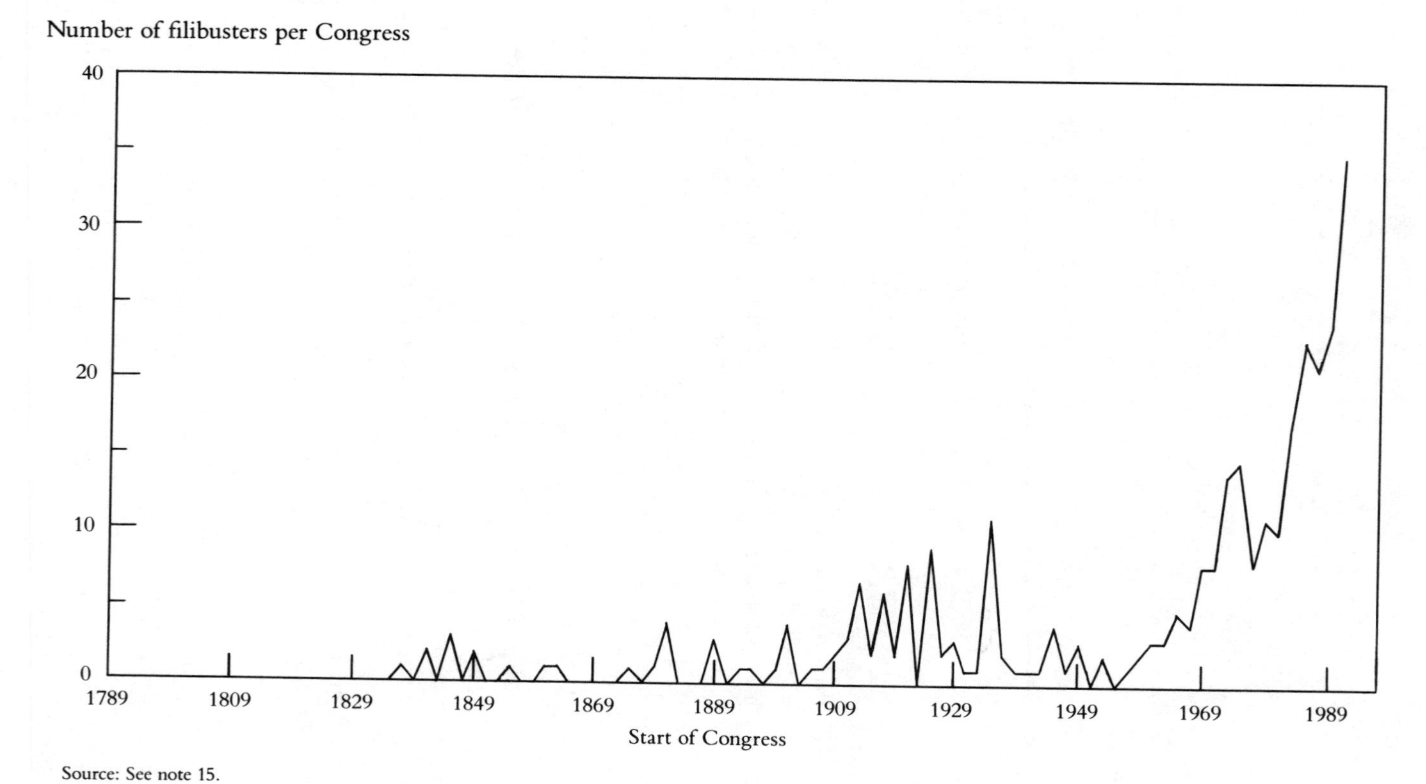

Source: See note 15.

and again after the 1960s (see chapter 4). Filibustering declined noticeably from the 1940s to the 1960s—the period in which the filibuster became intricately tied to the fate of civil rights measures. After 1967, however, it rose to unprecedented levels. Whereas only 23 manifest filibusters are recorded for the entire nineteenth century, the number totaled 191 between 1970 and 1994. Thirty-five occurred in the 102d Congress (1991–92) alone.

If the strategy of filibusterers is judged by the distribution of cloture votes, the target of obstructionism has expanded across the stages of the legislative game in recent decades. Whereas cloture motions on the motion to proceed were offered on only six measures in the 96th Congress (1979–80), the figure rose to thirty-four in the 102d Congress (1991–92).[16] Recently senators have also tried to filibuster motions to go to conference, as well as motions to appoint the conferees themselves. In 1994 a campaign finance reform bill was killed in the Senate when the majority failed twice to get cloture on a motion to request a conference with the House.[17] Also in 1994 cloture was applied to thwart filibusters on the motion to proceed on a major California wilderness bill, on a motion to disagree with House amendments, and on the final conference report as well. Circumstantial evidence suggests that the increase in cloture as a means of managing the floor reflects something more than a change in leaders' legislative styles (see chapter 5). Senators, it seems, have grown much more willing to threaten filibusters across a host of issues and throughout the stages of the legislative process.

Less amenable to quantification is the rise of "holds," the practice of registering objections to bills slated for floor consideration. Because Senate leaders so often rely on unanimous consent agreements to lend order to Senate floor activity, a single senator can delay or block Senate action. Often, senators place holds simply to ensure that a measure will be scheduled to their convenience. At times senators use holds to extract concessions they might otherwise have little leverage to obtain or to keep a measure off the floor altogether. At the extreme, in the early 1980s, Senator Howard Metzenbaum (Democrat of Ohio) had so perfected the practice of holds that even Republican leaders would directly consult with him before bringing measures to the floor.[18]

The use of holds rose in the 1970s, when Senate leaders began to rely on increasingly complex time-limitation agreements to structure floor debate.[19] Although data are unavailable on the number of such holds registered and honored by the two parties over time, the *effects* of holds have clearly changed since the 1970s. As the weight of Senate business and partisan conflict over salient issues increased in the 1980s, holds had the effect of keeping legislation off the floor, rather than simply warning senators in advance that measures of interest to them were headed to the floor. As one veteran Senate staffer noted in the 1980s, "Four or five or six years ago it started to mean that if you put a hold on something, it would never come up. It became, in fact, a veto."[20]

Equally difficult to measure is the increase in individual activism. Because Senate leaders so often need unanimous consent to structure floor proceedings, individual senators hold incredible leverage over a majority leader intent on pursuing a party agenda. Under the time constraints imposed by a large workload or by the approach of the end of session, party leaders often give in to pressure from obstructive senators, even if those senators are too few to block cloture. Such senators are not likely to back down simply because they lack enough votes to prevent cloture. As discussed in the next section, the external rewards for blocking even marginal measures far outweigh the costs to many senators of bogging down the Senate for endless days and angering Senate colleagues. Metzenbaum (admittedly an extreme example) was willing to filibuster a water rights bill in 1982 even though a unanimous consent agreement limiting the time for debate had already been reached.[21] Most of Metzenbaum's amendments that day had already been rejected by the Senate in previous floor votes, but that did not stop him from offering them again; eager to recess, his colleagues gave in to most of his demands.

A 1982 supplemental spending bill illustrates a less extreme and more typical Senate encounter with individual activism. Seeking to pass the supplemental, the Senate found itself facing two nongermane amendments, neither of which was likely to pass but which still succeeded in tying the chamber in knots.[22] Richard Lugar (Republican of Indiana) sought an extra appropriation for emergency housing assistance for his state, a provision that Lugar knew would spark a presidential veto. In response, William Armstrong (Republican of Colorado) threatened to obstruct the passage of any spending bill containing the Lugar funds by offering an amendment to repeal federal law governing union wages on federal projects, an amendment he knew would spur a filibuster. After the Senate spent four days on the minor spending bill, Armstrong agreed to test support for the Lugar provision with a cloture vote. Although the provision passed, Ronald Reagan vetoed the bill (twice) before it was eventually enacted some four months after the House Appropriations Committee had first acted. Armstrong himself admitted that he knew he could not defeat the bill in the first place: "We started out with only five or six opposed to it. Twenty-seven ended up voting against it. . . . We created an issue where none existed before."[23] One Republican senator groused during the debate, "If this is the world's greatest deliberative body, . . . I'd hate to see the world's worst."[24] According to most accounts of Senate politics in the 1980s, such exploitation of Senate rules is more routine than not. There is little doubt that obstructionist behavior in the Senate has left any remaining tradition of deliberation in tatters.[25]

Why So Many Filibusters?

Filibustering can be a costly legislative strategy. At times those costs are physical, as, for example, when the floor is held continuously for several hours. At other times the costs are more political, as filibustering senators may provoke their colleagues to retaliate on favored legislation in the future. The exact costs of filibustering range across policy issues considered by the Senate and vary over time—depending on the mix of incentives and constraints senators face both inside and outside the chamber. As the following chapters show, changes in the Senate's policymaking environment have consistently influenced senators' legislative behavior. When incentives to filibuster increase and disincentives decline, senators become more than willing to adapt their legislative strategies and press obstructive tactics. Not surprisingly, for a set of purposeful, goal-directed political actors, when the rewards for obstructive activity increase, senators are generally more willing to incur the costs of filibustering; when the political costs of filibustering rise too high, senators have shown themselves remarkably willing to limit their obstructive behavior.

The explosive growth in filibustering after the 1960s can be explained by an examination of the range of factors most likely to reduce the costs of filibustering and increase the rewards for obstructive behavior. Changes in workload, partisanship, procedural strategies, and political and electoral demands on senators together fueled the remarkable increase in obstructionism. Just as a mix of incentives and constraints slowly encouraged the growth of filibustering at the turn of the 20th century and then helped to depress filibustering between 1937 and 1967, changes in the policymaking environment of the Senate have continued to influence senators' legislative strategies in more recent decades.

The expansion of the Senate's workload in recent decades has no doubt made it easier for senators to obstruct chamber business. Although there is no perfect measure of the Senate's workload over time, most indicators suggest that the level of legislative activity has increased markedly since the end of World War II. To be sure, the move to more omnibus bills

Table 1-3. *Senate Workload, 1947–94*

Congress	Bills passed	Time in Session			Total pages of statutes (public bills)	Number of recorded votes
		Days	Hours	Hours per day		
80 (1947–48)	1,670	257	1,462	5.7	2,236	248
81 (1949–50)	2,362	389	2,410	6.2	2,314	455
82 (1951–52)	1,849	287	1,648	5.7	1,585	331
83 (1953–54)	2,231	294	1,962	6.7	1,899	270
84 (1955–56)	2,550	224	1,362	6.1	1,848	224
85 (1957–58)	2,202	271	1,876	6.9	2,435	313
86 (1959–60)	1,680	280	2,199	7.9	1,774	422
87 (1961–62)	1,953	323	2,164	6.7	2,078	434
88 (1963–64)	1,341	375	2,395	6.4	1,975	541
89 (1965–66)	1,636	345	1,814	5.3	2,912	497
90 (1967–68)	1,376	358	1,961	5.5	2,304	595
91 (1969–70)	1,271	384	2,352	6.1	2,927	667
92 (1971–72)	1,035	348	2,294	6.6	2,330	955
93 (1973–74)	1,115	334	2,028	6.1	3,443	1,138
94 (1975–76)	1,038	320	2,210	6.9	4,121	1,290
95 (1977–78)	1,070	337	2,510	7.4	5,403	1,151
96 (1979–80)	977	333	2,324	7.0	4,947	1,028
97 (1981–82)	803	312	2,158	6.9	4,343	948
98 (1983–84)	936	281	1,951	6.9	4,893	673
99 (1985–86)	940	313	2,531	8.1	7,198	740
100 (1987–88)	1,002	307	2,342	7.6	4,839	799
101 (1989–90)	980	274	2,254	8.2	5,767	638
102 (1991–92)	947	287	2,291	8.0	7,544	550
103 (1993–94)	682	291	2,513	8.6	7,542	724

Source: Norman J. Ornstein, Thomas E. Mann, and Michael J. Malbin, *Vital Statistics on Congress, 1995–96* (Washington, D.C.: Congressional Quarterly Inc., 1996), pp. 160–61, 165.

instead of numerous small bills masks some of the increase in workload, but the time consumed by the Senate's agenda has clearly increased in recent decades (table 1-3). Between the 1950s and 1960s the length of Senate sessions increased from 271 days to 357 days on average. Senators spend more hours in session each day, the average increasing from fewer than six hours a day in the 80th Congress (1947–48) to nearly nine hours a day in the 103d (1993–94). In addition, the number of recorded votes has increased sharply since the 1940s (peaking in the 1970s), as has the number of pages of statutes enacted in each Congress.

The increase in demands on the Senate is important for several reasons. First, it has created more targets for senators to filibuster. The broader the agenda, the greater the opportunity to filibuster and the wider the range of senators likely to find that obstructive tactics serve their interests. Second, it has imposed strict time constraints on the chamber.[26] Such constraints affect the strategies not only of rank-and-file senators but also of the majority and minority party leader. Senators seeking to block action on a particular measure know that increased time pressures will often work in their favor: the heavier the agenda, the less likely that party leaders will be able to afford the time to wait out filibustering senators. As agendas expand and time constraints increase, other senators' legislative agendas are likely to be squeezed as well. Under these conditions, most senators—including majority party leaders—have an incentive to give in more swiftly to filibustering senators and even to those simply threatening to filibuster.

Ironically, the efforts of Senate Democratic leaders in the 1970s to reduce these time constraints and the filibustering that ensued may have further fueled filibustering. Under Majority Leader Mike Mansfield (Democrat of Montana), a "tracking" system devised by then majority whip Robert Byrd (Democrat of West Virginia) was put into place to better structure the consideration of legislation on the floor. Tracking allows the majority leader—with unanimous consent or the agreement of the minority leader—to have more than one bill pending on the floor as unfinished business. Before the introduction of tracking, a filibuster would stop the Senate from moving on to any other legislative activity. With a two- (or more) track system, the Senate simply puts aside the filibustered measure and moves on to other legislation. To some degree, this flexibility enabled the Senate to cope with its burgeoning workload in the 1970s. But by making filibusters more tolerable and less costly to the filibustering senators—other senators would no longer be forced to hold the floor continuously to block legislation—tracking also seems to have sparked an increase in filibustering.[27] The increase in legislative business, in other words, has made filibustering more successful and less costly—and hence more common—despite the tactical adjustments of party leaders.

A greater opportunity to filibuster, however, is in itself insufficient to encourage obstructionism; minority coalitions also need a strong enough political incentive to exploit their rights. Thus, just as the increase in partisanship in the late 1800s helped to fuel filibusters by partisan minorities, increasing partisanship appears to have encouraged more obstructive behavior in recent decades. Although absolute levels of partisanship remain low compared with their levels at the turn of the century, differences between the two parties have climbed fairly steadily since 1967 (figure 1-2).[28] Polarized conflict between the two parties, particularly in the 1980s, certainly encouraged the minority party to exploit its parliamentary rights. As the two parties became internally more cohesive and the differences between them grew larger, holding together a party-backed filibuster became significantly easier. The result is seen clearly in the distinctly partisan

Figure 1-2. *Senate Party Differences, 1947–90*

Party difference scores

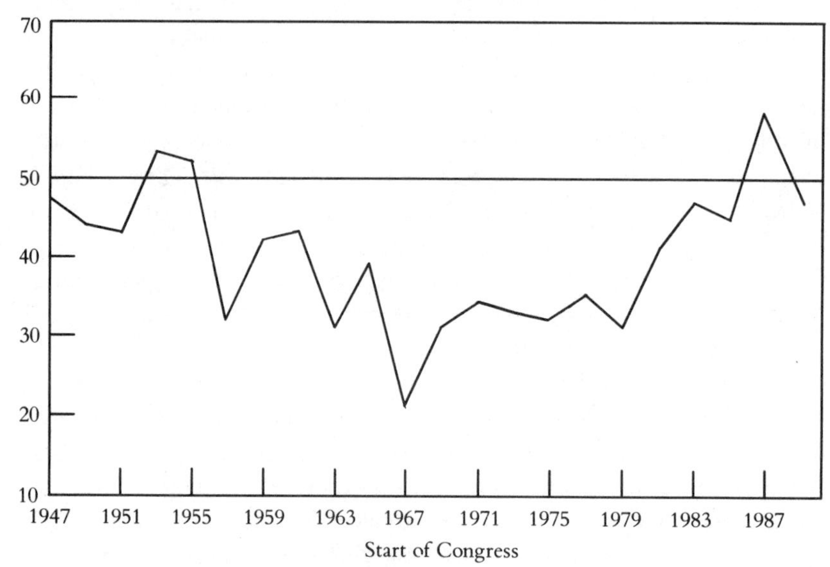

Source: Senate roll-call votes (ICPSR File #00004).

a. Party differences are calculated as the mean percentage of the majority party voting Yea minus the mean percentage of the minority party voting Yea across all roll-call votes for each Congress.

alignment of senators on filibustered bills after 1980 (see chapter 4). Although an expanded workload makes possible obstructive strategies that might otherwise have little bite in a chamber with a limited legislative agenda, the polarization of senators' preferences in recent decades has helped to increase party-based obstructionism against the majority party.

Such partisanship has also helped to fuel what might be called a parliamentary arms race. Republicans, for example, defended their use of the filibuster to block much of President Bill Clinton's congressional agenda in 1994 on the grounds that the Democrats had done the same to George Bush and the Republicans in 1992. And Democrats filibustered regulatory reform, congressional term limits, and other aspects of the Republican agenda in 1995 and 1996, knowing that Republicans had used the filibuster effectively against the Democrats in 1994. As one Senate observer noted, "Once parliamentary strategies such as these have been unleashed, they—like the atom bomb—cannot be uninvented."[29] What seems like an extreme use of the filibuster at one time often becomes a routine strategy later on. Such a dynamic likely fueled the initial increase in filibustering in the early 1970s. As some senators started to filibuster measures other than civil rights bills—such as liberal Democrats filibustering Nixon administration initiatives—other senators quickly followed suit.

Another striking characteristic of the Senate's political environment in recent decades has been the explosive expansion in the Washington policy community.[30] As government involvement in the economy expanded with the advent of Great Society programs in the 1960s and the tackling of other economic, consumer and environmental issues in the 1970s, these new programs spawned innumerable interest groups—each with a stake in the continued involvement of the federal government and the health of the programs it created. Expansion of the national agenda—and the conflict it often engendered—after the prosperity following World War II, in other words, helped spur the development of an immense, active, and interested policy community. The increased activism (and obstructionism) of senators in recent decades can be attributed in part to the demands of this "transformed" policy community. The rewards for legislative activism from those interests outside the chamber have vastly reduced the costs incurred by senators seeking either to shape or to block the course of Senate action. Encouragement from external groups, in other words, has given senators an incentive to exploit their procedural rights, sometimes leading them to block legislation with the filibuster or with holds and at other times leading them to use procedural prerogatives to force the Senate to consider issues of importance to parochial, partisan, or national constituencies. Increased time constraints within the Senate have only made it easier for senators to exploit chamber rules to pursue their political goals.

Still other features of the Senate's political environment encourage senators to strike out on their own.[31] Modern Senate campaigns are run on contributions from thousands of individuals and hundreds of political action committees. Free time on television—interview programs, evening news programs—is in short supply. This environment gives senators an extraordinary incentive to strike out legislatively on their own and to distinguish themselves in the legislative arena. Filibusters and other forms of legislative obstructionism provide a means for individual senators to champion a cause and attract support, and they may encourage one-upmanship among senators. Only when the effects of such activism run counter to the political interests of enough senators has the Senate been willing to protect specific policy matters from the uncertainty of a future filibuster. Budget, trade, and a host of other issues have been protected from filibusters by placing into statute strict limits on their debate (see chapter 6). Such expedited procedures have become an increasingly popular tool for the Senate to limit potential damage of a filibuster.

To be sure, the pressures from a nationalized political environment and a polarized partisan environment might turn out to be contradictory. At the extreme, political parties might completely dictate senators' floor strategies, leaving little room for other groups to influence senators' floor behavior. Except in such an extreme case, however, senators have ample room to pursue their separate legislative agendas in their quest for national political attention and campaign support. If senators are spurred by their own political goals and partisanship in the chamber to take advantage of such opportunities, obstructionism is likely to increase. On some issues, senators will feel pressures from both sides, which may limit their ability to respond to external political incentives. But not all issues, even in a polarized partisan environment, provoke party-backed filibusters. This leaves room for senators to exploit their rights independently of partisan pressures. Whatever the balance of pressures from partisanship or a nationalized political environment, filibusters have increased greatly since the 1960s.

As can be seen by the reaction of senators on both sides of the aisle, obstructionism has left the Senate at times nearly unmanageable and its leaders extremely frustrated. This view was echoed by former Senate majority leader George Mitchell (Democrat of Maine) in 1993:

> The reality is that getting anything done in the Senate now has become extremely difficult, and the propensity, the tendency, the growing pattern of offering amendments that are not related to the pending bill is increasing. . . . The ability to offer amendments unrelated to the bill provides all Senators an outlet to have the issue that they are concerned about raised, if it is not otherwise to be raised. . . . Since I became majority leader . . . I have tried very hard to accommodate every single Senator, without regard to party. . . . The schedule which I announced to accommodate Senators with families . . . was that we would not vote after 7 p.m. on Tuesdays and Wednesdays. But that assumed that we would be voting prior to 7 p.m. This is a Wednesday, and we have reached 7 p.m., and there have been no votes. Well, obviously, if we cannot vote before 7 p.m. and we cannot vote after 7 p.m., we cannot ever vote. And the result is that it takes several days to enact legislation or to act on legislation that ought to take several hours. . . . The Senate cannot continue to function in a manner in which it has so far.[32]

Even Robert Byrd, perhaps the most often-quoted defender of the filibuster, advocated numerous changes to Rule 22 as majority and minority leader between 1977 and 1988. Although he had backed away from more stringent changes to Rule 22 in the 103d Congress (1993–94), Byrd still supported banning the filibuster on motions to proceed: "I no longer see a need to retain the right to filibuster on a motion to proceed. There was a time in the past when that may have had its merits, but that has been abused."[33] Across the aisle, a Pearson-Ribicoff commission in 1983 and a Quayle commission in 1984—in addition to the bipartisan Joint Committee on the Organization of Congress in 1993—recommended banning the filibuster on motions to proceed to reduce senators' exploitation of Rule 22 for political gain.[34] Increases in obstructionism, in short, have not gone unnoticed in the Senate. Neither have its consequences and costs been ignored: "Unless we recognize that things are out of control and procedures have to be changed," Senator Dale Bumpers (Democrat of Arkansas) argued in 1982, "we'll never be an effective legislative body again."[35]

Revisiting the Received Wisdom

Despite these concerns about the adverse effects of Rule 22, efforts to reform the filibuster have essentially been stalled since the last major reform in 1975 and the modest adjustments in 1979 and 1986. As this book demonstrates, the received wisdom about the filibuster works strongly in favor of preserving the status quo. It is said that the filibuster can do no harm and in fact has done much good. Furthermore, some argue, the Senate would be unable to meet its responsibilities as envisioned by the framers of the Constitution without the filibuster.

To date, such claims have gone unchallenged. Indeed, they are so untarnished that even the explosive growth in Senate obstructionism has failed to prompt procedural reform. Although majority-party Democrats in the Senate between 1987 and 1994—particularly under a unified government in 1993 and 1994—were frustrated numerous times by Republican-led partisan filibusters, the election of a Republican Congress in the 1994 elections swiftly led the new Democratic minority to forget the frustrations of trying to govern under Rule 22.

Most senators still find the rules convenient for pursuing their short-term political interests, even though they may defend their support of the filibuster on the basis of more principled commitments to the history and traditions of the Senate. This book focuses on five claims made by defenders of the filibuster. They are briefly examined in the remainder of this chapter, along with the sources of their weaknesses. The rest of the book more rigorously tests the soundness of these faulty propositions about the Senate filibuster and shows that senators' political interests, not philosophical commitments, lie at the heart of the Senate's resistance to change.

Designing the Senate

Perhaps the most common assumption about the filibuster concerns its origins. Many consider the filibuster to be an original feature of the Senate and the essential factor distinguishing the two chambers of Congress. In such a view the House was intended to reflect the interests of a simple majority and the Senate, the interests of the minority. The right of unlimited debate is considered critical to preserving that essential difference. Without the power to filibuster legislation, the minority would too often find its interests trampled by a rash majority. Some even believe that the cloture provisions of Rule 22 (first adopted in 1917) were an original feature of the Senate. "Yet, hardly a week goes by that we do not have a cloture vote," says Senator Phil Gramm (Republican of Texas). "It is part of the fabric of American democracy. It was part of the process making the Senate the deliberative body of Congress that George Washington described to Thomas Jefferson when Jefferson came back from France."[36] The conventional wisdom, in short, endows the filibuster with a constitutional basis, making it considerably more difficult to revamp Senate rules.

There is little evidence, however, to support such an interpretation (see chapter 2). First, the framers of the Constitution left decisions regarding rules of procedure entirely up to the members of the House and Senate. Second, what is known about the framers' views on legislative procedure suggests quite the opposite, namely, that empowering a minority to veto the preferred policies of the majority would produce undesirable legislative outcomes. Neither the framers nor the early senators expected that filibusters would be invented for obstructive purposes or that more than a majority would be needed for the passage of measures, outside of treaties and nominations. Third, the differences between the House and the Senate are not so clearly a matter of intentional design. On the whole, House and Senate rules and practices are a result of political developments in the two chambers over the course of their first few decades. In those early years, members anticipated neither the emergence of the filibuster in the Senate nor the strict limits on debate in the House. Thus nothing in the framers' intentions argues against reforming Senate rules to permit a simple majority to bring debate to a close.

Senate Tradition

The view that Senate tradition demands unlimited debate can also be called into question. It is sometimes argued that the absence of Senate rules restricting debate in the nineteenth century reflected the philosophical positions of senators before and after the Civil War. The Senate failed to limit debate during that century because most senators were committed to the institutional tradition of extended debate.

In fact, the absence of rules limiting debate has a quite different explanation (see chapter 3). First, it is important to note that use of the filibuster developed relatively slowly in the nineteenth century, primarily in response to changes in the Senate's policymaking environment that made obstructionism an increasingly effective legislative strategy. Perhaps more important, unrestricted debate was a contentious issue. Not only did Henry Clay (one member of the "Great Triumvirate" that led the Senate before the Civil War) advocate strict limits on debate, but numerous Senate leaders before and after the Civil War argued that limits on debate would vastly improve the Senate's legislative capacity. Without debate limits, a coalition of almost any size could oppose procedural change by filibustering the proposed reforms. Although senators no doubt believed in the value of unlimited debate, a principled commitment to institutional traditions was not responsible for preventing changes in Senate rules.

Sectionalism, Partisanship, and the Filibuster

Perhaps the greatest myth about the Senate filibuster is that it was once reserved for a few issues of utmost national importance, primarily the issues of slavery and civil rights, but that it has been used for increasingly narrow partisan and parochial purposes in recent decades. Modern exploitation of Senate rules for parochial purposes, it is said, masks the more noble, bipartisan history of the filibuster. Although there is little question about the use of the filibuster for less important matters in recent decades, the received wisdom glorifies the history of the filibuster (see chapter 4). There is little empirical support for the conventional view about the past use of the filibuster: partisan and parochial filibusters flourished in the nineteenth century just as they do today.

Conventional views about the historical use of the filibuster are often based on the rather atypical period between 1937 and 1967. At that time, the filibuster was almost exclusively associated with southern Democrats and Republicans seeking to block passage of civil rights measures. The dominance of a sizable bipartisan conservative majority in the Senate dampened the use of the filibuster for other measures, since conservatives could block more liberal initiatives in committee and liberals were generally willing to settle for conservative legislation over nothing at all. However, a close examination of the nature of the issues subject to filibusters before and after this period and of policy preferences on filibustered measures reveals its partisan and parochial past and present.

The changes in the political nature of the Senate filibuster can also be assessed from senators' votes on cloture reform, as explained in chapter 4. These votes show that senators' views about the rules vary systematically with their short-term political interests. Indeed, support for and opposition to procedural reform in the twentieth century turn predictably on their policy interests. As the ideological and sectional weights of the two parties shift over time, the distribution of preferences over Senate rules changes as well.

The Filibuster and the Little-Harm Thesis

According to the "little-harm" thesis, few measures supported by a majority have ever been killed by the filibuster. The filibuster is also said to be a moderating influence, which ensures that public policy will better reflect the preferences of the popular majority. Not only does it preserve minority interests, but it somehow also protects the interests of the majority. Such views about the filibuster are based mainly on anecdotal evidence. A more systematic test (see chapter 5) shows that the filibuster has been responsible for killing or delaying enactment of a considerable body of legislation that was otherwise likely to be enacted into law. To be sure, the filibuster seems to have been more successful in recent years in blocking passage of legislation favored by the president and a majority of both chambers, but there is scattered evidence of its effect on majority-favored legislation even in the late nineteenth and early twentieth centuries.

The proposition that the filibuster moderates legislation in the Senate is more difficult to test. Certainly, the filibuster has forced compromises in measures that have subsequently been supported by a bipartisan majority of the Senate. But supermajority requirements do not necessarily make legislation more reflective of dominant public opinion or more moderate than it would be under simple majority rule. The moderating effect of the filibuster depends on many factors, including the position of the policy status quo, the type of measure being filibustered, the distribution of public opinion, and the alignment of preferences within the Senate. Indeed, a successful filibuster against a bill to reauthorize a popular federal program can have an extreme effect on the policy status quo by preventing existing federal programs from being renewed. There is no necessary connection between the filibuster and the moderation of legislation.

Senate Majorities and Procedural Reform

Has a majority ever been thwarted in reforming the Senate? The received wisdom says no: the Senate resists reform because a majority of senators wants extended debate preserved. That is only a partial accounting of the Senate's efforts to change its rules, as discussed in chapter 6. First, an analysis of past votes on reform suggests that strategic considerations have at times foreclosed anything more than incremental procedural reform. In the past, filibustering minorities have often agreed to modest changes in Rule 22 to prevent a majority from pressing forward with more stringent reform. Because a Senate minority can filibuster changes in Rule 22, the preferences of a majority are insufficient to dictate the shape of reform in the face of a determined minority. Second, senators have proved quite willing to restrict the right of extended debate when it serves their interests. Expedited procedures—for instance, those banning the filibuster on budget measures and some trade agreements—precommit potential Senate minorities to desist from filibustering future legislation. In creating these special floor procedures, senators have only rarely complained that their parliamentary rights were being taken away. Even the most ardent defenders of extended debate have acquiesced to (and, at times, advocated and designed) expedited procedures. When pragmatic interests prevail, the Senate has quietly sacrificed tradition for more practical procedural rules.

A Perspective on Institutional Change

The distinction between politics and principle in this book reflects a more general theoretical view about the dynamics of institutional change: the character of the Senate today represents the sum of choices senators have made about institutional arrangements since the very first Senate met in 1789. How senators make those choices—and how the Senate as an institution has consequently evolved over time—is the central concern of this book. If senators' choices are based primarily on "principle," the history of the filibuster should reflect senators' shared, long-term commitments to the protection of minority rights and free speech and to ideas about the role of the Senate in American politics. If instead senators base their choices primarily on "politics," the rules and practices of Senate debate should more closely reflect senators' short-term strategic policy and political considerations. Thus the question to keep in mind throughout this discussion is, How do lawmakers choose the procedural rules under which they will collectively forge public policy?

Since it is assumed that individuals are motivated by their calculations of the costs and benefits of those changes, then the objective here will be to determine the nature of those costs and benefits. Some argue that it is the *collective* interests or general welfare of the institution that weighs heavily in these calculations. Others suggest that institutional choices are shaped by their effect on individual or group interests within the institution. The determining factor, in other words, would be how legislative and political advantages and disadvantages would be *redistributed* within the institution.[37] Rules and practices would be preferred if they secured outcomes favoring some particular interests over others.

Whether the development of the Senate better reflects the influence of redistributive or collective interests—politics or principle—is not simply an arcane matter for political scientists. This issue has implications for the political future of the filibuster—for when and how the Senate is ever likely to reform the rules that grant extraordinary power to individual senators and chamber minorities.

Reforms aimed at securing collective interests may take different forms. Some are designed to maximize the welfare of the community affected by the institution: rules are chosen to ensure that the institution protects the greatest gains for the entire community. Other changes are designed to be Pareto optimal: they are expected to improve the welfare of at least one member or faction without hurting any other member or faction. In some contexts, collective interests might be secured by opposing any change at all. If the institution adequately serves shared principles or goals, few of its members would have an incentive to violate the rules, and no change might be preferred. In this case, a stable institution would be expected.

In contrast, when change is designed to redistribute advantages and disadvantages within the institution, political competition between groups or factions takes on an important role. In this case, institutional change is governed by self-interest. Rules are chosen because they protect the winning coalition's most preferred outcomes. Any one institution, of course, might be a product of both approaches to change. Particularly in a legislative environment, where political disagreements often focus on which version of change will best serve the collective interests of the institution, institutional change will often disproportionately favor one set of chamber interests over another. In the world of politics, meaningful change will seldom produce Pareto optimal outcomes: it is rare that everyone can be made better off and no one worse off by changing the rules of the game.

The filibuster's defenders argue that the institutional interests of the Senate have been paramount in shaping its political past. For one thing, they say, the filibuster ensures policy outcomes that serve the collective interests of the Senate and thus does little harm. For another, supermajority requirements are said to foster the compromise and moderation needed to protect the interests of popular majorities. In other words, by opposing filibuster reform, senators ensure that policy outcomes are Pareto optimal—everyone's lot is improved and no one's is harmed. All the evidence, however, strongly suggests that senators prefer changes in the rules of debate that best protect their preferred political and ideological outcomes. Even when senators are concerned about the consequences of institutional change for the collective interests of the Senate, they never lose sight of the consequences for their own political and often partisan agendas.

If the choice of rules reflects how well those rules enable senators to pursue and secure their political goals, then those rules should change when two conditions hold.[38] First, a coalition or coalitions of senators must believe that their interests are no longer well served by existing rules, either because of some change in the policymaking environment of the Senate or because old rules are producing unanticipated consequences. Second, a shift must occur in the relative power of contending coalitions within the chamber: this shift in the balance of power must be large enough to overcome the Senate's traditionally high threshold for change. Institutional change, under this view, occurs not simply because most senators might be seeking greater collective goods, but because a sizable coalition finds procedural change necessary to achieve the political objectives of its members and because it gains at least a momentary advantage over its opponents.

Such institutional reforms are likely to be rare in the Senate, given the chamber's exceedingly high threshold for procedural change. Because the majority party or dominant policy coalition has rarely been strong enough to overcome minority opposition to changing the rules, the alignment of partisan and policy interests alone will not be sufficient to predict the timing of major Senate reform. The likelihood of reform is bolstered, however, when political goals beyond mere policy preferences produce a supermajority willing to adopt meaningful reform. In fact, neither collective interests nor policy preferences alone can account for the Senate's rare, but significant, episodes of reform.

Soon after the Republicans took control of the Senate following the 1994 elections, Action Not Gridlock, an interest group supporting reform of Rule 22, locked its doors and shut down. Its labor union sponsors decided that a filibuster wielded by Democrats against a Republican majority might not be such a bad thing. The predicament of Action Not Gridlock is not unlike the politics of congressional reform. Rules of procedure often bias policy outcomes to some degree. As a result, it is often difficult to disentangle reformers' procedural preferences from their political interests. "Procedural principles," intoned an editorial in the *Washington Post*, "tend to follow self-interest."[39] This is precisely what one would expect when senators choose rules because of the way they will redistribute advantages and disadvantages in the chamber.

Reforming the Senate

The prescriptions for reform offered in this book presuppose that no particular party will maintain control of the Senate and that the ideological tenor of the two parties will not remain fixed over time. The proposed reforms are expected to enhance the power of Senate majorities over Senate minorities, but they would not exclusively benefit one party or another over the long run. The objective of these reforms is to ensure that the U.S. Senate operates under workable majority rule that nevertheless retains the chamber's comparative advantages over the House. Those advantages certainly include the power of a Senate minority to raise issues swept underfoot by a hasty House majority (whether germane or not) and the ability of a small legislative body to more carefully deliberate controversial measures. These proposed reforms would not affect the framers' intentions for the Senate: small and large states would remain on equal footing, senators' reelection would continue to depend on pleasing broad state constituencies rather than narrow district interests, and the system of staggered Senate elections would continue to dilute the impact of strongly partisan electoral waves. As pointed out in chapter 7, calibrating procedural reform to preserve the traditional advantages of the Senate is difficult, but both possible and desirable.

Helping to shape the rules of the early Senate:
Aaron Burr (left), vice president of the United States, and
John Quincy Adams of Massachusetts

2

The Original versus the Traditional Senate

"THE PURPOSE of the Senate is entirely different from the purpose of the House of Representatives," argued Senator Royal Copeland (Democrat of New York) in 1926. "From the very beginning it was intended to be a deliberative body where the expenditure of time and the exchange of views should determine judgment in any pending matter."[1] Like Senator Copeland, many observers contend that the framers intended the Senate to be a body of unrestrained debate. Yet there is nothing to suggest that the right to filibuster was a feature of the original Senate. The framers of the Constitution did envision and prescribe different structures and roles for the two chambers, but they had little to say about the rules of procedure in either one. The procedural uniqueness of the Senate was instead a central feature of the *traditional* Senate, a result of developments in its first few decades and not a result of the framers' or first senators' vision for the upper chamber.

This chapter explores the differences between these two Senates, the original and traditional. Members of the original Senate—acting only after the House had acted, meeting at first behind closed doors, and representing almost exclusively the economic elite—seem not to have been preoccupied with questions of procedural rights. Only in the traditional Senate was a norm of extended debate vigorously articulated and defended, earning that

Senate a reputation for having its galleries "crowded to overflowing with fashionable Washingtonians eager to listen to scintillating brilliance."[2] Members and observers of the Senate alike tend to confuse these two Senates. Thus distinguishing between them is a necessary first step in assessing the politics of the filibuster.

The distinction is an important one to make for two reasons. First, opponents of reforming Rule 22 often defend extended debate on the grounds of its prominence in the original design of the Senate; without the filibuster, they argue, the Senate could no longer fulfill its original function of cooling the passions of hasty and rash House majorities.[3] However, if the Senate was actually designed with little attention to procedural matters, then a substantial reform of Rule 22 would hardly destroy the framers' original intent. Second, if procedural differences between the House and Senate were not part of the original design but evolved over time, the persistence of rules protecting extended debate in the traditional Senate might reflect considerations other than a commitment to principles motivating the framers. Indeed, broad concerns about the collective interests of the Senate are clearly absent from senators' early decisions regarding institutional arrangements for the Senate. Those decisions shed considerable light on the framers' vision for the original Senate, the procedural beginnings of unlimited debate, and the nature of early Senate floor practices.

The Framers and the Design of the Senate

"The use of the Senate," noted James Madison during the Constitutional Convention in 1787, "is to consist in its proceedings with more coolness, with more system, & with more wisdom, than the popular branch."[4] Toward that end, as is well known, delegates to the convention debated numerous institutional features of the upper chamber. The solutions they chose were intended to create a more distinguished membership and to ensure more measured consideration of legislation in the Senate than in the popular and populous House.[5] A quick review of those solutions indicates that designs for internal procedural rules for the upper chamber were decidedly absent.

First, senators were to be older than House members and subject to a citizenship requirement of at least nine years, which was two years longer than the requirement for members of the House. Such provisions, argued

Madison in Federalist no. 62, would ensure that senators had a "greater extent of information and stability of character."[6]

Second, six-year staggered terms for senators—in contrast to the concurrent two-year terms to be served by House members—were crafted with an eye to buttressing the stability of the upper chamber against the "impulse of sudden and violent passions, and . . . factious leaders."[7] Longer terms and infrequent election by state legislatures, according to Madison in Federalist no. 63, would be essential to bolstering order and stability in the new government. Not only would the upper chamber restrain intemperate majorities from the House, but it would also serve "as a defence to the people against their own temporary errors and delusions."[8]

Third, although Madison fought long and hard in the convention against state-based representation in the Senate, the adoption of the Connecticut Compromise providing for two senators from each state actually gave Madison and the Federalists "a justification for the upper house that they had not anticipated."[9] Equal representation of the states in the upper chamber meant "a constitutional recognition of the portion of sovereignty remaining in the individual states" and made the Senate "an instrument for preserving that residuary sovereignty."[10] Moreover, by granting each state two votes in the Senate, the upper chamber would provide a means of protecting the small states from the ambitions of the large.[11]

But the delegates were concerned with more than simply the contours of the Senate; they also wanted to secure the place of the Senate in a larger republican system so as to ensure political stability and protect the status quo. To this end, it was important not only to establish a bicameral system, but also to differentiate between the two chambers, and thereby to prevent the accumulation of power in any single set of governmental hands as well as to limit the powers of government. "As the improbability of sinister combinations [between the House and Senate] will be in proportion to the dissimilarity in the genius of the two bodies," argued Madison in Federalist no. 62, "it must be politic to distinguish them from each other by every circumstance which will consist with a due harmony in all proper measures."[12]

Although Madison clearly thought it was imperative to distinguish between the composition of the two chambers, there is no evidence that the delegates sought to do so procedurally. Strikingly absent from Madison's records of the convention and from the Federalist Papers is any mention of procedural matters in either chamber. That task delegates were willing to leave to Congress in Article I, section 5, of the Constitution: "Each House may determine the rules of its proceedings." The rule-making clause was approved by voice vote, without opposition.[13] Only on two matters did procedural challenges occur. Gouverneur Morris of Pennsylvania tried (but failed) to allow any individual, rather than one-fifth of the chamber, to demand that the yeas and nays be entered on the journal, while Madison persuaded his fellow delegates to require a two-thirds vote, rather than a majority, to expel a member from either house. "The right to expulsion," argued Madison, "was too important to be exercised by a bare majority of a quorum: and in emergencies of faction might be dangerously abused."[14]

Thus the delegates did not stipulate constitutional protection for the rights of individuals or legislative minorities in the Senate and apparently did not think such procedural protections would be necessary to ensure that it remained the more temperate of the two chambers. Both Madison and Alexander Hamilton warned that the costs of procedurally protecting legislative minorities would be unbearable. As Madison pointed out,

> It has been said that more than a majority ought to have been required for a quorum, and in particular cases, if not in all, more than a majority of a quorum for a decision. That some advantages might have resulted from such a precaution, cannot be denied. It might have been an additional shield to some particular interests, and another obstacle generally to hasty and partial measures. But these considerations are outweighed by the inconveniences in the opposite scale. In all cases where justice or the general good might require new laws to be passed, or active measures to be pursued, the fundamental principle of free government would be reversed. It would be no longer the majority that would rule; the power would be transferred to the minority.[15]

It is important to remember that the delegates had already experimented with supermajority requirements under the Articles of Confederation. In the Continental Congress, a two-thirds vote of the states was required to pass certain categories of legislation, including revenue, spending, and military matters.[16] As a result, on numerous occasions gridlock ensued, as a majority of the states in the Congress found themselves unable to muster the requisite supermajority to pass favored legislation. Reflecting on the earlier Congress's supermajority rule, Hamilton in Federalist no. 22 made clear his opposition to such cumbersome restraints on the majority: "To give a minority a negative upon the majority (which is always the case where more than a majority is requisite to a decision) is in its tendency to subject the sense of the greater number to that of the lesser number. . . .

The necessity of unanimity in public bodies, or of something approaching towards it, has been founded upon a supposition that it would contribute to security. But its real operation is to embarrass the administration, to destroy the energy of government, and to substitute the pleasure, caprice or artifices of an insignificant, turbulent or corrupt junto, to the regular deliberations and decisions of a respectable majority."[17]

The records of the convention and the arguments in the Federalist Papers give no indication that the framers either anticipated or desired procedural protection for Senate minorities. The vision of the Senate as a body of unrestrained debate and amendment simply cannot be attributed to the framers of the Constitution. Protection of the status quo was not to be lodged in Senate rules and practices but instead was to result from the very composition of the Senate. By stipulating that the Senate was to have longer terms than the House and was to be filled by older men, by insulating senators from popular election, and by giving each state equal representation, the framers of the Senate trusted that these novel features would by themselves distinguish the upper and lower chambers and guard against the passions of rash and intemperate majorities in the House. Unlimited debate for senators was absent from that scheme.

Procedural Choices in the Original Senate

Free to choose their own rules of procedure and to change them whenever and however they saw fit, the first senators could easily have fashioned the chamber to ensure that parliamentary rights were unrestricted in every way. As representatives of the sovereign states, they were in a position to readily promote or block new federal legislation. But did their procedural choices reflect such parliamentary principles?

Early Senate rules provide few clues to the value of extended debate in the original Senate. Instead senators seemed surprisingly unconcerned about setting the foundations for unlimited debate and expected a simple majority would be adequate to close debate. Even the rule change in 1806 that made possible the filibuster—by eliminating the Senate's previous question motion (a motion the House would soon thereafter revamp into a tool for limiting debate)—did not spring from a desire to institutionalize a novel way of conducting legislative business in the Senate.[18] Although that rule change left subsequent majorities powerless to cut off debate in the face of a determined minority, members of the original

Senate expressed no commitment to a right of extended debate in making this change.

Original Senate Rules

What is striking about the first rules adopted by the House and Senate is not how different they were, but how similar. The committees appointed to draft initial sets of rules for each chamber both chose rules intended to limit members' liberty to speak on their respective chamber floors. In the House, the second standing rule stipulated that no member could speak more than twice on the same question without permission of the House.[19] In the Senate, the fourth rule prohibited members from speaking more than twice in any one debate on the same day, again without the permission of the chamber. In addition, under the sixth Senate rule no motion could be debated unless it was seconded by another senator. Neither chamber placed a time limit on debate. Although the rules of both chambers provided for a previous question motion, in neither chamber (as discussed in the next section) was it originally used by the majority to force votes on favored bills. Although the Senate made some minor changes to its rules in its first decade, none affected the rights of members on the floor to speak or offer amendments.[20]

The close similarity between the rules of the two chambers suggests that early senators harbored no unique conception of Senate procedure.[21] To be sure, senators were at first occupied with matters of decorum and protocol in an effort to emphasize its superiority over the House.[22] This somewhat aloof attitude is reflected both in the Senate's initial lack of a public gallery and in its decision to close its doors to the public. Procedurally, however, no senators tried to amend chamber rules to ease the formal limits on floor debate. Senators might have been expected to do so, as suggested by an entry in the diary of John Quincy Adams (Federalist of Massachusetts), noting that the Senate's two-speech rule was at times enforced and prevented senators from talking.[23] In the Eighth Congress, Adams also observed, Vice President Aaron Burr showed some partiality in his willingness to enforce the rule: "In this debate the President suffered Mr. Giles to speak three times without checking him as he did Mr. Bradley last week. Indeed, his partialities to Giles have been frequent and obvious this session."[24] Despite evidence of unevenness in the enforcement of the rule, members of the early Senate apparently were not motivated—with one critical exception—to tamper with the chamber's original limits on debate. That exception—the decision to eliminate the previous question rule in 1806—merits a closer look.

The Previous Question in the Original Senate

The rules adopted by the first Senate in 1789 allowed any senator to offer a previous question motion; if the motion was seconded, the chair would ask, "Shall the main question now be put?" In the modern House, approval of a previous question motion brings the House to an immediate vote on the pending matter, cutting off further debate and amending activity; defeat of the motion allows debate to continue and by precedent grants the minority control of the floor. That is to say, the previous question motion provides the majority party with a means of managing and controlling the floor agenda. Once members of the majority party determine that enough debate has taken place and that they have the support of a floor majority, they simply move the previous question to bring the House to a vote.

Such an effect was not expected of either the original House or Senate rule. During the House's first two decades, speakers ruled on several occasions that approval of the previous question motion did *not* bring an end to debate. Only in 1811, during the buildup to the War of 1812, did a partisan majority intent on securing its wartime agenda over the objections of an obstructionist minority revamp the motion into a tool for limiting debate.[25] In the Senate, no such revision occurred. In fact, senators invoked or tried to invoke the motion only ten times between 1789 and 1806, when it was wiped from the Senate's rule book.[26]

Not only was the motion seldom used in the Senate, but it also did not have a single, consistent use.[27] According to *Jefferson's Manual*—a compilation of procedural precedents assembled by then Vice President Thomas Jefferson in 1797–1801 for the Senate's future use—the previous question was to be used to avoid undesired discussions. "The proper occasion for the previous question," noted Jefferson, "is when a subject is brought forward of a delicate nature as to high personages, etc., or the discussion of which may call forth observations which might be of injurious consequences."[28] Jefferson further explained that if the previous question motion were defeated—that is, if the Senate answered in the negative the question "Shall the main question be now put?"—the pending discussion would temporarily be displaced for a single day.[29] According to Jefferson's reading of the British and American precedents, the previous question was to be used to postpone temporarily consideration of delicate *discussions*; approval or disapproval of the motion was not intended, according to Jefferson, to affect consideration of Senate *decisions* (that is, votes).

Almost immediately, however, senators appear to have ignored Jefferson's highly principled definition of the previous question procedure. Senators wishing to avoid a vote on controversial legislation would move the previous question to put off *decisions*, as well as *discussions*. The motion thus came to serve the same purpose as a motion to postpone. A senator opposed to a particular measure would move the previous question—hoping that the nays would prevail—and thereby push the main question off the agenda at least temporarily.[30] Jefferson himself complained that senators were abusing the previous question motion by adapting it beyond its traditional purpose: "The use of it has been extended abusively to other cases, but in these it has been an embarrassing procedure. . . . [I]t should [be] restricted within as narrow limits as possible."[31]

This is clearly a case in which a rule intended to spare the Senate a delicate discussion was used for political advantage. An example of senators' willingness to manipulate the previous question motion for parliamentary advantage comes from 1798.[32] In April of that year, Senator James Lloyd (Federalist of Maryland) offered a resolution to permit the publication of instructions to the special envoy to France (John Jay). The documents in question helped vindicate the Federalists in the aftermath of the XYZ affair. John Hunter (Republican of South Carolina)—opposed to the printing of the instructions and seeking to prevent a vote on Lloyd's resolution—countered by offering the previous question motion, hoping that it would be defeated. Hunter was one of eleven senators voting against the previous question motion, but it passed 15-11.[33] Had Hunter's strategy succeeded, the effect of defeating the previous question motion would have been to postpone action—temporarily, if not permanently—on Lloyd's resolution. Instead, the previous question motion having passed, the Senate voted directly on Lloyd's motion, passing it 16-11.[34] Every senator voting in favor of the previous question motion voted with Lloyd to order the printing of the instructions; ten of the eleven senators (including Hunter) who had tried to derail the Lloyd vote (by voting against the previous question motion) voted against the Lloyd motion.[35]

Hunter's move was clearly consistent with the procedure that Jefferson laid out, but inconsistent with the intent of the procedure as Jefferson saw it. The use of the previous question motion before 1806 suggests that early senators did not hold a principled commitment to the niceties of Senate procedure. Politics clearly superseded principle in the Hunter case, as in other cases of the use of the previous question before 1806. Senators exploited chamber rules of procedure to shape policy and to serve their political interests.

Note, however, that this use of the previous question motion bears little resemblance to its later use in the House. Although today it is used by *proponents* of a measure seeking to cut off debate and reach a final vote, the motion in the early Senate was clearly used by *opponents* of legislation to *postpone* action. But the motion was ill suited as a tool for proponents seeking to limit debate and bring a vote on favored legislation. First, because defeat of the motion postponed a decision on the main question, proponents of a measure were pursuing a risky strategy in choosing to move the previous question. If supporters of a measure underestimated chamber opposition and the previous question was defeated, the favored bill would be put off for at least a day, so it was hardly a reliable tool for ending debate and reaching a final vote. Second, subsidiary questions—such as motions to adjourn, amend, or postpone—took precedence over the previous question motion. Consequently opponents of a measure could also obstruct a vote on the previous question. In that case, moving the previous question would hardly be an effective way for supporters of a bill to secure a vote on the main question. Without doubt, the original previous question rule provided opponents of legislation with a tool for delaying action on a bill, but it provided proponents of legislation scant means of forcing a vote on favored legislation. Counter to Jefferson's expectations about the proper use of the previous question motion, senators adeptly exploited the previous question rule to serve their obstructionist purposes.

Aaron Burr and the Revision of Senate Rules

The decision of the Senate in 1806 to drop the previous question motion from its rule book must be viewed in the context of the original Senate's use of the motion. Because the rule had not been used as a means of limiting debate, its deletion could not have signaled a commitment to the principle of extended debate, a view that is borne out by the circumstances of the rule change. Even so, conventional treatments of the rule change are loath to accept this interpretation. Senate observer William S. White, for one, has argued: "In 1806, in order to be absolutely certain about it, the Senate went vigorously on record for no limitation whatever."[36] Which interpretation better fits the turn of events in 1806, of course, has important implications for our claim that political advantage—rather than collective interests—governs the choice of Senate rules.

What prompted the Senate to eliminate the previous question rule seems to have been a recommendation by Vice President Aaron Burr in his farewell speech to the Senate in March 1805, after his indictment for the murder of Alexander Hamilton. Burr stated that the previous question motion was simply not needed in the Senate. Although the *Annals of Congress*, the official record of debates, glossed over the details of Burr's speech, John Quincy Adams recounted them in his memoirs: "He [Burr] mentioned one or two of the rules which appeared to him to need a revisal, and recommended the abolition of that respecting the *previous question*, which he said had in the four years been only once taken, and that was upon an amendment. This was a proof that it could not be necessary, and all its purposes were certainly much better answered by the question of indefinite postponement."[37] It seems the motion was not used to limit debate but had become a tactical means of postponing decisions.[38] Burr concluded his speech by praising the Senate for its conduct in preventing the impeachment of Justice Samuel Chase earlier that month, and he commended the Senate as well for its "habits of order and regularity, which upon experience are found to be intimately connected with important principles."[39] By simultaneously making a case for preserving "order and regularity" and advocating elimination of the previous question, Burr's speech suggests that a right to extended debate had little bearing on the impending rule change.

Unfortunately, little else is known about the circumstances surrounding the Senate's revision of its rules the following year. Adams was appointed to a temporary select committee to recommend changes in the rules, and at least three members of the committee (two Federalists and one Republican) met twice between January and March of 1806.[40] In his accounts of those meetings, Adams made no note of any substantive decisions or difficult issues, which suggests that the revision sparked no controversy. The *Annals* show no record of the floor debate during their adoption on March 10, or of the votes on the rule changes. The Senate *Journal*, however, indicates that although the previous question rule was dropped, most of the existing Senate rules were recodified and nearly twenty new ones adopted.[41] To be sure, most of these new rules concerned minor matters of decorum and procedure. But the Senate did adopt one new rule preventing debate on motions to adjourn. This move suggests that senators, far from endeavoring to protect unlimited debate, felt that new limits on debate were necessary to help the Senate overcome obstructionism on a simple procedural motion.

The principles of free speech were hardly at stake in the 1806 decision to eliminate the previous question rule. Nor were the early senators trying to create a procedurally unique upper chamber. Their actions show that they were aiming for nothing more than a simple majority, perhaps through the motion to postpone, to stem debate. In making the most critical procedural choice in the nineteenth century, the collective interests of the chamber seemed far from senators' minds.

Legislating in the Original Senate

Yet the 1806 decision gave obstructing minorities an important new tool. Majorities seeking new procedural limits on senators' rights to debate and amend legislation were now powerless to force the chamber to cast a vote on favored procedural innovations. As a result, even a small minority willing to insist on its right of extended debate was able to prevent action on measures it opposed.

In contrast, the House—revamping its own previous question motion in 1811 to allow majorities to force votes on favored measures—followed a different procedural path. Subsequently majorities were able to force votes on additional rules aimed at limiting minority obstructionism and boosting majority control of the chamber. The House's decision to move in this direction has been attributed to the flare-up of partisanship in the chamber and persistent obstructionism by the Federalist minority over the impending war with England.[42] But neither the level of partisanship nor the behavior of the Federalist minority reached such precipitous levels in the Senate—where the War of 1812 bill passed without any effort to restore the previous question rule.

The Senate not only weathered the war with England without a major procedural innovation but also showed no effects of the 1806 rule change. Legislative deliberation proceeded in the very same manner before and after the elimination of the previous question rule. Although the lack of a previous question motion after 1806 meant that any minority could theoretically obstruct passage of pending legislation, no real filibusters took place until the late 1830s. Senator William Maclay (Federalist of Pennsylvania) did note in his diary that during consideration of a bill to select a permanent site for the capital "every endeavour was used to waste time [and] lengthy . . . speeches were made," but that does not really constitute a conscious move to exploit procedural rights to prevent the passage of legislation.[43] To reiterate, floor practices in the original Senate bear little resemblance to Senate debate in the later tradition of the mid–nineteenth century. Why filibustering arose only then can be explained by the character of the early Senate, most notably its legislative role, practices, and working conditions.

Legislative Role and Working Conditions

As noted in chapter 1, contemporary theories of Senate politics suggest that conditions in the modern Senate foster obstructionism. A heavy workload and the pressure for Senate activism from audiences outside the chamber have conspired to decrease the costs of filibustering and increase its rewards.[44] The more work that needs to be done, the greater the incentive chamber leaders have to accommodate the wishes of senators threatening to obstruct legislation—either by delaying consideration of the measure or making concessions to gain their support. If they fail to accommodate the preferences of obstructing senators, they place the rest of the agenda at risk and increase the likelihood that the legislative priorities of other senators will be pushed off the agenda. Whereas a large workload makes it easier to obstruct through delay, the attention of an audience outside the chamber can *increase* the benefits of such obstructionism. The more that senators see obstructionism inside the chamber reaping rewards outside it, the more they are likely to filibuster.

Conditions in the original Senate—in terms of both workload and outside pressures—were quite different. Moreover, senators had little opportunity to exploit their rights to the fullest by obstructing a simple majority from governing the chamber. By most accounts the original Senate acted primarily as a revisory body, initiating only a small proportion of Congress's workload and preferring to refine House-passed measures.[45] It was not unusual, as Senator John Quincy Adams (Federalist of Massachusetts) recorded in his diary in 1803, for its relatively inactive members to walk to the House chamber to hear its debates after the Senate had adjourned.[46] As late as 1827, the Senate enjoyed a rather leisurely schedule: "The Senate used to meet at noon and generally conclude its day's work by three o'clock," noted Washington correspondent Ben Perley Poore—adding that adjournments from Thursdays to Mondays were quite common.[47]

A comparison of the legislative business initiated by each chamber also suggests that the Senate generally deferred to the House in tackling legislative issues (figure 2-1).[48] The House initiated an overwhelming share of legislative business for the first seventeen Congresses (1789–1823). Over the course of the first thirteen Congresses (through the end of the War of 1812), the House originated nearly three times as many public bills as did

Figure 2-1. *Comparison of House and Senate Workload, 1789–1823*

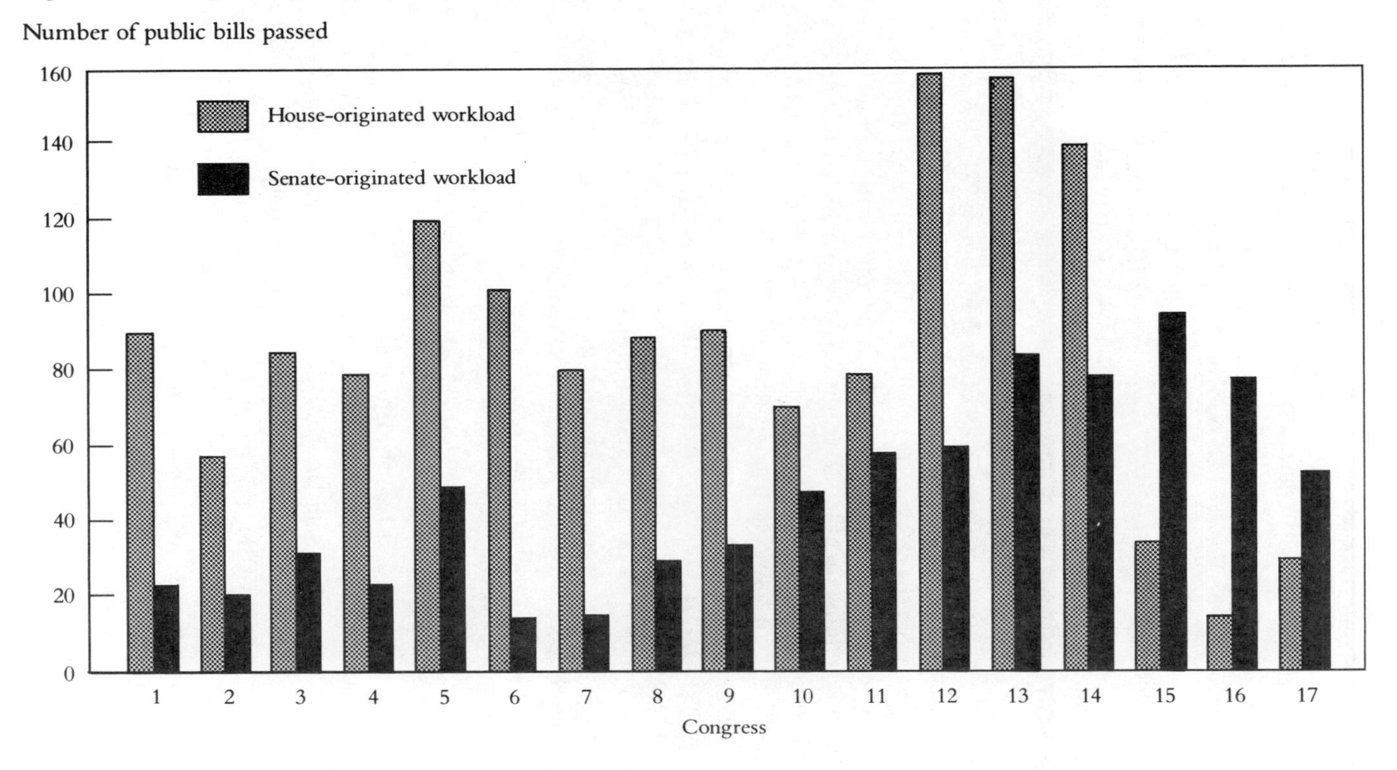

Source: House *Journal*, 1st–17th Congresses.

the Senate. Their floor voting records also differed over the same periods (figure 2-2). Over the first seventeen Congresses, the House averaged more than 160 recorded votes per Congress, whereas the Senate averaged 130.[49] For the shorter period, 1789–1814, the number of votes cast in the House significantly exceeded that of the Senate.[50]

Changes in Senate activity over time are equally revealing. To begin with, senators cast few floor votes in comparison with the levels of the mid–nineteenth century (figure 2-3). As a first proxy for time spent on the floor considering legislative business, the pattern of recorded floor votes confirms the relatively small workload and inactivity of the original Senate. Similarly, the length of each Congress over the course of the nineteenth century suggests the early Senate spent little time in session in comparison with the majority of Congresses after 1840 (figure 2-4).[51] Although the length of Senate sessions varies somewhat, there is a discernible upward trend in the number of days spent in session between 1799 and 1919. Unlike conditions in the Senate even by the mid–nineteenth century, chamber conditions in the early 1800s clearly would have made it difficult for senators to obstruct measures by relying on the size of the legislative agenda. Hardly in a rush to conclude business on a host of pressing issues, Senate majorities would have had the liberty of sitting out any set of obstructive senators, knowing that they would not be putting a heavy agenda at risk.

The Senate was eclipsed by the House in other ways as well.[52] The Senate's sessions were closed to the public until 1795, and its original chamber in New York even lacked a gallery for visitors. Members were seemingly concerned that the Senate would no longer be insulated from popular pressures and its role as an "executive council" would be threatened if it were opened to the public, and thus exposed to the same public criticism experienced by the House.[53] Even after the public was allowed to attend the Senate's sessions, on several occasions before 1802 reporters were not permitted to record the debate from the floor, the only place in the chamber with good acoustics. It was not until the Republicans ascended to their first majority in the Seventh Congress (1801–03) that a Senate majority permitted reporters to sit on the Senate floor to record debate. Senators had voted along a strictly partisan line to open the chamber to reporters—the new Republican majority voting in favor and the Federalist minority uniformly opposed.[54] The Federalists seemed to emphasize a theme important to the framers—that the Senate should remain distant from public opinion—whereas the Republicans sought to move beyond the original vision of the Senate, in what may have been an initial edging away from the designs of the framers and early senators. Once again, senators'

Figure 2-2. *House and Senate Floor Votes, 1789–1823*

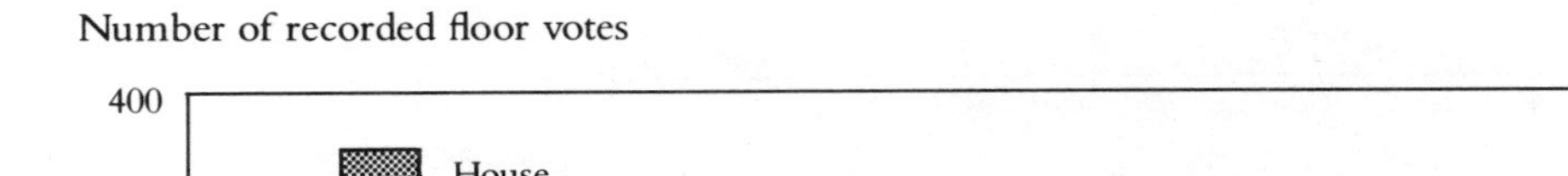

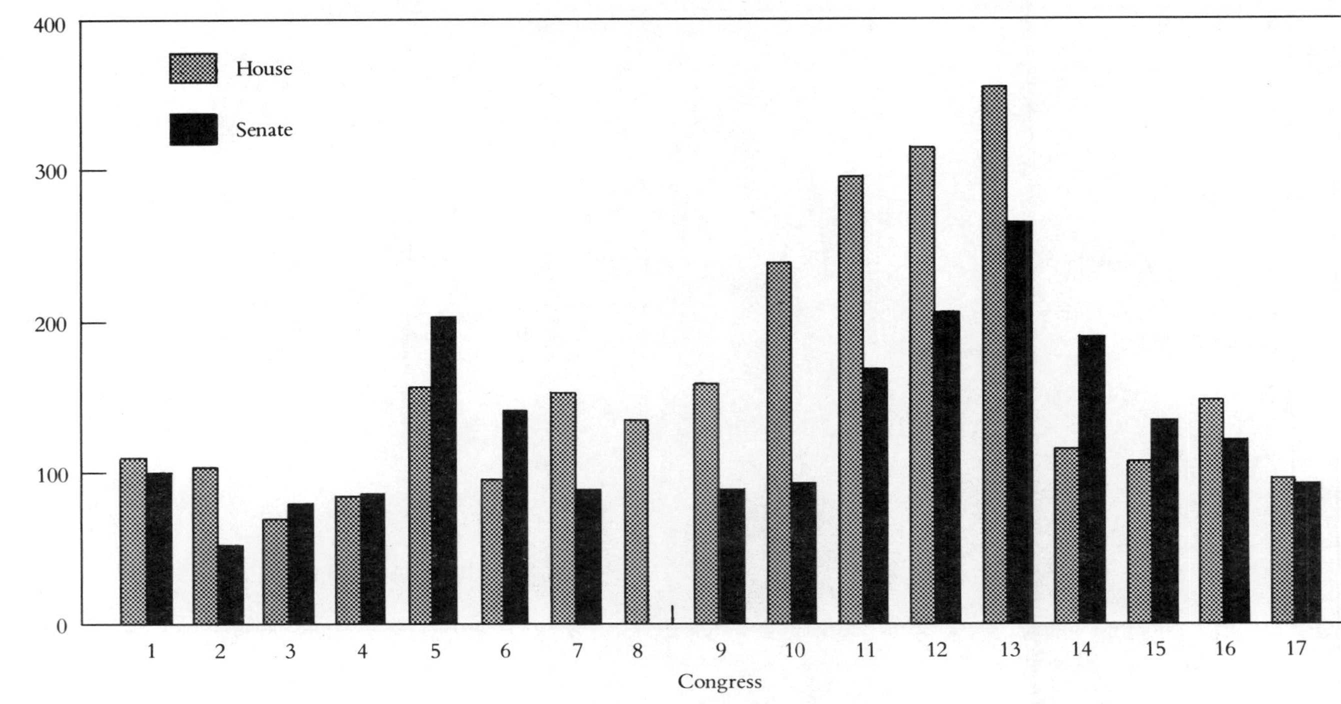

Source: Senate roll-call votes (ICPSR File #00004). Eighth Senate data indefinitely unavailable from ICPSR.

Figure 2-3. *Senate Floor Activity, by Congress, 1789–1991*

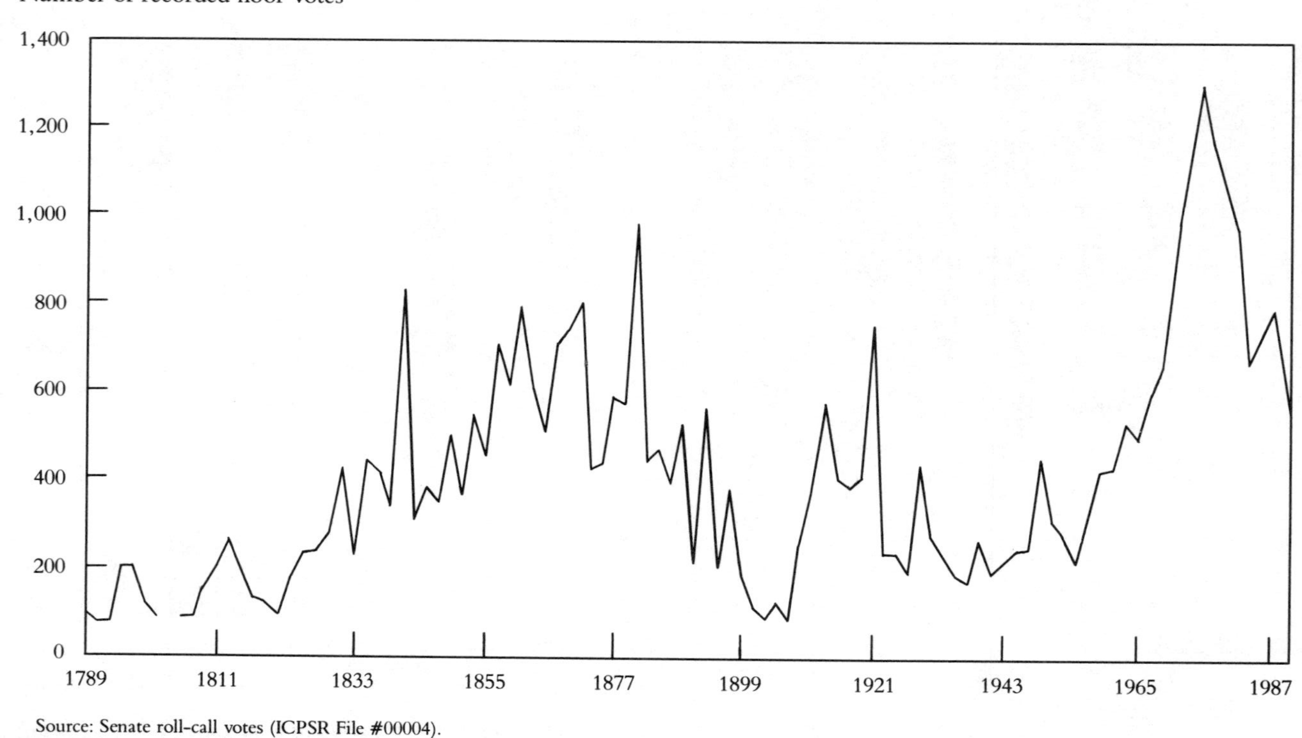

Source: Senate roll-call votes (ICPSR File #00004).

Figure 2-4. *Length of Senate Sessions, 1789–1921*

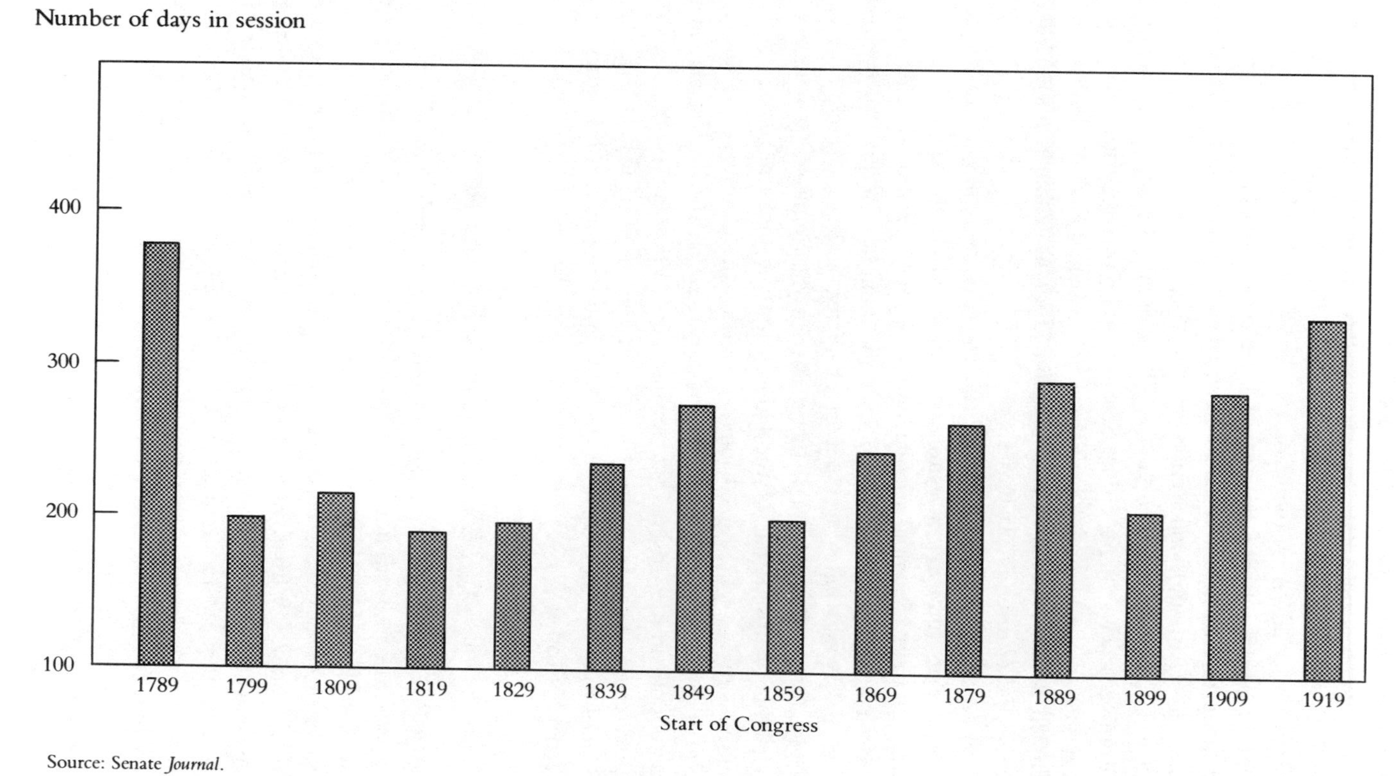

Source: Senate *Journal*.

views about appropriate institutional arrangements did not reveal an underlying consensus about the collective interests of the Senate.

Still, relatively little attention was paid to activity in the Senate in its first decades. Even by the second session of the Eighth Congress (1804–05) the Senate received only about 1 percent of nonelection news coverage in the prominent *National Intelligencer*, whereas the House accounted for 27 percent.[55] Although nonelection news coverage of the Senate had increased to 9 percent by 1829, the House still accounted for nearly 32 percent in prominent newspapers.[56] The Senate was ignored physically as well. In contrast to the House's "handsome" chamber, the room the Senate occupied in Washington in 1807 was noted for its falling timbers, leaking roof, and crumbling plaster.[57]

In this environment of low visibility, senators were unlikely to feel public pressure to filibuster measures they opposed. It would also have been difficult to use potential popular support for their positions to gain concessions from a chamber majority. Even the thought of seeking such external support would have been out of character, at least as far as the early Federalists were concerned. In contrast to the traditional Senate (whose visibility eclipsed that of the House) and the modern Senate (with its ample supply of organized interests outside the chamber), conditions in the original Senate provided few incentives for obstructing legislation and few opportunities to hold the Senate's agenda hostage to one's legislative preferences. As a result, floor practices in the early Senate bear little resemblance to either the Senate of the mid- and late nineteenth century or the Senate of today.

Floor Practices in the Early Senate

It is difficult, given the lack of reporting on early Senate business, to reconstruct in detail floor practices in the early Senate. With such a small workload and membership (averaging fewer than thirty-four senators for its first twenty years), there seems to have been little competition for access to the floor.[58] With the permission of the chamber (granted either by a majority vote or unanimous consent), senators could introduce bills, which, along with reports, were usually considered on the floor in the order in which they were reported. At times, however, the Senate did vote by majority to make some exceptions to this practice. In some instances senators would even specify a particular day for consideration of a specific measure.[59] But without formal leadership positions to set an agenda, the Senate's agenda as a whole moved in no particular direction.

Over the course of any given session, the Senate's legislative agenda was instead routinely influenced by the legislative pace and actions of the House. As early as the Second Congress some senators even proposed a joint House–Senate committee to parcel out legislative assignments to the two chambers, a proposal intended to distribute legislative work more evenly, both between the chambers and across the session.[60] Senators, reacting to the lack of business early in the session and the small logjam at the end, were rebuffed by the House, which no doubt resented the Senate's attempt to infringe on its institutional independence.[61] In any case, the size of the logjam at the close of any Congress was relatively small, legislative loads being so light in the first place.

What is striking about floor procedure in the original Senate, but perhaps not surprising, is that members seemed to have made little or no use of the procedural strategies employed by supporters and opponents of legislation certainly by the mid-1800s. Although senators today consider unanimous consent agreements essential to the deliberate character of the Senate, its leaders in the early period showed no signs of resorting to such time limitation agreements to govern legislative business on the floor.[62] And, as mentioned earlier, there is also no evidence that opponents of legislation routinely sought to exploit their rights of extended debate to prevent the chamber from casting votes on pending measures. If anything, restraint was the order of the day in those first two decades. Looking back on this period, Senator Willie Mangum (Whig of North Carolina) remarked in 1852: "In the older and better times of the Senate . . . it was supposed that the representatives of sovereign States, from a proper sense of what was due to themselves, as well as what was due to this body . . . would restrain themselves from the excessive use of irrelevant talking. Modern experience, however, has shown that this feeling, as a restraint, is utterly insufficient for the purpose of correcting this abuse."[63]

By the mid–nineteenth century, however, the Senate had begun to give way to the purposive exploitation of chamber rules. This is not to say that early senators were parliamentary angels. They were certainly not beyond trying to delay consideration of measures they opposed. Their creative use of the previous question motion has already been mentioned. Another common tactic used to delay Senate action was the motion to adjourn. When the frequency of dilatory motions to adjourn is compared with the frequency of filibustering in the nineteenth century, a striking pattern emerges (figure 2-5).[64] For the first two decades of the Senate, dilatory motions to adjourn never rose above 5 percent of the total number of roll-call votes taken. In the next two decades, dilatory motions accounted for

Figure 2-5. *Senate Obstructionism, by Congress, 1789–1992*

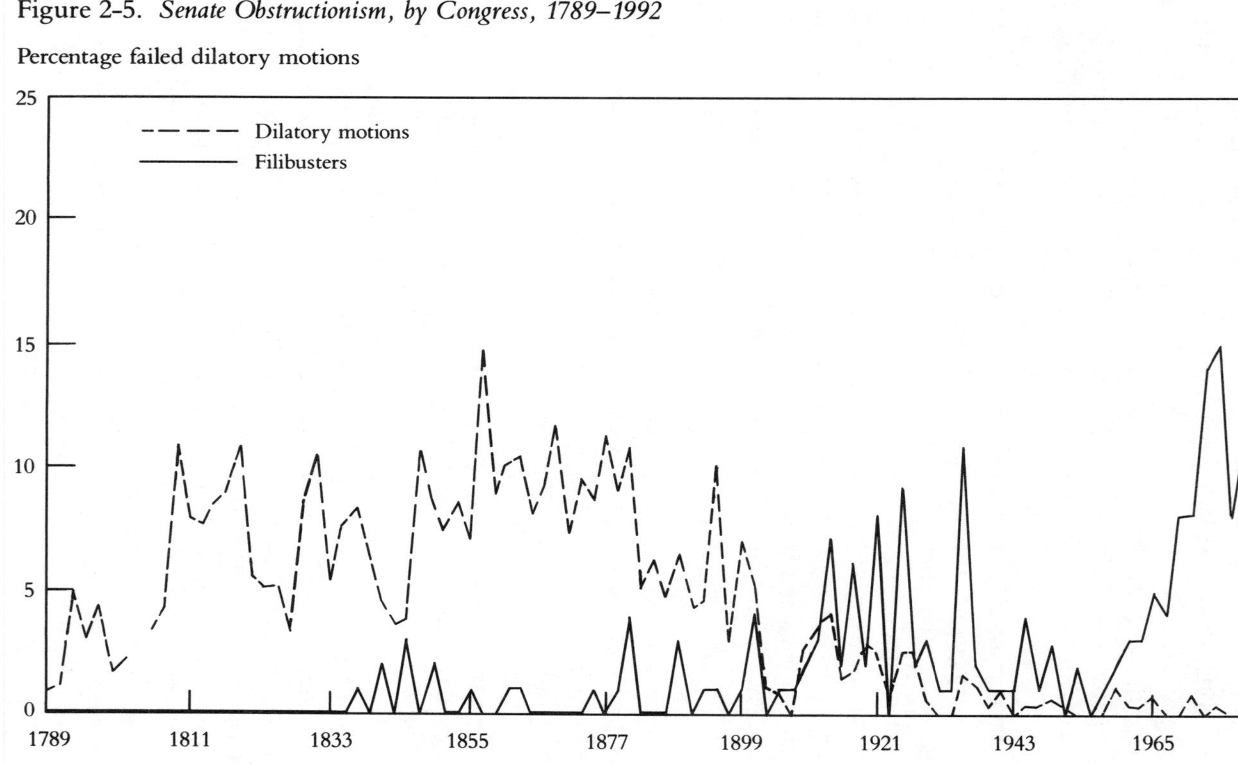

Source: Dilatory motions counted from Senate roll-call votes (ICPSR File #00004).

11 percent of the total votes during two Congresses that experienced particularly controversial legislation: the embargo bills against the British in the Eleventh Congress (1809–11) and the Missouri Compromise in the Sixteenth (1819–21). Even so, dilatory motions before the 1830s do not appear to have been unduly concentrated on particular measures, as was the case in the mid–nineteenth century. In the earlier period senators would offer only one or two such motions during the entire course of a controversial debate; by contrast, during the more partisan debates of the 1830s senators began offering repeated motions to adjourn during consideration of controversial measures.[65]

The general absence of blatant obstructionism is difficult to interpret, given the lack of contemporary commentary on the procedural tactics used in those early years. It may be that some norm of restraint prevailed: senators may have assumed a civil and orderly consideration of pending bills and expected that final votes would be cast, even on controversial legislation. It seems likely, however, that practical considerations, as much as norms, influenced senators' behavior. Given a relatively uncrowded agenda in the Senate, efforts to delay floor consideration of legislative business were much less likely to succeed. With few other measures pending, senators would no doubt have felt little pressure to either shelve disputed bills or make concessions to speed their consideration on the floor.

Moreover, voting alignments in the early Senate were never as polarized as they were in the House, and thus senators probably felt little incentive to exploit their procedural prerogatives. From the Eleventh through the Seventeenth Congresses (1809–23), for example, the level of partisan differences was generally lower in the Senate than in the House (figure 2-6). This was especially true for the war Congresses (Eleventh through Thirteenth) between 1809 and 1815. It was during that period that the Republican House majority moved to tighten procedural rules in its interests by revamping the previous question rule. As noted earlier, however, no such changes occurred in the Senate. Indeed, "it may well be argued that it would have taken at least as severe a set of experiences as the House underwent before the Senate would have allowed cloture to be imposed on its minorities."[66] The low public visibility of Senate floor activity would have further reduced the incentive for its members to alter or exploit the chamber's rules.

No doubt, norms, working conditions, and political interests provided reinforcing constraints on members of the original Senate. Knowing that legislation would be considered in an orderly and dignified manner, unable to manipulate the floor because of the small agenda, holding only mildly

Figure 2-6. *Comparison of House and Senate Partisan Differences, 1789–1823*

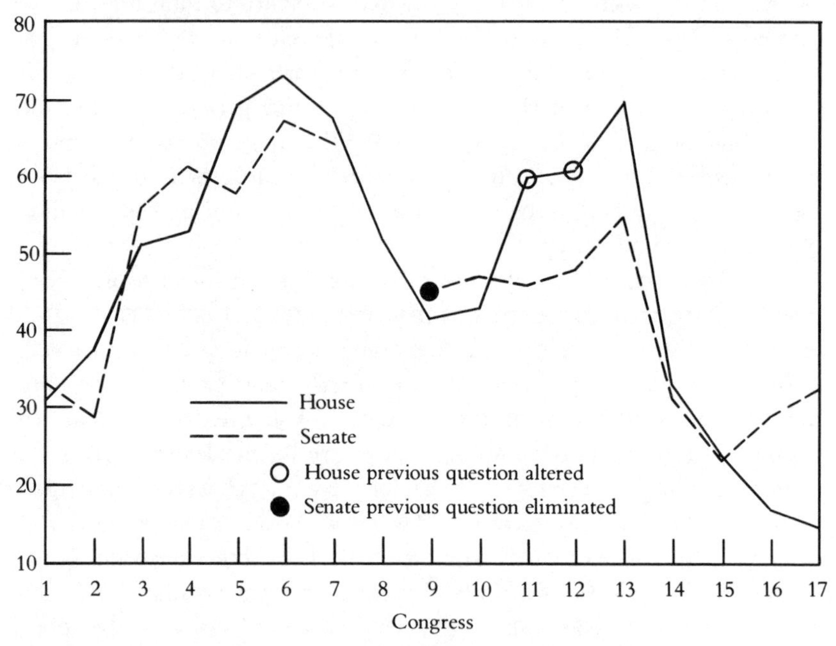

Source: Calculated from ICPSR roll-call data (File #00004). 8th Senate data indefinitely unavailable from ICPSR.

polarized views for much of the period, and insulated from public pressures, early senators would have felt little incentive—and many disincentives—to exploit chamber rules to pursue policy or other objectives. As a result, there were none of the glorious debates that the Senate would later become famous for, and certainly none of the filibusters. By and large, senators had little trouble coming to a final vote on salient matters. Even without a previous question rule after 1806, they managed their agenda with little recourse to the obstructive tactics that would emerge among the partisan tensions of the mid–nineteenth century.

Conclusions

Floor strategies in the Senate's first decades bear little resemblance to practices that developed toward the middle of the nineteenth century. Contrary to conventional views about the traditions of the Senate, senators seemed to assume that final votes—even on contentious legislation—would be taken as a matter of course, capping consideration of measures on the floor. Had senators negotiated unanimous consent agreements to govern bill consideration on the floor, it might be inferred that they were willing to push the rules to their limits and to exploit their rights to obstruct debate. The lack of recognizable filibusters, repeated dilatory motions, or time limitation agreements suggests that no such problems plagued the original Senate.

Furthermore, senators assumed that approval of legislation would require no more than a simple majority vote. There is no evidence that supermajorities were envisioned by the framers nor demanded by the first senators in order to ensure that the Senate could temper immoderate legislation passed by House. In fact, the available evidence concerning the framers' views strongly suggests just the opposite. Requiring supermajorities for passage of legislation would protect the narrow interests of minorities at the expense of reasoned and representative majorities in Congress. The delegates to the Constitutional Convention knew full well from their experiences in the Continental Congresses that requiring supermajorities was a recipe for stalemate and indecision.

By the middle of the nineteenth century, however, a different policymaking environment had taken hold. With increases in the size and workload of the chamber, the emergence of highly polarized voting alignments (along both sectional and partisan lines), and the broader visibility of the upper chamber, the mix of incentives and constraints on senators began to shift. Far from depressing the incentives to exploit their procedural rights, the new mix of forces set the stage for a more assertive Senate membership, turning obstructionism into a less costly and more rewarding strategy for opposing undesired legislation. Not surprisingly, changes in the policymaking environment also brought calls for stricter limits on Senate debate. It seems that principled institutional commitments to free speech and minority rights were not as embedded in Senate tradition as is commonly claimed. Chapter 3 turns to these new parliamentary strategies and senators' periodic attempts to reverse them.

All-star senators of the nineteenth century.

3

Senate Tradition Revisited

HAVING OUTGROWN the chamber that had served its needs for nearly half a century, the Senate in 1859 took possession of a new legislative hall at the north end of the U.S. Capitol. Minutes before proceeding to their new wing, senators of the Thirty-Fifth Congress gathered in their old chamber to hear the remarks of their presiding officer, Vice President John Breckinridge. His observations provide a striking account of the changing character of the Senate at midcentury:

> At the origin of the Government, the Senate seemed to be regarded chiefly as an executive council. The President often visited the Chamber and conferred personally with this body; most of its business was transacted with closed doors, and it took comparatively little part in the legislative debates. The rising and vigorous intellects of the country sought the arena of the House of Representatives as the appropriate theater for the display of their powers. . . . [S]o late as 1812, the great debates which preceded the war and aroused the country to the assertion of its rights, took place in the other branch

Senators, left to right from the top: Nelson Aldrich, William Allison, Henry Anthony, Thomas Hart Benton, Jesse Bright, John Calhoun, Lewis Cass, Henry Clay, Stephen Douglas, George Edmonds, Arthur Gorman, William Rufus King, Henry Cabot Lodge, Willie Mangum, Ambrose Sevier, John Sherman, Charles Sumner, Lyman Trumbull, Daniel Webster.

> of Congress. . . . But now, the Senate . . . assumes its full share of duty as a coequal branch of the Legislature; indeed, from the limited number of its members, and for other obvious reasons, the most important questions, especially of foreign policy, are apt to pass first under discussion in this body, and to be a member of it is justly regarded as one of the highest honors which can be conferred on an American statesman.[1]

By 1859 the transformation of the Senate from its original to its traditional form was well under way. The quiet, often secretive, revisory council envisioned by the framers and nurtured by the first senators now served as a highly visible forum for the great debates over slavery and national expansionism in nineteenth-century America.

Conventional treatments of Senate politics glorify the mid–nineteenth century as the "golden age of the Senate," an era in which filibusters were reserved for the great issues of the day and senators of all political stripes cherished the tradition of extended debate.[2] These treatments misread a fundamental conflict in the nineteenth century over the nature and character of the Senate. Although most senators valued the freedom of debate, it was their short-term pragmatic political interests—and not their normative principles—that prevented adoption of rules to limit debate. Throughout the nineteenth century, reform-minded Senate leaders sought to bring some order to the conduct of Senate debate, but found themselves unable to counter obstructionist uses of the filibuster that allowed a minority to block changes in the rules. On both sides of the debates over institutional reform, political interests helped shape senators' views about appropriate rules of procedure: majorities—not always partisan ones—seeking policy change often advocated stricter limits on debate, and legislative minorities preferring the status quo opposed changes in the rules.

A case for reforming Rule 22 cannot be built without scrutinizing Senate tradition, since that tradition is what defenders of the filibuster invoke to block reform. In their view, changing chamber rules today would destroy the inherited character of the Senate.[3] These appeals to Senate tradition must be corrected to tell the full story. A more accurate account of the traditional Senate will suggest that old Senate rules collided with changing political conditions over the course of the nineteenth century, leaving the Senate poorly equipped by century's end to meet the escalating demands on its members and leading many of them to recognize that radical reform of the filibuster was overdue.

Contours of Senate Tradition

What is Senate "tradition"? For most observers, it usually refers to two aspects of legislative life that took root in the antebellum Senate: the ironclad protection of minority interests and enduring norms of comity and restraint. These two characteristics were said to reinforce each other; senators claimed that they needed no limits on debate because of the dignity and decorum with which they conducted themselves in their exchanges.[4] In contrast to the nineteenth-century House, whose partisan majorities eventually gained significant procedural powers over the minority and put a premium on swift action at the expense of minority rights, the Senate is usually described as an arena in which thoughtful deliberation of vexing issues was inherently and consistently fostered. Most important, defenders of the filibuster argue, that tradition would not have developed under rules limiting the right of extended debate. "Abolish closure," warned one, "and the Senate will gradually sink to the level of the House of Representatives where there is less deliberation and debate than in any other legislative assembly."[5]

Protecting Minority Interests

There was no single conception of minority interests at stake in the nineteenth-century Senate. At least in their rhetorical justification for opposing debate limits, senators suggested that the type of minority protected by the right of unlimited debate was immaterial. As suggested by Senator Jefferson Davis (Democrat of Mississippi) in 1851, such a parliamentary privilege was inseparable from the integrity of the constitutional system; lacking the right of unlimited debate in the Senate, a minority—however constituted—might be trampled under foot by a tyrannous majority. In opposing the effort by Henry Clay (Whig of Kentucky) to conclude consideration of a rivers and harbors appropriation bill in 1851, Davis asked his colleagues: "Is it unfair in a Government of limited powers, of a carefully devised system of checks and balances, and forms of proceeding designed to secure them, for a minority to resort to the parliamentary advantage which under the rules of the body they possess, to prevent a dominant majority from forcing upon them measures violative of their sense of right and constitutional opinions?"[6] The Senate, according to Davis and other senators before and after him, was simply a microcosm of the broader polity. If the framers intended to disperse and check political power, then by extension any minority in the Senate was justified in trying to temper or halt the designs of a dominant majority.

Not only were senators willing to read into the Constitution a veto power for Senate minorities, but many also claimed that individual senators themselves retained such power as a matter of constitutional privilege. Consider, for example, the reaction of Senator Thomas Hart Benton (Democrat of Missouri) to Clay's proposal in 1841 to limit Senate debate. "With respect to debates," Benton asserted, "Senators have a constitutional right to speak; and while they speak to the subject before the House, there is no power any where to stop them. It is a constitutional right. . . . I go against the things themselves—against the infringement of the right of speech—and against the annihilation of our legislative faculties by annihilating the right of making amendments."[7] A minority as small as one senator could read into the Constitution a fundamental right of unlimited debate.

The proclivity of members of Congress to claim that individuals and minorities had a constitutional right to free speech was not, of course, limited to members of the Senate. Members of the House as well were perfectly willing to assert such a parliamentary privilege.[8] But only senators, elected by state legislatures, could claim that protecting their right of unlimited debate directly protected the interests of the states against the power of the federal government. Indeed, in arguing that unlimited debate was essential to preserving minority rights, senators often meant that state or sectional interests were at stake. "It was objected that on one amendment seven speeches had been made on this side of the House," noted John C. Calhoun (Democrat of South Carolina) in 1841, during debate over Henry Clay's proposals to curb debate in the Senate. "And what if there were? Was it anything extraordinary in the fact that seven Senators from different parts of the Union should have different views and different interests to consider?"[9] The direct and equal representation of the states in the Senate gave senators a unique advantage over their colleagues in the House in claiming a constitutionally grounded right of extended debate.

Doctrine of the Concurrent Majority

It was Calhoun who drew together claims about protecting minority interests into a more focused theoretical argument. His doctrine of the concurrent majority bears note because it was Calhoun, along with other southern senators, who placed the protection of minority interests at the heart of Senate tradition. It is therefore difficult to separate southern senators' justification for their right of unlimited debate from Calhoun's theory of the concurrent majority. Under both, minority interests were to be protected from a potentially tyrannous majority. The aim, according to

Calhoun, was "to prevent any one interest, or combination of interests, from using the powers of government to aggrandize itself at the expense of the others"; the solution was to take "the sense of each interest or portion of the community [and to] give to each division or interest, through its appropriate organ, either a concurrent voice in making and executing the laws, or a veto on their execution."[10] Arguing that the states delegated only a portion of their political power to the federal government, Calhoun reasoned that any state could constitutionally call a convention to nullify any new law deemed counter to state interests. Just as a single senator on behalf of his state could exploit his procedural rights to prevent action on measures he opposed, a state, too, could interpose its will against that of a congressional majority.

Calhoun's theory was based on the distinction between two majorities: numerical and constitutional. The numerical majority, in Calhoun's view, assumed that a community had only a single interest throughout; therefore collecting the sense of a numerical majority of the community would be sufficient to gauge its interest. But if a community had multiple and conflicting interests, then a numerical majority tended toward absolute government; only by taking the sense of each portion's interest could the community decide the proper course of action without harming the interests of any section within it. In contrast to the numerical majority, the concurrent majority "compels the different interests, or portions, or orders, to compromise—as the only way to promote their respective prosperity."[11] To ensure such protection of minority interests, Calhoun reasoned that each section needed a veto over every other: "It is this mutual negative among its various conflicting interests, which invests each with the power of protecting itself—and places the rights and safety of each, where only they can be securely placed, under its own guardianship."[12] Unwilling to admit that there was any common national interest between the North and South, Calhoun could thus argue that the South's threat to secede was justified under the doctrine of the concurrent majority: the South was simply exercising the veto that was essential to establishing a concurrent and constitutional majority protective of southern interests.[13]

In defending minority rights, southern senators such as Calhoun had little interest in broadly protecting free speech. In a portrayal of Calhoun, one historian draws the distinction clearly:

> Not in the slightest was he concerned with minority rights as they are chiefly of interest to the modern liberal mind—the rights of dissenters to express unorthodox opinions, of the individual con-

> science against the State, least of all of ethnic minorities. At bottom he was not interested in any minority that was not a propertied minority. The concurrent majority itself was a device without relevance to the protection of dissent, but designed specifically to protect a vested interest of considerable power. Even within the South Calhoun had not the slightest desire to protect intellectual minorities, critics, and dissenters. . . . It was minority privileges rather than rights that he really proposed to protect. He wanted to give to the minority not merely a proportionate but an *equal* voice with the majority in determining public policy.[14]

Principles of free speech—seemingly unrelated to the decision to drop the previous question rule in 1806—once again cannot fully account for the persistence of procedural traditions in the nineteenth-century Senate. When the tradition of extended debate began to take form in the Senate, the most fully developed and probably decisive theoretical justification offered in its defense relied mainly on political interests and little on principles of free speech. Southerners, under the intellectual guidance of Calhoun, defended rules of debate that would best protect their interests: here, their region's interest in protecting a culture and economy based on slave labor.

Tradition and the Status Quo

At this point a word about the evolution of chamber practices into chamber traditions is in order. Not all practices become legislative traditions. By midcentury the parliamentary protection afforded minority interests in the Senate clearly had come to be considered an institutionalized practice of the chamber. As time passed, it arguably became easier for senators to defend their right of unlimited debate on the basis of tradition. Appeals to constitutional rights were, in effect, no longer necessary. The longer Senate rules remained unchanged, the stronger the basis for keeping them. Thus as early as 1841 senators could defend extended debate simply on the grounds that it was the well-worn practice of the Senate. "Was it fit or becoming, after fifty years of unrestrained liberty," asked William Rufus de Vane King (Democrat of Alabama), "to threaten it [the Senate] with a gag law?"[15] Fifty years later, "tradition" had gained all the more weight. As argued by Senator George Gray (Democrat of Delaware) on the floor in 1891 against a majority cloture proposal by Nelson Aldrich (Republican of Rhode Island), "It was a violation of all the precedents that have obtained in this body for a hundred years. Nothing had occurred in this body in the course of the debate upon the elections bill that was any warrant for turning back the current of history, violating American traditions, trespassing upon that liberty of all liberties . . . the freedom of speech in this body."[16] Tradition, one might argue, was simply a more lofty label for the procedural status quo.

Not all senators, however, believed that chamber practices were inviolable once they attained the status of "tradition." By 1850 some senators had begun to question whether chamber traditions were quite so untouchable. Consider the exchange between Daniel Dickinson (Democrat of New York) and Lewis Cass (Democrat of Michigan) over a proposal to allow the Senate to table amendments without killing the underlying bill. When Dickinson warned that he had "great distrust as to the propriety of invading any old parliamentary custom which has been practiced so long," Cass directly attacked his logic. "I think we have no right to say that we will not change it [parliamentary law] because it has been practiced in the House of Representatives and in the Senate," argued Cass. "We should make a rational inquiry into the matter, and not avow that we will support the present rule because it has been long in use."[17] Cass's argument was echoed some years later by George Wright (Republican of Iowa), who had sponsored a resolution directing the Rules Committee to consider the adoption of debate restrictions for the Senate: "It is said . . . that the policy and practice of the Senate have been, for sixty years, so and so. A great many things are quite as old as the matter to which Senators have referred that were better changed. If by our practice and experience here we do not improve, we live to but little purpose."[18]

With the emergence of the traditional Senate came numerous changes in the Senate's legislative environment. By century's end, the policymaking environment—both inside and outside the chamber—presented senators with a new set of incentives and constraints that in all likelihood affected their willingness to exploit their traditional procedural rights. Over the course of the nineteenth century, filibustering became a less costly and more attractive parliamentary strategy. At the same time, Senate leaders increasingly called into question institutional rules they had inherited from the past. These changing political conditions had a decided effect on senators' parliamentary strategies.

Legislating in the Traditional Senate

Perhaps because its procedural traditions seem so durable, popular portraits of the Senate tend to emphasize its unchanging and timeless character.

"To [the Senate] the movement of time is of time upon a belt; the yesterday that has just gone is just arriving," argued the *New York Times* chief congressional correspondent, William S. White, in 1957. "This is a body that never wholly changes and never quite dies . . . where the national past and the national future meet and soundlessly merge."[19] Despite such perceptions of the Senate's "timelessness," what is striking about the Senate's political environment in the nineteenth century is how little things stood still.[20] Few aspects of the Senate—from the size of its workload to the quality of air in its chamber—remained unchanged over the course of the nineteenth century. Far from being a timeless, unchanging body—the typical portrait of the traditional Senate—the chamber by century's end was a nearly unmanageable institution, one that many senators believed had forfeited much of its claim to being the world's greatest deliberative body.

Changes in the Senate's policymaking environment in the nineteenth century altered the set of incentives and constraints facing senators inside the chamber. Transformation of the Senate occurred along numerous dimensions: the scope of the legislative agenda, the physical environment of the Senate, the character of electoral pressures, and the alignment of partisan preferences. These changes had the cumulative effect of making it easier and more rewarding for senators to exploit their procedural rights in pursuit of their legislative goals. Institutional rules and political interests—rather than closely held philosophical principles—seem to explain changes in senators' legislative styles in the nineteenth century.

Parliamentary Strategies in the Traditional Senate

Although the filibuster is commonly taken to be a central component of Senate tradition, there is considerable variation in the frequency and intensity of filibustering over the course of the nineteenth century. During the pre–Civil War Senate, relatively few filibusters were undertaken. Only nine filibusters are on record for this period, six of which occurred between 1845 and 1860 (figure 3-1). Filibustering remained sporadic until the 1880s, after which almost every Congress began to experience at least one bout of obstructionism. Not only did filibusters become more commonplace by the end of the century, but they were also more likely to succeed. Of the thirteen filibusters between 1837 and 1879, only four were successful (31 percent); of the thirty filibusters between 1880 and the adoption of Rule 22 in 1917, sixteen were successful (53 percent).[21] Clearly, the last two decades of the nineteenth century were measurably different from the decades that

Figure 3-1. *Frequency of Filibusters in the Traditional Senate, 1831–1917*

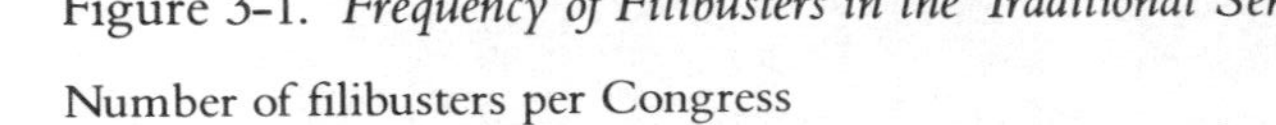

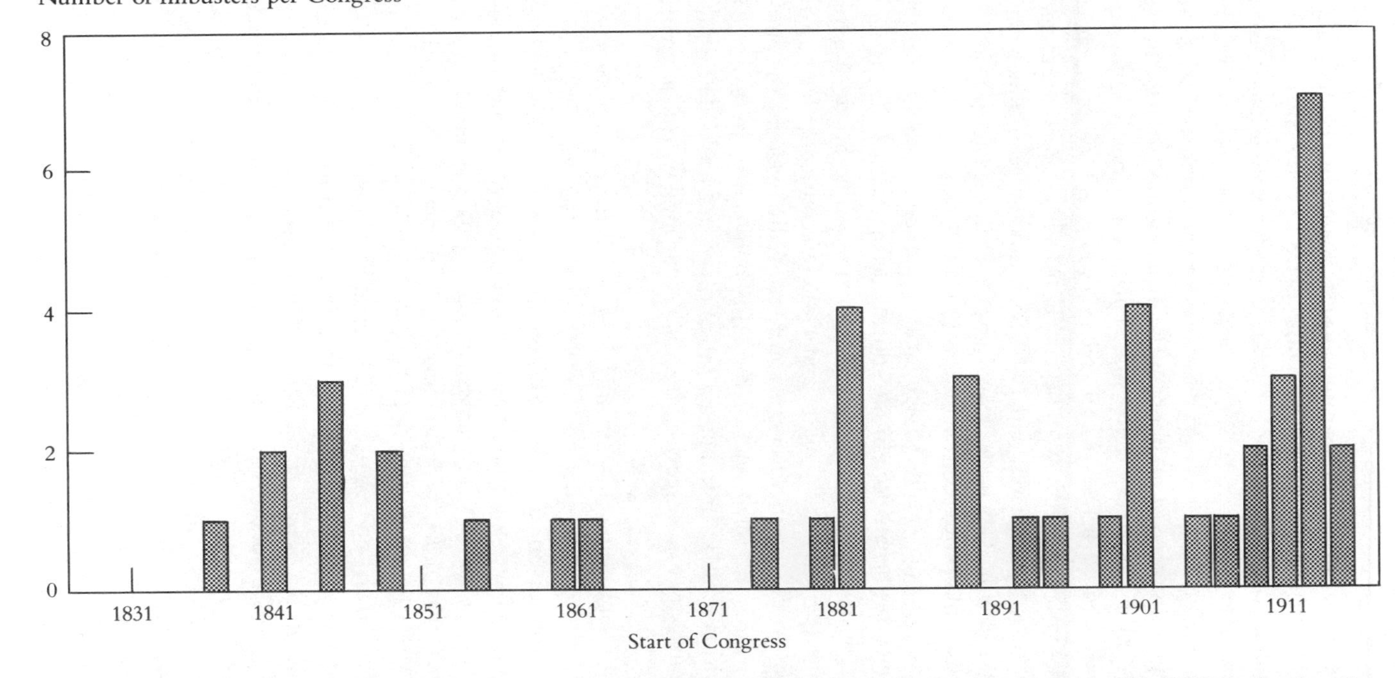

Sources: Franklin Burdette, *Filibustering in the Senate* (Princeton University Press, 1940); Richard S. Beth, "Filibusters in the Senate, 1789–1993," Memorandum, Congressional Research Service, February 18, 1994. See also note 15, p. 220.

preceded them, enough so to be described as a period of unrestrained filibustering.[22]

Even before the number of filibusters increased near the end of the century, senators had already become more inventive in their efforts to obstruct legislative majorities. In addition to presenting long speeches and offering endless amendments, senators exploited their right to offer motions to adjourn in an effort to force the majority to postpone action, at times staying in session past midnight as the majority tried to make progress on favored measures (recall figure 2-5). Dilatory motions to adjourn, which had exceeded 10 percent of all roll-call votes only twice in the twenty Congresses before 1831, were beyond 10 percent in nearly a quarter of the Congresses between 1831 and 1900. Such motions fell below 5 percent of all votes in only 20 percent of the Congresses in the later period. Dilatory motions could prove decisive in defeating a bill, particularly if undertaken at the close of a session. As Lyman Trumbull (Republican of Illinois) argued on the Senate floor in 1865 during debate over whether to recognize the Reconstruction government of Louisiana, "The Senate was ready to vote upon it on Saturday night, and a vote was only prevented by dilatory motions made . . . in a factious spirit, avowedly made for the purpose of delay. . . . I ask, shall one third of this body be permitted by factious opposition to delay an important bill of this character?"[23] In this instance, the strategy proved successful: Louisiana statehood was not approved until 1868.[24]

The disappearing-quorum trick—in which the minority would refuse to be counted for a quorum, thereby often preventing a majority of the Senate from casting a vote—was another favored tool of legislative minorities in the nineteenth-century Senate. In 1856, during a filibuster over the admission of the state of Kansas, majority senators complained that the minority was unfairly obstructing Senate business. The Senate, noted James Bayard Jr. (Democrat of Delaware), has "always supposed that every Senator who was present would, when necessary for the purpose of making a quorum, record his vote. There is no doubt that it is a plain violation of the rule of the Senate for a Senator to refuse to vote when he is not excused."[25] Senators had also discovered that they could exploit the rules at the end of the session to prevent action on measures they opposed, aided by the Senate's adjournment at a time and date certain. For the twenty-nine filibusters between 1880 and 1917 for which data are available on timing and outcomes, for example, end-of-session filibusters were markedly more successful than those that occurred earlier in the session (table 3-1).[26]

The "golden age" of the Senate then was short, and those who lived

Table 3-1. *Effect of Timing on Filibuster Success, 1880–1917*

Filibuster outcome	*End of session?*	
	Yes	*No*
Success	11	5
Failure	2	11

Source: Success rates compiled from Franklin Burdette, *Filibustering in the Senate* (Princeton University Press, 1940), chaps. 3–4.

through it did not necessarily like it. Had filibustering truly reflected a principled commitment to free speech, it seems unlikely that there would have been such variation in senators' behavior over time or such innovation in their legislative obstructionism. This variation could not have been due to the appearance of more divisive issues alone. Slavery-related measures that were not filibustered before the Civil War were certainly as divisive as measures filibustered after it. Also probably influencing parliamentary strategies at this time were several changes in the Senate's policymaking environment.

Increased Incentives for Obstructionism

As noted in chapter 2, the original Senate, with its uncrowded agenda, low visibility, and generally low levels of party division, did not encourage senators to manipulate chamber rules to their advantage or to obstruct the legislative agenda. By 1859, however, the legislative role of the Senate had changed significantly. No longer a simple revisory body, the Senate's legislative profile increased measurably throughout the first few decades of the nineteenth century. Some even said that the Senate had become not only the more visible but also the more capable of the two chambers.[27] As the Senate load grew larger and more visible, senators had more incentive to exploit their parliamentary rights.

One sign that the agenda had become far more crowded and individual senators more active was that the Senate spent more time in session after the Civil War than before (see figure 2-4). In the Sixth Congress (1799–1801), the Senate spent 198 days in session; in the Fifty-First Congress (1889–91), 291 days.[28] In addition, Senators on average gradually introduced more public and private bills per Congress, peaking at nearly 120 per senator in the Sixty-First Congress (1909–11) (figure 3-2). The actual number of bills passed by the Senate increased as well. The number nearly doubled between 1800 and 1840, doubled again by 1870, and doubled once more by 1890 (figure 3-3); whereas the Senate had passed fewer than a hundred public bills in the First Congress, the number had climbed to more than eight hundred in the Fifty-First.[29] Longer sessions and increased

Figure 3-2. *Rate of Bill Introduction in the Traditional Senate, 1847–1919*

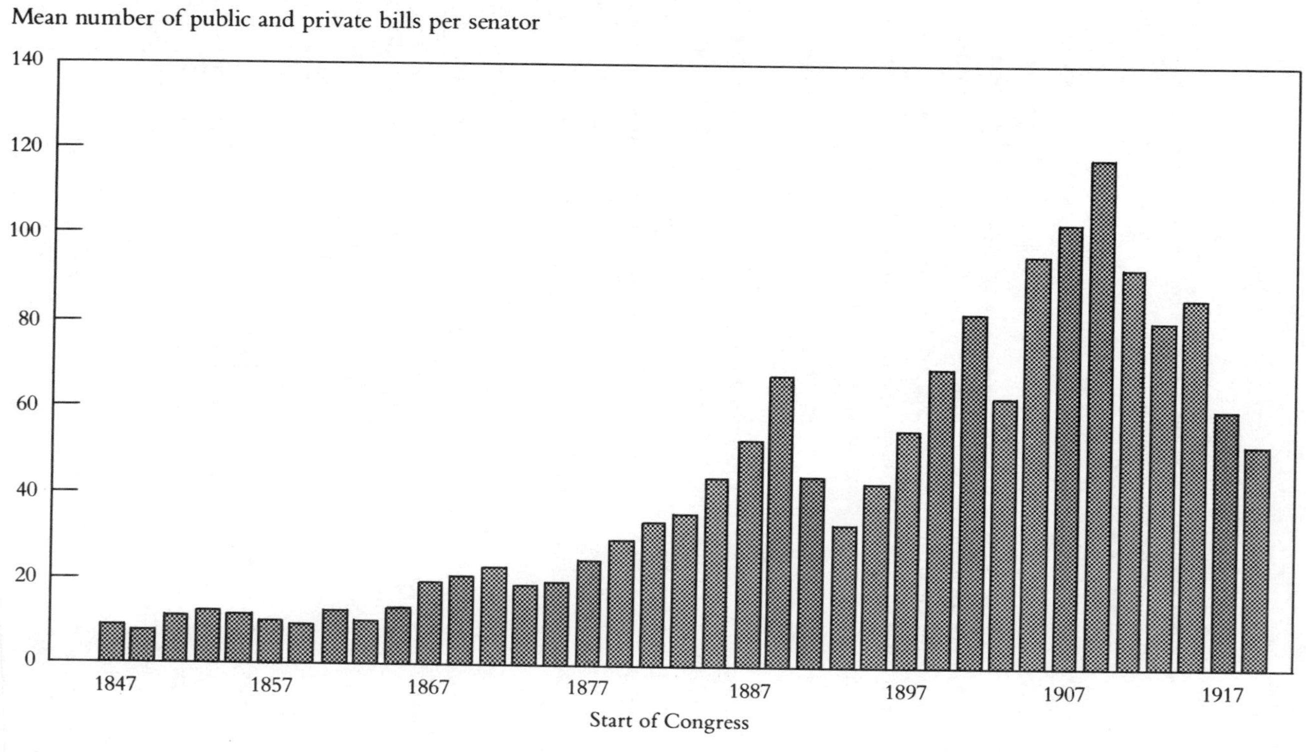

Source: Senate *Journals*. See note 29, page 228.

Figure 3-3. *Legislative Activity in the Senate, Selected Congresses, 1789–1909*

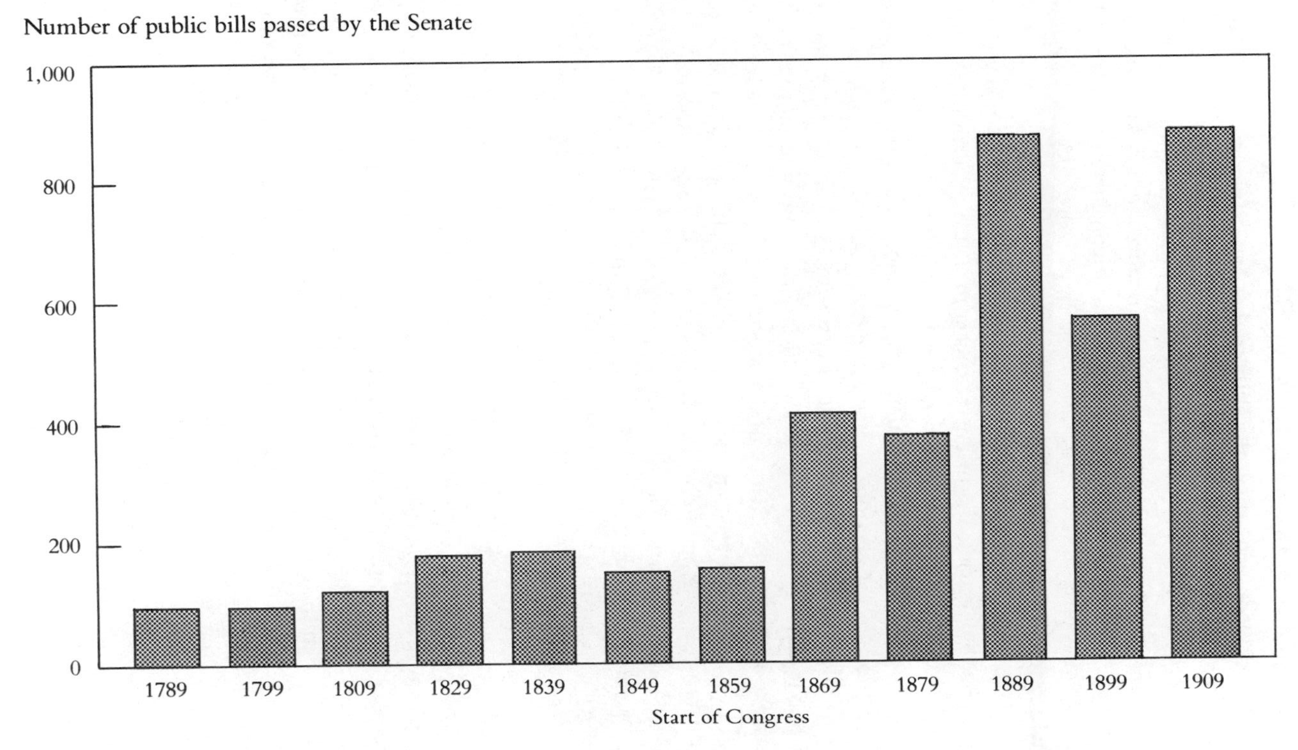

Source: Senate *Journals*. See note 29, page 228.

legislative loads brought many more demands for recorded roll-call votes (figure 2-3). Over the first forty years of the Senate, roll-call votes averaged around 150 votes per Congress; over the next forty years, more than 500 votes were cast on average in each Congress.[30]

In an environment of significantly higher legislative activity, the opportunity and ease of filibustering clearly increased. A larger agenda meant that there were simply more measures to filibuster. And an expanding workload meant that obstructionism had more bite. Taking the Senate hostage, whether to kill a bill or to gain floor consideration of some other favored measure, was significantly easier and more effective in a policy-making environment in which Senate leaders had a sizable unfinished agenda at stake. Senator John Sherman (Republican of Ohio) suggested as much in 1865 during the filibuster over a measure to recognize the post–Civil War government of Louisiana. "Let me state the condition of the public business," pleaded Sherman: "At this hour we are within five days of the close of the session, and we have not acted upon a single appropriation bill finally. . . . Under these circumstances I cannot, with my sense of public duty, allow the Louisiana question to consume more time. . . . I have looked into the history of the sessions of Congress for several years, and I do not find that at any period there was such a vast accumulation of public measures demanding attention as there is during this week."[31] End-of-session filibustering clearly became a more formidable tool of legislative opponents as the press of public business climbed sharply throughout the nineteenth century.

Reduced Disincentives to Obstruct

Complaints about conditions in the Capitol led senators to renovate their chamber several times during the nineteenth century. These changes probably reduced the disincentive to obstructionism in the antebellum Senate. An expanding workload had meant, of course, that senators spent more time in the chamber as the years wore on. Today, senators can work through the night and through hot, humid Washington summers in relative comfort. This was certainly not the case in the nineteenth century, at least until the Senate moved into a larger chamber in 1859 with its state-of-the-art ventilating system.[32]

A debate in 1833 over whether to cancel the daily recess from 3:00 to 5:00 P.M. in order to avoid an evening session reveals much about toiling in the Senate before the days of ventilation and electricity. Henry Clay often found it "impossible to breathe the impure air of the Senate Chamber after dinner," while Calhoun saw the evening sessions as "a great inconvenience to members" because of the bad atmosphere, which could produce "serious injury to health."[33] One senator blamed his poor performance in the Senate on the "mephitic air" there. "Out of that hall I feel I have the power to do it," explained Senator James Hammond (Democrat of South Carolina). "In it, I am stupefied by the infernal air."[34] Such an environment could hardly have been conducive to filibusterous tactics with much regularity or intensity.

Despite the installation of a new ventilating system in 1859, senators continued to complain that the chamber was an "unhealthy, uncomfortable, ill-contrived place" injurious to one's health.[35] Since the chamber lacked windows that opened to the outside, senators were unable to draw in fresh sources of air. In very hot weather "sessions of the Senate held in a chamber that has no window opening outdoors makes a stay of six hours in it very oppressive," noted Senator Benjamin Harrison (Republican of Indiana).[36] Even so, it was not until the early 1890s that significant technological changes were made in the ventilation of the Senate chamber that measurably improved working conditions there.[37] This increased comfort in the chamber might have contributed to the take-off in filibustering at the turn of the century.[38]

In the new and noticeably larger chamber—built to accommodate a growing and geographically dispersed membership—senators' interactions with one another probably also became increasingly impersonal. In such an atmosphere, senators would not have been as reluctant to be obstructive as they were in the informal and intimate chamber of old. Furthermore, whereas oratory had flourished in the intimate grandeur of the old hall, in the new chamber—vast and acoustically poor—a new style of debate emerged.[39] The Senate was certainly no longer a small group of men gathered around a fire, as accounts of the early Senate suggest. As the Senate became larger and more impersonal, informal restraints on obstructionism likely weakened as well.

Electoral Pressures

The increased visibility and prestige of the Senate and its members as the century wore on were bound to affect senators' parliamentary strategies inside the chamber. Unlike the original Senate, whose members seemed to have prized their distance from public opinion, the traditional Senate had a much more visible public profile. Between 1829 and 1841, major political newspapers for the first time gave the House and Senate nearly equal nonelection news coverage.[40] Also, around the time of the Civil War senators gradually began to earn some independence from state legislatures.[41] First, the use of legislative instructions to senators had all but disappeared by the 1840s, thereby reducing the leverage of state legislators over their respective senators. Second, the development of mass political parties brought a new claim on one's legislative position: reelection became increasingly dependent on a senator's ability to please state partisans.

Increased contact between senators and their constituencies is seen most clearly in the rise of the public canvass after the 1830s.[42] Senators used to canvass to campaign for state legislators who were essentially pledged to vote for them for the Senate. Before the 1830s, senators would only have canvassed state legislators after the election of the state legislature. Although the canvass appeared only sporadically starting in the 1830s, by the 1880s it had become a "regular feature of senatorial elections."[43]

The rise of the public canvass had important implications for senators' political constituencies. "Gradually," one student of the practice explains, "voters came to choose between rivals for the state legislature, not on the basis of their capabilities as lawmakers, but rather on the basis of the vote they would cast in senatorial elections."[44] By campaigning for state legislators, senators began developing their own electoral bases outside the state legislature. Such popular bases of support certainly helped build the public profile of the Senate. By the end of the century senators' interests were more closely tied with those of their state constituencies than those of the state legislatures that ostensibly elected them. Thus the ratification of the Seventeenth Amendment in 1913 mandating direct election of the Senate essentially cemented a trend that had been under way for several decades.

Unlike the original Senate, which had shielded itself from public attention, senators by 1900 had developed a significant public audience for their actions within the chamber. Exploiting parliamentary rights in pursuit of legislative victories arguably became a more attractive strategy as senators' electoral fortunes became more tightly linked with the preferences of their state constituencies.

Alignment of Preferences and Chamber Partisanship

By the close of the nineteenth century, partisanship in both the House and Senate had become increasingly intense. In nearly half the Congresses between 1889 and the introduction of Rule 22 in 1917, partisan differences had risen beyond 60 percent.[45] By contrast, only 15 percent were above that threshold between 1837 and 1889. This marked shift in senate preferences was accompanied by more filibusters, as well as by more efforts to counter them. At least eight resolutions imposing various types of debate limits in the Senate were proposed in the Fifty-First Congress alone (1889–91).[46]

By 1915 the filibuster had clearly become a tool to protect distinctly partisan interests, as pointed out by Senator Robert Owen (Democrat of Oklahoma): "I call attention to the large calendar, which we have . . . representing hundreds of measures of importance, which we never arrive at; and even aside from the calendar there are matters of the greatest possible importance, which are not being considered by the body . . . because it is well known that to make reports upon them would be perfectly useless in view of this now apparently well-established custom of a continuous filibuster against everything desired by the majority party."[47] This parliamentary strategy had been tried only intermittently before, primarily by the minority party during Whig-Democrat debates over fiscal and land policies in the 1830s and 1840s.[48] As noted earlier, however, filibusters were far more prevalent and successful after 1890. Coupled with the increased workload and expanded visibility of the Senate, partisan conditions in the Senate after 1890 appear to have fueled filibustering of "astounding proportions."[49]

Intense partisanship had also become a feature of House politics and was helping to centralize that chamber under the majority party. By 1900 the Speaker and the Rules Committee had nearly complete control of the agenda on the House floor. But no such centralization took place in the Senate, as filibusters against proposed debate limits in both 1890 and 1893 forced reformers to abandon efforts to impose procedural limits on the right of extended debate. Once House minority parties lost their easy means of obstructing the majority after the adoption of the restrictive Reed Rules in 1890—for instance, by offering dilatory motions or refusing to be counted for a quorum—obstructionism in the Senate became all the more imperative, especially during periods of unified government. Partisanship, in other words, had different manifestations in the two chambers directly as a result of their contrasting institutional contexts.[50] Inherited rules allowed majority parties to dominate outcomes in the House, while easily permitting minority vetoes in the Senate.

During the nineteenth century marked changes took root in the Senate's legislative ways. New working conditions and shifting political interests altered parliamentary responsibilities. Any norm of restraint that had flourished in the early Senate was severely strained by the end of the century. Where senators had earlier functioned as ambassadors of the states, now that diplomatic sensibility had all but disappeared. That measures would be brought to a final vote or that a simple majority would suffice to act on controversial bills could no longer be taken for granted. In response to these changes in their political environment, senators turned increasingly to exploit their parliamentary rights to secure legislative and political victories.

Tradition Viewed from Within

In our view, Senate tradition looks very different from what its defenders have led us to believe. A critical question remains. How did nineteenth-century senators see Senate tradition? We argue that our reconstruction of Senate tradition is not simply a function of hindsight. There is instead evidence that many nineteenth-century senators were frustrated with inherited practices and were openly critical of Senate practice. Many of the most notable senators of the nineteenth century held a more critical view of Senate tradition and moreover sought to change it. Although the lack of votes on reform makes it difficult to determine how Senate majorities viewed the filibuster, the fact that reforms were not adopted cannot be taken as support for the filibuster. In place of radical reform, chamber leaders turned to incremental adjustments to manage the Senate.

"Great Senators" and Extended Debate

Indeed, one must look to the chamber leaders to understand the forces at play in Senate tradition. By virtue of either their seniority or their long-term commitment to the Senate's institutional interests, these leaders should have reflected, if anyone did, the prevailing views about Senate tradition and the practice of unlimited debate. Most notable among them in the nineteenth-century Senate debates were the "Great Triumvirate": Henry Clay, John C. Calhoun, and Daniel Webster. Their procedural preferences provide a good first indication of how institutional giants perceived the rules and practices under which they forged legislation. If they preferred rules making it easier to limit debate, a reasonable inference is that something besides a commitment to minority rights and free speech underpinned their views about desirable institutional arrangements.

Table 3-2 presents a survey of nineteen recognizably great nineteenth-century senators, ten from the period before the Civil War and nine from the period after. The list reflects the judgments of a nineteenth-century congressional observer, modern U.S. senators, and prominent political historians. It consists in part of senators who were "prominent upon the Senate's floor" when legislative crises were pending. When they spoke, as one historian has noted, the Senate listened.[51] Some names are also drawn from the report of a select Senate committee chaired by John F. Kennedy in 1959 (Democrat of Massachusetts), which had been charged with selecting the five "outstanding senators" whose portraits would be hung in the Senate Reception Room. Kennedy polled former presidents, sitting and former senators, and political historians to determine those in whom the "high traditions of the Senate [are] best exemplified."[52] A list of ten greatest senators compiled by political historians polled in 1982 provided an additional name (Charles Sumner) for our list.[53] And three others (Benton, Aldrich, and Henry Cabot Lodge) were included because of their appearance in notable accounts of the nineteenth-century Congress.[54] Seven of the nineteen senators once served as president pro tempore of the Senate—another potential sign of their affinity for the Senate as an institution and its traditions.[55]

Most striking about the list is the preponderance of senators who clearly favored reforming the Senate tradition of unlimited debate. In the pre–Civil War period, positions on Senate debate can be established for seven senators: four are clearly on record as being in favor of imposing limits on Senate debate. Senators Clay and Stephen Douglas (Democrat of Illinois), although members of opposing political parties, both sought to create a previous question motion to empower a Senate majority to cut off debate. "Far from the rule being condemned," Clay would venture to say in 1841, "it would be generally approved. It was the means of controlling the business, abridging long and unnecessary speeches, and would every where be hailed as one of the greatest improvement[s] of the age."[56] Other proposals included one supported by Willie Mangum to ban debate on motions to proceed to legislative business, Mangum having declared that the "desire for much speaking" had "become almost a complete nuisance" in the Senate.[57] Even William King, who had opposed Clay's previous question proposal in 1841, conceded in 1848 that the minority had an obligation to fold once a strong chamber majority had formed.[58] No less an ardent foe of debate limits than John C. Calhoun led the fight in favor of the "gag law," a Senate rule adopted in 1836 to prevent consideration and discussion of abolition petitions. Only

Table 3-2. *Great Nineteenth-Century Senators on the Right of Extended Debate*

Period	*Senator*	*Position on debate limits*
Pre–Civil War	Thomas Hart Benton (D-Missouri)	Opposed debate limits in 1841: "When the previous question shall be brought into this chamber . . . I am ready to see my legislative life terminated."
	Jesse Bright (D-Indiana)	
	John C. Calhoun (D-South Carolina)	Opposed debate limits in 1841 but led the fight for the gag law in 1836 that prohibited the receipt and discussion of abolition petitions on the Senate floor. Also voted in favor of revamping the previous question motion into a tool for suppressing debate when he served in the House in 1811.
	Lewis Cass (D-Michigan)	Voted in 1852 to allow a majority to lay amendments on the table without killing the underlying bill. Stated in 1852 that "it is absolutely essential . . . that a power should exist with the majority by which at times they shall force to a determination important public measures." Supported proposed rule change in 1856 to confine senators to the question under debate.
	Henry Clay (W-Kentucky)	Sponsored proposals to impose a one-hour debate limit on senators and to create a previous question motion in the Senate in 1841.
	Stephen Douglas (D-Illinois)	Sponsored proposal to create a previous question motion in the Senate in 1850.
	William Rufus deVane King (D-Alabama)	Opposed debate limits in 1841 but voted to prohibit debate on motions to proceed in 1851. Also stated in 1848 that the minority had an obligation to fold in presence of a determined majority: "He . . . appealed to his friends . . . who could not be more opposed to the bill in its current shape than he was—to let the rules be suspended, that this bill . . . might go to the president."
	Willie Mangum (W-North Carolina)	Voted to prohibit debate on motions to proceed in 1851. Stated in 1852 that "this 'desire for much speaking' has become almost a complete nuisance in this body. . . . We must . . . resort to some mode of arresting this eternal talking."
	Ambrose Sevier (D-Arkansas)	
	Daniel Webster (W-Massachusetts)	

Post–Civil War	Nelson Aldrich (R-Rhode Island)	Proposed majority cloture rule to limit debate in 1891.
	William Allison (R-Iowa)	Voted to instruct the Rules Committee to consider a rule permitting debate limits in the Senate in 1873 (but stated that he opposed debate limits). Paired in favor of proceeding to consider a majority cloture motion in 1891. Proposed debate limits on appropriations bills in 1885 and 1890.
	Henry Anthony (R-Rhode Island)	Voted to instruct the Rules Committee to consider a rule permitting debate limits in the Senate in 1873. Author of the Anthony Rule imposing debate limits on noncontroversial bills.
	George Edmunds (R-Vermont)	Voted to proceed to consideration of a majority cloture motion in 1891.
	Arthur Gorman (D-Maryland)	Voted against proceeding to consider a majority cloture motion in 1891.
	Henry Cabot Lodge (R-Massachusetts)	Supported proposal to permit majority cloture in 1893. Stated in 1893 that "there is another right more sacred in a legislative body than the right of debate, and that is the right to vote. . . . To vote without debating may be hasty, may be ill considered, may be rash; but to debate and never vote is imbecility."
	John Sherman (R-Ohio)	Voted to instruct the Rules Committee to consider a rule permitting debate limits in the Senate in 1873. Voted to proceed to consideration of a majority cloture motion in 1891. Argued in 1873: "That we must change our rules is to me a matter of clear necessity. . . . The practice that has grown up in the Senate of engaging in desultory debate about everything in the world, when we have a specific proposition before us, is an abuse that ought to be corrected."
	Charles Sumner (R-Massachusetts)	Opposed debate limits in 1862 on measures considered in secret session during the Civil War, but noted that "if I saw any specific good surely to be accomplished by such a limitation . . . I certainly should be one of the last to hesitate."
	Lyman Trumbull (R-Illinois)	Opposed debate limits on appropriations bills in 1872 ("It is the beginning of striking down freedom of debate in the Senate of the United States"), but complained about dilatory tactics during a filibuster in 1865 ("Shall one third of this body be permitted by factious opposition to delay an important bill of this character?").

Sources: Senators' positions on reform were identified by surveying relevant floor debates on procedural reform in the *Congressional Globe* and *Congressional Record*, several secondary source accounts of those reform battles, and through their recorded floor votes (ICPSR File #00004).

a. Unable to locate views on extended debate. No votes cast on major reform proposals.

Senator Thomas Hart Benton seems to have held a consistent position in favor of preserving the Senate tradition of extended debate.

In the post–Civil War set of great senators, at least six of the nine senators had either voted or expressed support for measures to limit the practice of extended debate.[59] Even William Allison (Republican of Iowa), who in 1873 had opposed new rules limiting Senate debate, changed his mind: in 1891 he paired off in support of considering Aldrich's majority cloture proposal. Although Lyman Trumbull opposed debate limits on appropriations bills in the 1870s, he, too, had complained about obstructionism, particularly about a factious minority that in 1865 had unfairly prevented a majority from passing the Louisiana statehood bill. In our sampling of recognizably great nineteenth-century senators, then, a clear majority favored changes to inherited Senate rules, urging their colleagues to allow a majority of the Senate to decide when sufficient floor debate had elapsed. Those senators who "best exemplified" Senate tradition also seem to have been proponents of reform.

Filibustering Reform

If notable senators both before and after the Civil War favored limits on Senate debate, why were no such reforms enacted? As explained in chapter 6, the Senate voted only once in the nineteenth century—in 1873—on a proposal even remotely related to empowering a simple majority to close debate. On that occasion, the Senate voted down the resolution, 25-30, although at least some Republican senators likely did so to avoid provoking a protracted filibuster over a matter so uniformly opposed by minority Democrats.

Roll-call votes therefore are of only limited value in determining the views of rank-and-file senators on debate limits in the nineteenth century. Although reform permitting majority control over Senate debate was again proposed and abandoned in 1841, 1850, 1891, and 1893, it would be premature to conclude that it lacked the support of a chamber majority.[60] In the absence of roll call or other evidence, the most that can reasonably be inferred from the cases is that an actual or threatened filibuster led reformers to abandon their efforts, even though a majority may have been in favor of reform. Two of the cases merit a closer look.

In both 1841 and 1891 proposals to adopt a means to limit debate were raised but quickly withdrawn.[61] In the 1841 episode—in which Henry Clay first advocated a one-hour individual debate limit and then a previous question motion—a majority in favor of reform was apparently forced to retreat in face of a determined filibustering minority. Called to a special session of Congress, the Whig majority had a full legislative agenda ranging from public lands and appropriations to tariff and banking measures: "Whig majorities in both houses of Congress . . . supported by a Whig president offered an unparalleled opportunity for party government," as one historian of the period has noted.[62] Facing minority obstructionism over the Whigs' agenda, however, Clay had turned to procedural reform in an effort to secure favored legislative victories. At first, Clay proposed a one-hour rule—a rule adopted days before in the House by a Whig majority—but met with opposition from within his party caucus. "Several Whig senators had refused to go with Mr. Clay for the hour rule and forced him to give it up."[63] Nevertheless, Whig senators were willing to support a previous question motion, "supposing the minority would take it as a 'compromise'; but when they found this measure was to be resisted like the [one-hour rule] . . . they withdrew their assent again."[64] Under the circumstances, their effort to adopt a previous question rule was bound to be thwarted. Thus, facing a filibuster and not willing to risk their party's agenda, the Whigs folded and abandoned procedural reform.

Similar circumstances appear to have surrounded a majority party effort to create a majority cloture rule in 1891. Offered in the middle of a highly partisan debate over a federal elections bill, a cloture rule proposed by Nelson Aldrich was never fully debated on the floor because of intense opposition from minority Democrats. The lack of a direct vote on the rule change, however, cannot be interpreted as a sign that Aldrich lacked a majority. On a motion to proceed to consider the rule change in January 1891, a majority prevailed 36-32.[65] Yet the cloture rule never made it to the floor, since the filibuster against it became intertwined with a filibuster against the elections bill. Not wanting to further endanger the elections bill, Aldrich and his supporters gave up their fight for procedural reform.[66]

These cases suggest that the resilience of the filibuster in the nineteenth century cannot simply be attributed to senators' desire to protect the collective interests of the Senate. The lack of reform should instead be attributed to the power of inherited rules to preserve the status quo. Great leaders of the nineteenth-century Senate were evidently caught in an inherited institutional context they could not change, absent near unanimous support for their reforms. Senate tradition, when viewed from within the Senate, more likely looked like the accumulation of obstructionist uses of the filibuster, to block policy and procedural change alike.

The Rise of Unanimous-Consent Agreements

Unable to secure meaningful rules changes, Senate leaders tried other procedural innovations to help them manage legislation on the Senate floor. One of these innovations at the end of the nineteenth century was the unanimous-consent agreement (UCA), often taken to be a long-standing Senate tradition. Such time-limitation agreements today are orders of the Senate, under which a time is sometimes fixed for closing debate on a bill and its amendments and for casting final votes on both. Because a single senator's objection can prevent their approval, UCAs are generally considered to be consistent with Senate tradition, in which individual rights triumph over the preferences of a majority. Since the Senate lacked a means of forcing a vote as far back as 1806, it is often assumed that UCAs filled that void. It appears instead that UCAs did not become a routinized method of organizing floor debate until the late 1800s, after the Senate had several times failed to adopt rules changes that would have helped a majority to better manage the agenda on the floor. Rather than being an original or traditional feature of the Senate, UCAs seem to reflect the chamber's efforts to adjust to new legislating conditions as the nineteenth century wore on.

One of the first UCAs was used in 1846, during the course of extended debate over the fate of the Oregon territory.[67] That arrangement, however, seems to have been simply a gentlemen's agreement to cast a final vote on a date later in the week, so that senators could better plan their schedules: "He was desirous that a day should be determined on, inasmuch as some of the members of the body would be unavoidably absent . . . within a few days, and they would like to time their absence so that it should not fall on that day when the vote should be taken." The novelty of the arrangement was clear to all, as suggested by a comment by James Morehead (Whig of Kentucky): "He had not the slightest objection to fixing upon some day for terminating the debate, provided it was not to be regarded as establishing a precedent."[68] Nor was the agreement terribly well enforced, as considerable debate and a few votes on other amendments delayed final passage on the designated day.[69]

What began as a seemingly casual means of organizing Senate floor votes evolved into a more formal means of allowing a majority to better harness floor debate. But it took more than fifty years for the UCA to appear, and then almost as long for it to become institutionalized as a routine practice of the Senate. Even as late as 1870, UCAs were still informal agreements negotiated on the Senate floor. During debate over a bill concerning the composition of the Georgia legislature during Reconstruction, for example, the consent agreement was repeatedly changed, and one senator was charged with flagrantly violating the agreement. "The first agreement was Monday at four o'clock," noted the vice president presiding over the Senate. "It was then extended to Monday at six o'clock; then to Tuesday at six o'clock, and again, by unanimous consent, to-day extended until the conclusion of the remarks of the Senator from Illinois."[70] Not until the early 1900s did UCAs appear in a more standard form. In 1902, for example, UCAs were regular enough features of Senate practice that a senator inquiring about the form of a proposed UCA could "presume it [was] the usual one."[71] In 1914 they were finally made technical orders of the Senate.[72]

As UCAs became more regular in form and use in the late 1800s, they also came to serve a new purpose. Although they still lent some needed predictability to senators' own schedules, they also became an essential tool for Senate leaders trying to manage an increasingly unmanageable workload. In debating whether a UCA could be reopened after its initial approval, for example, Senator Frank Brandegee (Republican of Connecticut) argued that how the Senate resolved the matter would affect "the possibility of the transaction of business by the Senate in its whole future, for almost all the business that is crowded up here at the end of a busy session can only be put through by unanimous-consent agreements, and if they are to be played fast and loose with . . . we would be in chaos."[73]

UCAs became particularly useful in helping leaders manage the agenda in the face of minority obstructionism. UCAs could, in short, be used to avoid filibusters in an era of an expanding legislative agenda and demand for floor time. Republican efforts to negotiate a unanimous consent agreement on a bill to reform naturalization laws in 1870 provide a case in point. As noted by Roscoe Conkling (Republican of New York), unless the Senate set a time certain for a vote on final passage, the bill would be lost:

> I have no wish or purpose touching this bill excepting that it is an important measure in my charge, which everybody sees must be considered presently if it is to be considered at all finally, at this session. Senators will understand, without my referring specifically to measures, that in executive session and in legislative session there are matters which, beginning at once next week, will be quite likely to absorb the whole week, despite this measure. . . . If there be a

> majority of the Senate in favor of the bill, I want the votes of the majority of the Senate upon the final passage of the measure before it is too late.[74]

Most important, Conkling made clear that UCAs not only provided a solution to managing a busy agenda but also gave the majority a leg to stand on against minority obstructionism. The alternative to a UCA, Conkling continued, was a filibuster: "I suggest to gentlemen on the other side who wish further to debate this measure, that we may . . . have an understanding by which at a certain time the vote is to be taken, in lieu of an attempt to weary out each other by vying with each other in the very poor feat of personal endurance, of the power to remain here as a matter of bodily fatigue, to reach a vote upon the bill. . . . [T]he occasion says that it must be acted upon now, or not at all."[75] Given the apparent connection between UCAs, workload, and obstructionism, it is not surprising that time-limitation agreements took root in the Senate with the great increase in obstructionism at the close of the nineteenth century. Changes in the Senate's policymaking environment meant that inherited rules no longer served the Senate's needs very well by century's end. Unable to change the rules because of repeated filibusters, Senate leaders appear to have turned increasingly to time limitation agreements as the next-best option for managing a chamber handicapped by seemingly self-perpetuating rules. Of course, UCAs required unanimous consent of the Senate, and thus were not a substitute for filibuster reform.

Toward Cloture

What some see as a consensus about the desired character of the Senate largely reflected the inability of Senate reformers to change the rules. To be sure, senators recognized that the power of the Senate stemmed in part from the deliberative character of its proceedings. But by the end of the nineteenth century, the right of extended debate was quickly becoming a liability rather than an asset, as one observer pointed out in 1893: "The Senate of the United States sells not only its rights, but also its sworn duties . . . for the ghost of a shadow, euphoniously called the 'courtesy of the Senate.' Let it beware! The people of the United States are the most patient people on the face of the earth . . . but there is, after all, a limit to their patience, and they are not fools. It [the Senate] will not long be permitted to shield itself by pleading that, willing or not, it cannot break loose from its allegiance to this ghost of a shadow, because to dethrone the exacting sovereign is rendered impossible by its rules."[76] In the end, it would take considerable pressure from President Woodrow Wilson and an attentive press and public to bully the Senate into revising its rules. Adopting Rule 22 in 1917, the cloture rule that allows a supermajority to limit debate, the Senate finally overcame inherited institutional obstacles to reforming its traditions.

The adoption of a cloture rule in 1917 conforms to the pattern of Senate reform—or lack thereof—in response to short-term, pragmatic political considerations. And, just as earlier reforms were defeated by filibusters, the 1917 rule owed its particular form to the minority's power to prevent more radical reform. Seeking authority from Congress to arm merchant ships against German attack, Wilson was unable to secure his policy in the face of a filibuster at the close of the Sixty-Fourth Congress in March 1917. The public spotlight on opponents of the bill and on their exploitation of Senate rules—coupled with the presence of a supermajority prepared to vote for the bill—led dissenting senators to give up their fight against both filibuster reform and the armed ship bill.

By voting to change Senate rules, the Republican minority clearly avoided further blame for blocking Wilson's bill; a supermajority of the Senate agreed, adopting the rule by a vote of 76-3.[77] However, at least forty senators were willing to support a majority cloture rule, a position they were forced to abandon when it became clear that cloture opponents would block any reforms that empowered less than a two-thirds majority to stem debate.[78] Indeed, an amendment reducing the threshold from a super to a simple majority was withdrawn when the proposed reform was considered by the full Senate, its supporters charged with breaching faith with the senators who had negotiated the compromise on behalf of the two parties.[79]

Tradition Revisited

"We must . . . resort to some mode of arresting this eternal talking. I know of one way which might possibly be applicable, although not very parliamentary. If we were to devolve upon the Chair the duty of sending for a surgeon to have our tongues slit, it might answer some good purpose in this respect; but, sir, I am afraid, that even in that case, decimation would not be sufficient, but am inclined to think the operation would have to be performed in cases—nine out of ten. [Laughter.]"[80]

That Senator Mangum felt compelled in 1852 to offer such a radical solution to the Senate's woes—even if offered tongue-in-cheek—suggests how seriously senators saw the need for reforming the Senate even before the Civil War. Unlimited debate in the Senate was contested through much of the nineteenth century, as senators exploited their procedural rights far beyond anything experienced by members of the early Senate. Yet significant reform proved impossible in light of the rules new majorities inherited from the past. Absent widely shared political incentives to revamp Senate rules, the exceedingly high threshold for change in the Senate foreclosed any real reform until extraordinary political pressures surfaced in the context of the first world war in 1917 (see chapter 7).

Of course, senators' inability to alter inherited rules only posed a problem when obstructionism first began to increase in the 1830s and then mushroomed at the end of the century. Such changes in legislative strategies are important because they suggest that senators' willingness to exploit their parliamentary rights and their refusal to change the rules was shaped by something more than the value they placed on the freedom of debate in the Senate. Without drawing on more pragmatic political considerations and the wider policymaking environment, it is difficult to explain either the rise of obstructive parliamentary strategies during the nineteenth century or the Senate's resistance to procedural reform. During this period the absence of rules limiting debate, it can be concluded, came to serve many senators' political interests. Although senators certainly valued the freedom of debate, such institutional commitments alone fail to explain the Senate's refusal to limit the right of extended debate. Closely held political objectives—not the long-term collective interests of the Senate—seem to have shaped senators' choices over chamber rules governing debate in this period. Competing factions—sometimes partisan, sometimes not—supported or opposed reform on the basis of how such changes would affect their political interests in the future.

As the political rewards for refusing to fold increased, senators recast Senate tradition. Assumptions about Senate practices inherited from the early Senate were rewritten in light of changing political conditions. In the traditional Senate, it could no longer be taken for granted that final votes would be cast after a reasonable time for debate had elapsed. Nor could it be assumed that a simple majority would suffice for determining when it had come time to vote. Inherited rules that empowered chamber minorities to dictate Senate outcomes also empowered them to reshape chamber practices, practices that swiftly became chamber traditions. Thus senate tradition came to be shaped as much by senators' pragmatic political interests (increasingly asserted over the course of the nineteenth century) as by their normative commitments to free speech. Senate tradition clearly offers a weak defense of the modern filibuster.

An energetic filibuster.

4

Politics, Principle, and the Trivialization of the Filibuster

IN RECENT DECADES, senators and commentators on both ends of the ideological spectrum have observed that the filibuster has been used or threatened for increasingly trivial purposes. Conservative columnist George Will used the term "trivialization" in 1982 on the occasion of an end-of-session filibuster conducted by Senator Jesse Helms (Republican of North Carolina) against an increase in the gasoline tax.[1] Liberal senator Thomas Eagleton (Democrat of Missouri) complained in 1985 that "the Senate is now in the state of incipient anarchy. The filibuster, once used, by and large, as an occasional exercise in civil rights matters, has now become a routine frolic in almost all matters. Whereas our rules were devised to guarantee full and free debate, they now guarantee unbridled chaos."[2]

Indeed, the received wisdom suggests that filibusters—once reserved for the momentous national issues of slavery, civil rights, and states' rights—have become a more routine tool of senators seeking to force concessions on minor, often parochial, matters. In 1982, for example, just before Senator Helms buried the gas tax hike, Senators John James Exon and Edward Zorinsky, both Nebraska Democrats, filibustered an administration-backed bill to fund a radio station to broadcast into Cuba because they feared that jamming measures taken in response by Cuba would interfere with the signal of a Des Moines radio station. Parochial and personal concerns, rather than issues "of deep national significance," as Senator Eagleton once put it, are now said to be at the root of the contemporary filibuster.[3]

Closely related to the trivialization thesis is the claim that filibusters have become a means for pursuing purely partisan interests—even petty partisan interests. This was noted as early as the late 1970s when President Jimmy Carter's program faced filibusters in the Senate. But 1993 brought another round of complaints. Senator George Mitchell (Democrat of Maine), then the majority leader, observed that

> the Senate rule with respect to filibusters went into effect in 1919. For more than a half century after that, into the 1970s, filibusters occurred here in the U.S. Senate less than once a year, on average. In some Congresses, an entire 2-year period was passed without a single Senate filibuster. The filibuster was not used as a political party device. It was used on matters which, by common consent, were of grave national importance. That has now changed in the U.S. Senate. . . . The question is not when it is used occasionally, but when it is used as a part of a deliberate pattern, an unmistakable pattern, an unmistakable record of filibuster after filibuster after filibuster after filibuster. It is not anymore reserved for issues of great national importance. It is not anymore limited to those matters which do not have anything to do with one party or the other, but, by consensus, affect grave national issues. It is virtually every major bill.[4]

An even stronger claim about partisan uses of the filibuster in 1993, President Bill Clinton's first year in office, is made by political scientist John Gilmour: "For the first time ever, the minority party seeks to block important elements of a president's program through filibuster. . . . Never before has the minority party used the filibuster against a president of the other party to block important initiatives. Indeed, for nearly all of its history, use of the filibuster has been thoroughly bipartisan."[5] Partisanship should not be equated with trivialization, of course, but the broader theme is the same: senators have been willing to exploit their parliamentary prerogatives for purposes other than the most important constitutional issues facing the country.

This chapter examines these claims about the trivialization of the filibuster and its corollary, the increasingly partisan use of the filibuster, in their historical context. Trivial and partisan uses of the filibuster are *not* new. What needs to be explained is why filibusters of any kind were so uncommon in the mid–twentieth century. The chapter also reviews the wider range of political forces that may have been influencing senators' views of cloture and procedural reform. By far the strongest correlates of voting on cloture and cloture reform are senators' positions on the major policy dimensions, a finding consistent with the suggestion in chapter 1 that calculations about political advantage (rather than collective interests) shape senators' views about institutional arrangements.

The Substance and Significance of Issues Subject to Filibusters

Historically, civil rights issues—extension of slavery to the West, voting rights, antilynching measures, and so on—have been the single most common subject of filibusters. Yet civil rights measures have *not* constituted even a majority of the measures that have been the targets of filibusters. Figure 4-1 shows the number of filibusters that aimed at civil rights and non–civil rights legislation in each Congress since the first known filibuster in 1837.[6] Overall, 45 civil rights measures and 289 non–civil rights measures were the targets of filibusters through 1992. Civil rights filibusters dominated in two periods—the period before 1880 and the years between 1937 and 1967—but the number of non–civil rights filibusters far exceeded the number of civil rights filibusters in the 1881–1936 and post-1967 periods.

If major civil rights bills constitute the most important issues, figure 4-1 suggests that many lesser issues were the targets of filibusters in the 1881–1936 period. Almost as much range in the significance of filibustered legislation can be found in that period as in recent decades. Several tariff and general appropriations bills were filibustered, most of substantial policy significance. Others involved truly narrow, parochial concerns. Two brief examples illustrate the range.[7]

The 1915 ship subsidy bill proposed by President Woodrow Wilson would have given the government authority to purchase merchant ships for the course of World War I in Europe. The president was prompted to make the proposal after administration efforts to jawbone private shipping companies to reduce their rates proved ineffective. The shortage of vessels had bid up rates and was hurting exporters who were eager to supply Europeans in need of the goods. Republicans and some Democrats came to the defense of the shipping industry and charged that the plan would involve the United States with belligerents. Proponents finally gave up their effort

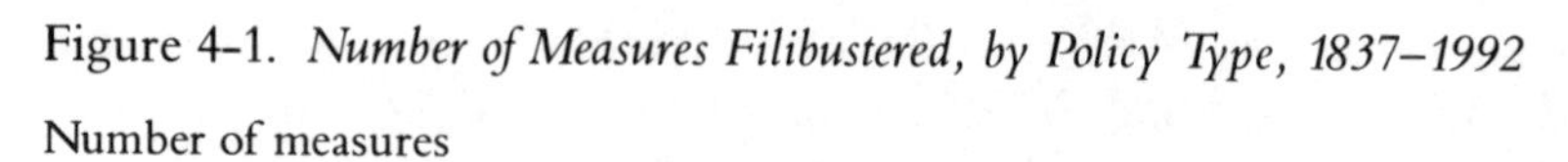

Figure 4-1. *Number of Measures Filibustered, by Policy Type, 1837–1992*

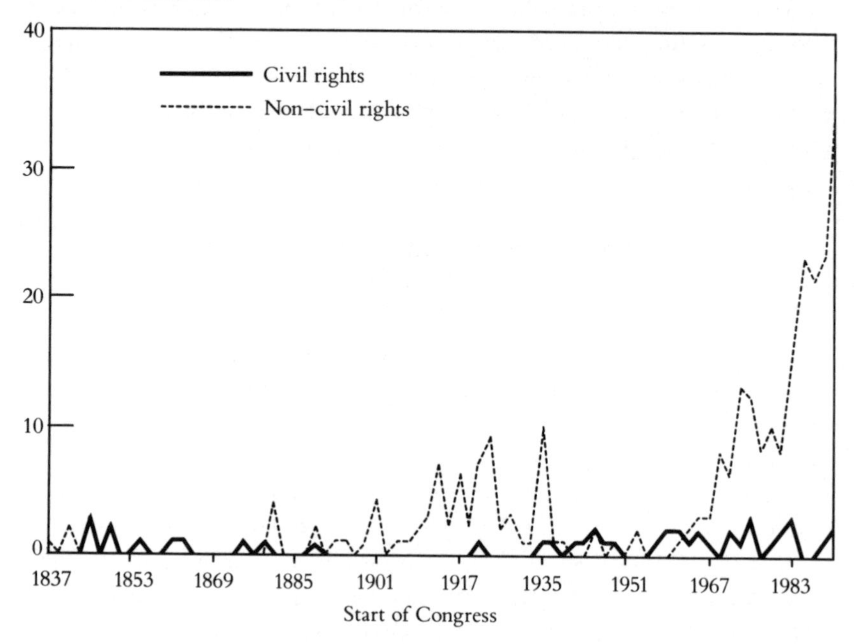

Sources: Richard S. Beth, "Filibusters in the Senate, 1789–1993," Memorandum, Congressional Research Service, February 18, 1994; Burdette, *Filibustering in the Senate*.

to overcome a filibuster that stretched over thirty-three calendar days.[8] By any standard, the ship subsidy bill was an important bill that had no connection to civil rights and yet was a reasonably significant measure in its day.

In contrast, Senator Nathaniel Dial (Democrat of South Carolina) threatened to hold up Senate action on a measure concerning mergers of meat packers if his separate bill to provide compensation to a former collector of internal revenue in his state was not considered. One senator indicated that he would object to the consideration of Dial's measure, so Dial objected to the consideration of the meat packers' bill, thus indicating that he was willing to disrupt the Senate by filibustering the meat packers' bill. Dial's threat appeared to be taken seriously, and the meat packers' bill was then pulled from the floor.[9] Because Dial was not compelled to follow through on his threat to filibuster, neither bill is on any list of filibusters. Dial's bill was at least as insignificant as the radio station bill blocked by Nebraskans Exon and Zorinsky and certainly more trivial than the Helms gas-tax filibuster that aroused commentators to complain about the trivialization of the filibuster in 1982.

Moreover, the incivility often associated with the use of the filibuster in recent decades is not new, as is evident from Senate activities during the last two decades of the nineteenth century:

> If dilatory tactics upon the Senate floor, increasing in turbulence and boldness for more than fifty years, had largely been fruitless expenditures of energy in a parliamentary sense, the closing decades of the nineteenth century reveal another story. Tactics remained essentially the same, but boldness gave way to ruthlessness, and obstruction began to be bounded only by the daring ingenuity of its designers. If courtesy required restraint, it was forgotten; if dignity demanded moderation, it was sacrificed to political or sectional advantage. With the determination never to surrender short of sheer physical exhaustion came success for the devotees of filibustering.[10]

In recent decades, the Exon-Zorinsky filibuster is only the tip of the iceberg. In fact, as discussed further in chapter 5, the effects of the filibuster on Senate policymaking have been so pervasive in recent decades that they cannot be easily quantified. What can be said, however, is that the emergence of filibusters on quite trivial matters in recent decades should not be taken to signify that all or most filibusters are without substantial policy import. To the contrary, the number of filibusters directed at major legislation, as nearly any congressional observer would define the term, has been substantially larger since the late 1960s than at any other time. They may not measure up to the Compromise of 1850 in importance, but many surely constitute major policy statements with substantial consequences for the nation.

As explained in chapter 3, intense partisanship, an expanding workload, and even the physical conditions in the Senate chamber may have contributed to the surge in filibusters at the end of the nineteenth century. Figure 4-1 adds something more to take into account: the quiet period between 1937 and 1967. During that period, filibusters were somewhat less frequent than at the turn of the century, and the majority of filibusters did indeed concern civil rights legislation. Why did filibustering fade during this period except for civil rights measures?

The answer, in our view, lies in the distribution of power within the Senate during the 1937–67 period: for most of this period, the Senate was dominated by the "conservative coalition."[11] Beginning in the late 1930s, southern Democrats became more conservative, in relation to other sena-

Figure 4-2. *Percentage of Conservative Coalition Victories on Votes Where Coalition Appeared,*[a] *1933–66*

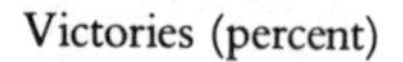

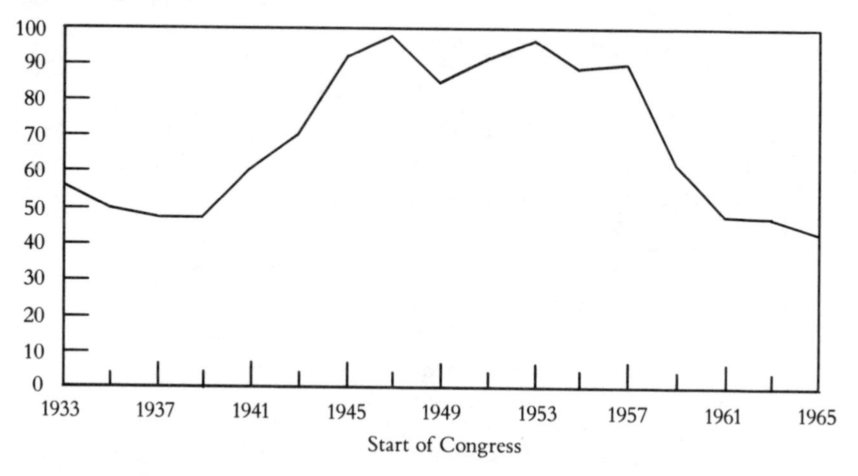

Source: Adapted from John F. Manley, "The Conservative Coalition in Congress," in Lawrence C. Dodd and Bruce I. Oppenheimer, eds., *Congress Reconsidered* (Praeger, 1977), p. 87.

a. Coalition appears when a majority of southern Democrats and a majority of Republicans vote against a majority of northern Democrats.

tors, on most issues, and more frequently joined with Republicans to form a conservative coalition against northern Democrats and a handful of Republicans.[12] Historian James Patterson observed, "So long as the New Deal did not disturb southern agricultural, industrial, or racial patterns, these leaders would support it, sometimes with enthusiasm. But if and when the northern wing of the party began to dominate (as it did after the 1936 election), a certain degree of friction was almost inevitable."[13] In fact, as the southerners shifted in a conservative direction after the 1936 election, the overall ideological balance in the Senate shifted in the same direction.[14] This conservative coalition proved remarkably successful (see figure 4-2).

This was also the "era of committee chairmen," during which an oligarchy of senior and disproportionately conservative Democratic senators chaired committees, enjoyed disproportionate influence over committee assignments and other sources of leverage with their colleagues, and generally dominated Senate decisionmaking.[15] On the surface, the Senate appeared to be a body governed by a set of unwritten norms that senators "go along to get along" with their colleagues. These norms may have been reinforced by the nation's preoccupation with the economic crisis of the 1930s and the subsequent external threats of the Axis powers and world communism. But a reasonable hypothesis is that the norms emerged, at least in major part, as a by-product of the exercise of power by southern Democrats, usually with the quiet support of Republicans, who opposed new federal initiatives in domestic policy and bottled up liberal legislation in committee whenever they could.

The conservative coalition was generally satisfied to have little new legislation pass and, because it constituted a majority of the Senate during much of this period, did not have to resort to the filibuster to block liberal legislation. Only on civil rights measures, which were attractive to many Republicans, did southerners regularly have to resort to filibusters or threaten filibusters to kill undesirable legislation (see chapter 5 for more detail on civil rights filibusters during this period). For liberals, it is reasonable to speculate, the absence of a majority on most issues reduced the incentive to be aggressive and perhaps made many of them conclude that cooperating with conservative committee leaders was the only way to make contributions of any kind. And with few major legislative initiatives emanating from the conservatives, liberals did not have occasion to filibuster. The behavior of Senate liberals might be interpreted as compliance with Senate norms, but it is more likely that the behavior reflected liberals' recognition of their weak political position.[16] So the futility of filibustering and its counterproductive consequences, rather than a deep commitment to inherited norms, seem best to account for the quiescent period during the mid–twentieth century.[17]

Some of those senators who argue for a return to the mid–twentieth century pattern may want to reconsider their arguments. Liberals such as Senator Mitchell surely would not want to return to the era of the conservative coalition's domination of congressional policymaking. Senate conservatives, when in the majority, may still have something to complain about. But in the late twentieth century (at the time of this writing) a conservative majority means a Republican majority and Republican leaders are in no position to reestablish and enforce the norms that once appeared to minimize obstructionism. In any event, Republicans, who have spent more time in the minority than the majority during the past half century, have not been nearly as eager as liberal Democrats to complain about a procedural weapon that protects the status quo more often than it facilitates its demise.

Partisanship and Filibusters

Two propositions about partisanship and filibusters have been suggested by observers, mainly critics of the filibuster: that filibusters have become quite partisan affairs in recent decades and that this trend represents a radical change from the historical pattern. The first proposition is easily confirmed, as discussed in the following paragraphs. While Senator Mitchell, then the Democratic majority leader, decried partisan filibusters in 1993, Senator Robert Dole (Republican of Kansas) as the Republican majority leader in 1995 lamented that "the Senate is stuck in a filibuster of the Cuba Liberty and Democratic Solidarity Act of 1995. Unfortunately, some have decided to make this a partisan issue."[18] Connecting filibusters with partisanship, even on matters of modest importance, had become routine.

The second proposition concerning the recent break from Senate tradition is used to cast blame on the Senate's minority party, whichever one that happens to be, and so might be more suspect than the first. Certainly the discussion in chapter 3 casts it in a suspicious light. Indeed, the first place to go for a history of the filibuster, Burdette's *Filibustering in the Senate*, published in 1940, suggests something quite different about the late nineteenth century. His chapter on the period, entitled "Filibustering Unrestrained," indicates that partisan interests frequently motivated obstructionism.[19] Burdette's commentary, summarized in table 4-1, makes it clear that a significant number of filibusters before 1917 concerned issues that divided the Senate primarily along party lines. Where the Senate voted on a measure, amendment, or motion that was directly related to the issue stimulating the filibuster, voting alignments were partisan on a significant number of the filibustered issues. Partisan divisions overlap with sectional divisions in the late nineteenth century because of the strongly sectional basis of the parties during that period. But, as a number of scholars report, many of the divisions were deeply partisan.[20] In any event, partisanship and filibusters frequently were a matched pair in the late nineteenth and early twentieth century, and they occurred on important, not-so-important, and trivial matters. Contrary to recent claims about use of the filibuster in the 1980s and 1990s, the partisan filibuster is not new to the Senate.

For the period since 1917, votes on cloture reflect the partisanship associated with issues subject to filibusters. To be sure, cloture votes are not ideal measures of partisanship. Some senators may have supported or opposed cloture on principle; others may have seen cloture as a way of

Table 4-1. *Political Division on Issues with Filibusters or Threatened Filibusters before Adoption of Rule 22, 1837–1917*

Year	*Measure filibustered*	*Political division*[a]	*Key vote*[b]
1837	Jackson censure removal	Partisan	
1841	Appointment of Senate printers	Partisan	Partisan
1841	Creation of a U.S. bank	Partisan	Partisan
1846	Oregon statehood		Partisan
1846	Wilmot proviso		
1847	Wilmot proviso		
1850	Organize Western territories	Sectional	
1850	California statehood	Sectional	
1856	Kansas statehood	Sectional	
1863	Habeas corpus indemnification	Partisan	Partisan
1865	Recognize Louisiana government		Partisan
1879	Army appropriation, election law		Partisan/sectional
1881	Organize Senate	Partisan	
1881	Nominations	Partisan	
1881	Nominations	Partisan	Partisan
1881	Officers of the Senate	Partisan	Partisan/sectional
1890	Education–Blair act		
1890	Force bill (federal elections)	Partisan/sectional	Partisan/sectional
1891	Cloture rule		
1893	Silver purchase	Sectional	Sectional
1897	Naval appropriation		
1901	Rivers and harbors appropriation		
1903	Statehood bill		Partisan
1903	Deficiency appropriation		
1903	Rivers and harbors		
1903	Columbia treaty (Panama Canal)		
1907	Ship subsidy	Partisan	Partisan/sectional
1908	Emergency currency, banking	Partisan	Partisan/sectional
1911	Canadian reciprocity		
1911	Arizona, New Mexico statehood		Partisan
1913	Labor Department		
1913	Nomination	Partisan	
1913	Nominations	Partisan	
1913	Public buildings		Sectional
1914	Rivers and harbors	Partisan	Partisan
1914	Panama Canal tolls		Partisan
1914	Federal Trade Commission		
1914	Clayton Antitrust Act		Partisan
1915	Ship purchase	Partisan	
1917	Armed ship resolution		

a. The entries reflect Burdette's characterization of the political divisions on the issue that stimulated the filibuster as partisan or sectional. Other divisions that Burdette mentioned are ignored. Burdette often failed to note the divisions on issues, so the absence of an entry in this column should not be interpreted to mean that we could not determine the division from other sources. See Franklin Burdette, *Filibustering in the Senate* (Princeton University Press, 1940).

b. For each measure, we attempted to identify a roll-call vote directly related to the issue that stimulated the filibuster or obstructionism. In many cases no appropriate vote was found. When a vote was found, we determined the division between the parties. Votes on which at least two-thirds of the voting members of one major party voted against at least two-thirds of the voting members of the other major party are listed as partisan. And votes on which at least two-thirds of one section (north versus south) voted against at least two-thirds of the other section are listed as sectional. We ignore other divisions, realizing that other sectional divisions are sometimes important. No entry means that either no appropriate vote was found or no partisan or sectional vote was found. All key votes identified and examined are listed in appendix 4-A.

avoiding a direct vote on the underlying measure. And yet, because filibusters often prevent a direct vote on the underlying issue, a cloture vote is in many instances the only behavioral measure of the alignment of senators on the issue.

Partisanship once again assumed a central place in cloture voting in recent years. Figure 4-3 shows a measure of party differences on cloture votes. The "party difference" measure used here is the difference between the percentage of Democrats voting yea and the percentage of Republicans voting yea on cloture votes. If 70 percent of the Democrats and 20 percent of the Republicans voted in favor of cloture, the difference is 50 percent. As figure 4-3 indicates, many cloture votes have been nearly straight party-line votes in recent years, a sharp contrast to the cloture votes of the mid–twentieth century.

So Senate history did not begin in 1917. The trivialization thesis and its partisanship corollary require heavy qualification in light of the experience of the Senate in the late nineteenth and early twentieth century. To be sure, filibusters have become very partisan affairs in recent decades, but this represents a far less radical change from the historical pattern than some recent discussion indicates. One might even argue that the decades of the mid–twentieth century serve as a break from a trend toward more numerous and more partisan filibusters that began in the mid–nineteenth century and regenerated in the late 1960s. But a more cautious approach, one that is attentive to the political incentives and disincentives for obstructionism, is more likely to produce an accurate account of the use of the filibuster.

Patterns of Support and Opposition to Cloture

The next, and essential, step is to ask a more general question: Has the relative importance of partisanship, sectionalism, *and* other forces that may have shaped senators' behavior about obstructionism changed over time? One possible additional influence is senators' commitment to a principle that favors or opposes simple majority rule on debate limits. The rhetoric of many senators over the decades certainly would suggest that their commitments to certain procedural principles would guide their behavior.

If unlimited debate is a matter of Senate tradition and high principle for senators, one might expect to find senators who are never willing to vote for cloture. Similarly, if other senators are adamant about the right of simple majorities to determine legislative outcomes, one might expect to find senators who always vote for cloture. How many purists have there

Figure 4-3. *Party Difference on Cloture Votes, by Congress, 66th to 103d Senate*

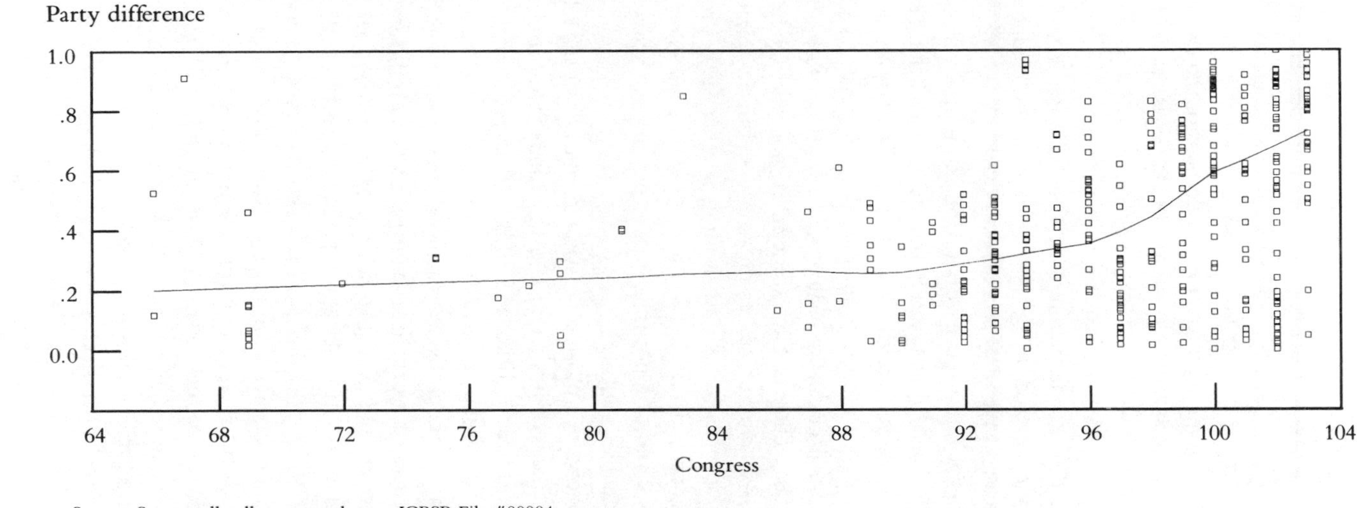

Source: Senate roll-call votes on cloture, ICPSR File #00004.
Note: Line is the lowess regression line.

been? Through 1990, 306 senators voted ten or more times on cloture motions, but only eleven always voted against cloture and only five senators always voted for cloture.[21] Many of those sixteen cases can be accounted for by the political circumstances in which they served. Some were southern Democrats serving in the middle decades of the twentieth century who voted repeatedly against cloture on liberal legislation. Those who always voted for cloture include Senator Robert Kennedy (Democrat of New York), who served for three-and-a-half years up to the time of his assassination in 1968, a period in which the filibusters were spearheaded by southerners against civil rights measures (for other interesting cases, see box).

Plainly, procedural purism is uncommon—the other 94 percent of the Senate's membership were not purists in their cloture voting. Political considerations beyond high principle appear to dictate the behavior of most senators most of the time. Understanding the changes in the mix of such considerations is critical to evaluating the current state of the Senate. Party and sectional influences have sometimes worked together and sometimes placed cross-cutting pressures on senators. But any analysis of party and sectional influences may be misleading if other factors influencing cloture votes are ignored. In fact, even the sharply partisan votes on cloture in the early 1990s cannot be put into proper perspective without an accounting of other possible influences.

What follows is a more sophisticated analysis of the relative influence of a somewhat larger number of considerations. Unfortunately, a direct test of the filibuster-as-politics and filibuster-as-principle perspectives is not possible. It is possible to identify measures of a variety of political considerations that might influence attitudes about filibusters and Rule 22, but direct measures of a principled commitment to unlimited debate and minority rights are not available. Moreover, some considerations that might influence senators' attitudes about filibusters and Rule 22 can be viewed as matters of both politics and principle. For example, senators with extreme views may oppose strict limits on debate both to preserve their personal influence and to protect the right of small minorities to be heard and to educate their colleagues. Plainly, political and principled motivations are not readily separated. And talented elected officials become quite adept at camouflaging politics with principle.

Nevertheless, it might be possible to demonstrate that some good measures of political considerations do, or do not, have expected effects on senators' behavior. For example, are policy views and majority/minority party status associated with voting on cloture or cloture reform? If so,

Senators with Perfect Records

Between 1917 and 1994, four senators never failed to support cloture and eleven senators never failed to oppose cloture (among senators who voted on cloture ten or more times). Senator Claiborne Pell (Democrat of Rhode Island) broke his run of votes in favor of cloture in 1995, when he voted against cloture to block action on a Cuban policy. He had voted against cloture only once before on the occasion of Senate action on a contested election outcome in 1964. Even for Senator Pell, the dictates of policy preferences eventually overcame a commitment to a procedural principle. Senator Pell remained in the Senate through 1996, when he retired. Nonvoting and voting present are not considered in this count.

Top Supporters of Cloture
Dennis DeConcini (D-Arizona)
Robert Kennedy (D-New York)
William Saxbe (R-Ohio)
Millard Tydings (D-Maryland)

Top Opponents of Cloture
William Borah (R-Idaho)
Harry F. Byrd Sr. (D-Virginia)
Allen Ellender (D-Louisiana)
J. Lister Hill (D-Alabama)
Olin Johnston (D-South Carolina)
Gerald Nye (R-North Dakota)
James A. Reed (D-Missouri)
Absalom Willis Robertson (D-Virginia)
Donald Stuart Russell (D-South Carolina)
Richard Russell, Jr. (D-Georgia)
Burton Wheeler (D-Montana)

Source: Senate roll-call votes (ICPSR File #00004).

then such a finding strengthens the circumstantial case that political considerations directly or indirectly—perhaps by shaping senators' attitudes about procedural principles—influence senators' behavior, even if it is impossible to directly weigh politics against principle as influences on senatorial behavior.

The analysis is limited to the period from 1919 to 1994, for which cloture votes are known and complete data are available on the variables representing the political forces that may influence senators' vote choices. The first step is to identify the considerations thought to structure senators' legislative behavior and examine the relationship between each of those considerations and voting on cloture. More sophisticated statistical techniques can then be applied to assess the relative importance of those considerations in voting on cloture, and thereby to determine who is voting on cloture in a manner inconsistent with his or her political characteristics.

Party and Section

Party and section have both played an instrumental role in the development of Senate rules and the divisions on both cloture votes and cloture reform votes. To show this, and the effects of the factors considered below, we have calculated for each senator who served during the 1919–94 period the percentage of measures on which a senator supported cloture for those measures subject to cloture votes. We have also calculated support of cloture for the separate periods of Democratic and Republican control of the Senate.[22]

The pattern of party and sectional support for cloture is shown in table 4-2. Party status clearly plays a major role: majority parties file and support cloture motions and minority parties tend to oppose them. On balance, both Republicans and northern Democrats supported cloture more frequently when they were in the majority party than when they were in the minority party. But southern Democrats opposed cloture by overwhelming margins during the period between the 1930s and 1960s. Since that time, civil rights issues have faded as a part of the filibustered agenda, and southern Democrats have become progressively more similar to other Democrats in the support for cloture. By the late 1980s, when the Democrats were in the majority, southern Democrats were quite close to northern Democrats in their overall high level of support for cloture.

Small-State Interests

While party and section structure cloture voting to a significant degree, other political forces may have a systematic influence on senators' views about cloture as well. One such force is state population size. The protection of the interests of small states is the essence of the Senate. By granting every state two Senate seats, and then by making the Senate a coequal partner with the House in legislating, the framers of the Constitution achieved the grand compromise that was required to gain the support of

Table 4-2. *Mean Support for Cloture by Party, Region, and Periods of Party Control of the Senate, 1919–94*

Percent[a]

	Majority party and years								
Party group	*1919–32 Republican*	*1933–46 Democrat*	*1947–48 Republican*	*1949–52 Democrat*	*1953–54 Republican*	*1955–68 Democrat*	*1969–80 Democrat*	*1981–86 Republican*	*1987–94 Democrat*
Northern Democrats	62.9	68.7	. . .	76.7	12.0	73.6	81.1	53.1	90.9
Southern Democrats	52.4	3.5	. . .	0.0	4.8	10.9	49.7	69.3	84.7
Republicans	72.4	48.3	. . .	85.4	91.3	50.3	58.9	79.7	42.8
Number of measures	11	7	0	1	1	12	53	36	93

Source: Senate roll-call votes (ICPSR File #00004).

a. Percentages are calculated on the basis of the number of measures on which a senator voted at least once in favor of cloture. Votes related to measures designed to amend Rule 22 are excluded.

small-state delegates to the convention for a stronger central government. Small-state delegates feared that the Congress, if composed of a single chamber in which seats were allocated to the states on the basis of population, would give large states too much power in the new government. The separation-of-powers system was later justified in the Federalist Papers as a means for reducing the probability that any one faction would dominate all institutions of government and for preventing a majority from imposing its will on a minority. The overall scheme of representation in the Senate, bicameralism, and the separation of powers held out some hope to small states that they would not be dominated by a central government under the control of large-state interests.

Small-state senators sometimes argue, usually implicitly, that the constitutional mechanisms for protecting their states' interests are inadequate and that supplementary rules are required to protect small states. Senator Harry Reid (Democrat of Nevada) has been among the more outspoken and explicit representatives from small states about the protection that small states find in Rule 22. In the brief 1995 debate about reforming Rule 22, Reid argued:

> I believe that the Founding Fathers were right in setting up the Constitution in the manner in which they did. I believe that if we are going to have the legislative form of Government that they set up, we do need to protect the integrity of States that are small in population like the State of Nevada. . . .
>
> Checks and balances and vetoes would not help the State of Nevada or the State of Alaska if the 52 Members of the congressional delegation of California decide they want to do something that would affect the State of Nevada. The only thing I can do to take on one of those big States is to exercise my ability to talk on this floor and explain my position in detail. Checks and balances has nothing to do with protecting a small State. Vetoes have nothing to do with it, unless you have the ear of the Chief Executive of this country. The filibuster is uniquely situated to protect a small State in population like Nevada.[23]

Small-state senators, it might be said, would generally oppose cloture so as not to establish a precedent that runs counter to their states' interests and would certainly oppose cloture reforms that reduce the barrier to limiting debate.

Arguments about cloture and small-state interests usually stimulate a little arithmetic about the potential influence of large states in the House and small states in the Senate. For example, in the 104th Congress, representatives from as few as nine states could constitute a majority in the House, while senators from states with little more than 10 percent of the nation's population could constitute a blocking minority under the Senate's cloture rule. The former is emphasized by senators from small states; the latter is emphasized by senators favoring cloture reform.[24]

To determine the distinctiveness of the behavior of small-state senators in relation to cloture and cloture reform votes, we define small states as those with three or fewer House seats in the 104th Congress.[25] Overall, small-state senators have not opposed cloture more often than other senators. In the 1918–88 period, small-state senators voted for cloture 64 percent of the time, while other senators did so 63 percent of the time.

Outliers within the Senate Parties

The filibuster is a tool not only of substantial minorities but also of individual senators. Individual senators cannot prevent cloture from being invoked, but under the Senate's rules a single senator can be heard and delay action. This parliamentary privilege may be more important for some senators than others. Personality, no doubt, plays a role here. But so may political circumstance.

Former Senator Lowell Weicker (Republican of Connecticut), a liberal Republican, once began a floor statement on the reform of Senate rules by observing: "When I came to the Senate in 1971 as a Republican, we were in the minority. When the Republicans took over the Senate in 1980, I found myself in the minority. [Laughter.] So I understand what it is like to be in terms of philosophy and partisanship in the minority."[26] The "laughter" insertion comes from the *Congressional Record* and indicates how widely recognized Weicker's predicament as a liberal in a conservative party was. Weicker went on to say: "I joined my friends in the main from the South when I first came to the Senate in 1971. There was an effort to reform. Many were surprised when I voted to retain the two-thirds requirement to cut off debate. I was thought of as a northeastern liberal Republican, and I should be against the two-thirds requirement in favor of a lower number to cut off debate. I was not. Even then I think I understood what was important to this institution in terms of an individual being able to express his or her views, in terms of the power it represented in that individual by virtue of the rules of the U.S. Senate."[27] And before concluding, Weicker noted, "I do not have allies in terms of numbers either on my side of the aisle or on the Democratic side. My allies are the rules of the U.S. Senate."[28]

All senators, whatever their position within their party, probably value the parliamentary prerogatives they enjoy under the Senate's rules. But Weicker's example suggests that senators who are outliers within their parties might benefit most from the preservation of individual rights under the rules. If so, they might be less supportive of cloture generally and, as Weicker indicates, less supportive of reducing the threshold for cloture.

Whatever Weicker's rationale and behavior, similarly situated senators do not behave on regular cloture votes as if they share his procedural perspective. We have examined the cloture voting of senators whose policy positions locate them at the extreme liberal or conservative ends of two policy dimensions, liberal-conservative and pro-anti civil rights. Extremists are defined as being located in the top 5 percent or bottom 5 percent of a party's senators on the two policy dimensions. Depending on party size, this criterion isolated one to three senators. If Weicker's claims are generally true of senators isolated on the extremes, the extremists would be expected to oppose cloture even if their policy interests dictate otherwise and the isolation of extremists would yield similar voting behavior among extremists on the left and right. This does not happen very often. Within both parties, when liberals favor cloture, so do the most liberal senators; when conservatives favor cloture, so do the most conservative senators, as is demonstrated below.

Experience and Seniority

An appreciation of the Senate's special role, and the significance of free debate for that role, is often said to be acquired with years of service in the institution. Henry Cabot Lodge Sr., Harvard University's first Ph.D. in political science and Republican senator from Massachusetts from 1893 until he died in 1924, is often cited as an example. During his first year in the Senate, Lodge noted in the prominent journal *North American Review*: "To vote without debating is perilous, but to debate and never vote is imbecile."[29] But in 1915, when a proposal to establish a cloture rule was again debated, Lodge observed that experience had changed his mind about limiting debate and rose to oppose the proposal.[30] Wisdom gained with experience, he intimated, produces support for unlimited debate. Perhaps some senators do not learn from history or experience, as Lodge claimed to have done, but their arguments suggest that seniority might be associated with greater patience for, and even an appreciation of, extended debate.

However, senators' seniority has no obvious relationship to their votes on cloture motions.[31] The correlation between seniority and support for cloture motions is very low, but in the predicted direction. In the 1955–68 period, however, the correlation is moderately strong and is statistically significant.[32] On closer inspection, seniority does seem to be related to cloture voting during that period, even when we control for other factors. Thus, in the middle part of the twentieth century, more experienced senators appear to have been modestly more opposed to voting for cloture than other senators.

Policy Positions

The most obvious consideration—senators' policy preferences—is also the most difficult to measure. Policy preferences reflect political preference. They are partly the product of personal beliefs and values and partly the product of political influences. Whatever motivates their preferences, senators are likely to vote on cloture or cloture reform with an eye to the consequences of such votes for policy outcomes and for themselves. Unfortunately, there are no reliable indicators of senators' policy preferences on the specific issues that are subject to cloture votes. No surveys have gauged the sentiment of senators on matters before the chamber. Perhaps other votes could be used to measure senators' policy views. But unless cloture is invoked, a filibuster usually prevents roll-call votes on the substance of the issue, so other votes will not capture senators' policy preferences on the issue creating the necessity of a cloture vote.

The absence of valid measures of senators' policy preferences on the specific measures subject to cloture is a serious constraint on drawing inferences about the basis of senators' cloture voting. For example, a straight party-line vote on cloture may lead some observers to assert that senators were being *merely* partisan. The assertion is that the vote reflected one party's interest in scoring political points against the other party, whatever the genuine views of senators or the diversity of constituency views within either party. However, it could be that the political forces (senators' personal views, constituency expectations, lobbyists' pressure) beyond partisan concerns led the senators of one party to line up against the senators of the other party. In the late twentieth century, southern conservatives are a rarity among congressional Democrats, and several southern conservatives have joined the ranks of congressional Republicans since the 1970s. The result is a more uniformly liberal Democratic party and more uniformly conservative Republican party in the Senate. Determining how much *merely* partisan considerations influenced senators' cloture voting is not possible without first determining how they would have voted in the absence of those considerations. That exercise is beyond the scope of this discussion, however.

Instead, we use measures of the relative positions of senators over the full scope of the Senate's roll-call agenda for the period through 1994. The measures are based on what political scientists call scaling techniques. Senators are arranged in a "space" of one or more dimensions in a manner that minimizes error in predicting how they would vote over the full set of votes in the two-year period of a Congress. A scale score is calculated to show a senator's position in relation to other senators on each dimension. Just one dimension—one that aligns senators in what everyone would recognize to be a left-right or liberal-conservative fashion—does very well in predicting votes throughout most of Senate history. A second dimension that sometimes is strongly associated with civil rights issues is important in many Congresses. In the twentieth century, the second dimension was clearly a civil rights dimension during the period after 1948. At other times, the Senate did not cast enough votes on civil rights measures for senators to be scored. We limit our focus to these first two dimensions and, for the second dimension, to the post-1948 period.[33]

Of course, many other cross-cutting divisions among senators—urban-rural, east-west, and so on—have produced statistically defined dimensions of their own. One or more of these minor dimensions in Senate politics may be important for some cloture votes, or even for votes on cloture reform. But never have these minor dimensions had much predictive power over the full array of votes. And we could never be quite sure which ones were relevant to the issue that is subject to a cloture vote. So, somewhat arbitrarily, we do not examine the relationship between these more minor dimensions of cloture voting and restrict ourselves to the more robust liberal-conservative dimension and, for some Congresses, the civil rights dimension.

Although senators' scale scores are indicators of senators' locations in the broad policy space defined by the voting record, extreme caution is required in any interpretation of them. Perhaps the most obvious interpretation of the liberal-conservative dimension is that it represents senators' ideologies. Such an interpretation would be far too strong. Personal beliefs, *along with many other political forces*, shape members' voting behavior. It is appropriate to characterize senators' *behavior* as more or less liberal, to relate their general pattern of roll-call voting to their voting on cloture and cloture reform, and to determine if the liberal-conservative spectrum (or the pro-to-anti civil rights spectrum) separates senators who on other grounds (party, region, and so on) might be expected to vote alike.

The record of Senate filibustering in the twentieth century suggests that liberals would favor cloture more frequently than conservatives and that they would certainly favor a lower threshold for cloture than conservatives. One might even argue that conservatives generally would favor rules that serve to block new policy proposals, as does a high cloture threshold. However, because political contexts change rapidly, proponents of the policy status quo may suddenly become proponents of a policy revolution and so alter their views of the use of rules. For that reason, we examine the relationship between policy preferences and cloture voting across the eras of party control of the Senate.

As table 4-3 shows, the correlation between civil rights policy positions and cloture voting is sizable until the 1980s. The left-right, or liberal-conservative, dimension became more important than the civil rights dimension in the 1970s and has since gained strength in its correlation with cloture voting. And as the party divisions reported in table 4-3 suggest, the signs of the large correlations for the liberal-conservative dimension flip back and forth with changes in party control of the Senate. Liberals oppose cloture more often when Republicans control the agenda; conservatives oppose cloture more often when Democrats control the agenda.

A Multivariate Perspective

Most senators appear to behave on cloture votes as their general party, regional, and policy interests suggest that they would. It appears that senators choose to play hard within the rules that they have inherited. But the observations to this point are incomplete. The factor-by-factor discussion does not provide a very precise view of the relative importance of the factors. To see that, one must use multivariate statistical techniques to estimate the importance of each of the factors controlling for the effects of the other factors. For example, one can determine whether policy positions or party labels are better predictors of voting on cloture when most liberals are expected to be Democrats and most conservatives to be Republicans. If commentators of the 1980s and 1990s are correct, party differences would appear to be significant even when the effects of policy differences among senators are taken into account.

Table 4-3. *Correlation*[a] *between the Mean Support (Percent) for Cloture and Policy Positions, by Party Control of the Senate, 1919–94*

Pearson r

	Majority party and years								
Policy preferences	*1919–32* Republican	*1933–46* Democrat	*1947–48* Republican	*1949–52* Democrat	*1953–54* Republican	*1955–68* Democrat	*1969–80* Democrat	*1981–86* Republican	*1987–94* Democrat
Left-right policy position	**.30**	−.14	. . .	.19	**.79**	**−.46**	**−.59**	**.75**	**−.93**
Civil rights policy position	**.23**	**.30**	. . .	**.67**	**.44**	**.75**	**.47**	−.08	−.14
Number of measures	11	7	0	1	1	12	53	36	93

Source: Senate roll-call votes on cloture (ICPSR File #00004).

a. Correlations are calculated on the basis of the number of measures on which a senator voted at least once in favor of cloture. All columns are calculated using NOMINATE scores (see text). Boldface numbers are statistically significant at $p < .05$.

Table 4-4 summarizes the results of the statistical analyses. The detailed statistical results are provided in appendix 4-B. Senators' policy positions dominate the statistical results. In the 1950s and 1960s, when civil rights votes were relatively frequent and constituted a clear second dimension to the dominant left-right dimension, a senator's position on the civil rights dimensions is far more important for cloture voting than any other consideration. After that point, civil rights differences fade as a source of division on cloture voting and eventually give way to the left-right differences and partisanship as predictors of cloture voting, although the second dimension remains reasonably important in the 1987–94 period.

Just as commentators have indicated, party emerges as a strong influence on cloture voting in the 1987–94 period. Party stands about even with the left-right dimension as a predictor of cloture voting, which indicates that partisan ties have an importance that extends beyond policy ties for at least a substantial number of senators. We must not ignore the partisanship of filibusters in the decades spanning the late nineteenth and early twentieth centuries, but these findings indicate that late-twentieth-century voting on cloture is strongly partisan in character.

Beyond policy positions and party status, no other consideration has an effect that is consistently significant and in the predicted direction. Region is highly correlated with position on the civil rights dimension, so it is difficult for both factors to be significant at the same time. Seniority is sometimes significant, but the substantive effect is always very small and the sign is sometimes of the opposite direction of that suggested by experienced senators in the 1987–94 period (that is, more senior senators were more likely than junior senators to support cloture). The outliers within the two parties generally do not show distinctive anticloture biases. The relationships are not always of the expected sign (that is, sometimes extremists are more likely to support cloture). Finally, senators from small states do not exhibit distinctive behavior on cloture votes.[34]

Patterns of Support and Opposition to Cloture Reform

Although politics appears to dominate principle in cloture voting, principle may have a more central place in senators' evaluations of proposals to reform Rule 22. At least that is what many senators claim. Senator after senator has proclaimed that he or she will take advantage of the full extent of his or her parliamentary privileges in pursuit of an important cause and yet argue, perfectly consistently, that he or she has an obligation to take

Table 4-4. *Political Factors Strongly Related to Votes on Cloture, Multivariate Results, 1919–94*

	Majority party and years								
Variable	*1919–32 Republicans*	*1933–46 Democrats*	*1947–48 Republicans*	*1949–52 Democrats*	*1953–54 Republicans*	*1955–68 Democrats*	*1969–80 Democrats*	*1981–86 Republicans*	*1987–94 Democrats*
Left-right policy position		−√	[a]	[a]	[a]			+√	−√
Civil rights policy position	+√					+√	+√		
Party status									+√
Region	−√	−√							
Small state		−√							
Seniority	+√					+√			−√
Extremism variables									
LR, Dem, Lib						−√			
LR, Dem, Con									
LR, Rep, Lib	−√						−√		+√
LR, Rep, Con								−√	
CR, Dem, Pro	−√					+√			
CR, Dem, Anti		−√						−√	
CR, Rep, Pro								−√	
CR, Rep, Anti									
Number of measures subject to cloture votes	11	6	0	1	1	12	53	36	93

Source: Senate roll-call votes (ICPSR File #00004).

a. Too few cases.

Note: √ signifies statistically significant; +, − are signs of the coefficient, indicating that the seniority and extremist variables are sometimes significant in opposite directions. LR refers to the left-right dimension; CR refers to the civil rights dimension; Dem refers to the Democrats; Rep refers to the Republicans. For the left-right dimension, Lib is the liberal end and Con is the conservative end. For the civil rights dimension, Pro is the pro–civil rights legislation end and Anti is the anti–civil rights legislation end. See appendix 4-B for the detailed statistical results.

into account the institution's long-term interests when considering a change in Rule 22. Indeed, it may well be that even the mix of political factors that shapes attitudes about the rule is different from the mix that shapes senators' cloture votes on substantive policy questions. After all, any change in the rule is likely to last for some time and may affect a wide range of policy choices and possibly even the character of the Senate.

The relationship between voting on cloture and voting on reform proposals suggests that voting on reform proposals is in fact quite political. And the first major battle over a new cloture rule in 1891 is consistent with that interpretation. The successful filibuster over the elections bill (see table 4-1) led the frustrated Republican leaders to propose a cloture rule. On a key vote related to the proposal, nearly perfect partisan division occurred. Thirty-six of thirty-nine majority party Republicans voted against all thirty minority party senators who voted. In fact, the effects of party and policy positions (as measured by the left-right alignment) cannot be separated for this vote because the three variables are very highly correlated in that Congress.[35]

To see the relationship between voting on reform and the factors whose effects on cloture voting we examined above, we have chosen a key vote to analyze for each major effort to reform Rule 22 since 1917. In some cases, the vote is on a procedural matter, such as on an appeal of the ruling of the chair (for a detailed review of these episodes, see chapter 6). In 1986, when it approved the resolution providing for televised floor sessions, the Senate changed the number of hours for post-cloture debate from 100 to 30, but did not cast a vote that concerned reform of Rule 22 to the exclusion of other important issues. Thus, the following analysis concludes with the reform-related vote in 1979.

As table 4-5 indicates, voting on cloture motions is strongly related to voting on the key reform votes. Table 4-5 shows the percentage of times that senators supporting and opposing reform had voted in favor of cloture previously over their career in the Senate.[36] Senators favoring reform usually exhibit more than twice as much support for cloture as senators opposing reform.

One might think, then, that the factors that shaped senators' behavior on cloture votes also influenced their behavior on votes associated with reform of Rule 22. Table 4-6 reports the results of a multivariate estimate of the effect of each of the factors on senators' behavior on one roll-call vote for each episode of attempted reform of Senate rules governing debate since 1917. Factors with a statistically significant relationship with the vote on reform, controlling for the influence of the other factors, are checked.

Table 4-5. *Mean Percentage of Previous Cloture Votes on Which Supporters and Opponents to Cloture Reform Voted Yea, for Selected Key Reform Votes,*[a] *1949–79*

Position	*1949*	*1953*	*1957*	*1959*	*1961*	*1963*	*1967*	*1969*	*1971*	*1975*	*1979*
Supported reform	70.7	92.0	65.4	62.4	83.0	81.5	86.0	86.6	80.8	79.6	75.0
Opposed reform	33.4	43.0	44.7	39.8	25.6	18.9	37.9	19.3	22.2	47.7	40.3

Source: Senate roll-call votes (ICPSR File #00004).
a. Calculated over all previous cloture votes for senators with previous cloture votes.

In eight out of the twelve models, senators' policy positions are the only statistically significant predictor of senators' reform votes. And in all but one of the twelve models (1975, discussed below), senators' policy interests appear to directly shape their views about new institutional arrangements. Over time, however, the importance of the two policy dimensions shifts. After the reform effort in 1918, which divided senators along the liberal-conservative spectrum, civil rights divisions took over as the basis for senators' response to reform efforts. Liberal-conservative differences sometimes were apparent as well, but positions on civil rights issues almost completely ordered senators' voting on cloture reform from the mid-1950s until the early 1970s. But by the mid-1970s, after filibusters against the major civil rights bills had become ineffectual, the civil rights dimension had lost its structuring influence on attitudes about reform of Rule 22.[37] At that point, the liberal-conservative dimension took over, supplemented by partisan considerations. This pattern is entirely consistent with the change in cloture voting patterns observed above. That is, since the late 1970s, both cloture voting and voting on reform have been ordered by the liberal-conservative continuum, which itself has become increasingly structured by party.[38]

As in cloture voting, region, state size, seniority, and policy extremism have little to do with voting on the reform of Rule 22. Even party status has no measurable effect independent of the differences between the parties on the two policy dimensions. And extremists generally show no proclivity toward defending extended debate; they behave in much the same way as senators who neighbor them on the policy dimensions. Small-state interests and extended experience may lead a few senators to appreciate extended debate, as those few senators have claimed, but such factors are not systematically related to senators' voting on key votes related to reform most of the time. In fact, in two instances in which small-state senators show some distinctiveness in their reform-related votes, they actually were more likely to support reform that limited debate than other senators, just the inverse

Table 4-6. *Factors Influencing Support and Opposition to Cloture Reform, from Multivariate Analysis, 1918–79*

Variable	*1918*	*1949*	*1953*	*1957*	*1959*	*1961*	*1963*	*1967*	*1969*	*1971*	*1975*	*1979*
Left-right policy position	√	√		√	√				√			√
Civil rights policy position	n.a.	√	√	√	√	√	√	√	√	√		
Party status												
Region											√	
Small state									√		√	
Seniority												
Extremists												
LR, Maj, Lib	—				√							
LR, Maj, Con	—											
LR, Min, Lib												
LR, Min, Con												
CR, Maj, Pro	n.a.											
CR, Maj, Anti	n.a.											
CR, Min, Pro	n.a.	√										
CR, Min, Anti	n.a.											

Source: Senate roll-call votes (ICPSR File #00004).
√ statistically significant at $p < .05$.
n.a.: Not available.
— senators in category did not vote.
Note: For the first vote, civil rights dimension scores are not available. LR refers to the left-right dimension; CR refers to the civil rights dimension; Maj refers to the majority party; Min refers to the minority party. For the left-right dimension, Lib is the liberal end and Con is the conservative end. For the civil rights dimension, Pro is the pro–civil rights legislation end and Anti is the anti–civil rights legislation end. See appendix 4-C for the detailed statistical results.

of the argument that small-state senators should want to bolster the political interests of their states by empowering Senate minorities to block legislation.[39]

Of course, the statistical models reflected in table 4-6 do not perfectly predict senators' behavior on reform-related roll-call votes. In 1975, for example, the statistical model incorrectly predicts that Senator Weicker would support reform, largely on the basis of his liberal voting record. And yet, as his comments about being an outlier in his party suggested that he would, he voted against reform. The inference must be that Weicker placed greater weight on that argument in his decision about reform than did other similarly situated senators. Consequently, one cannot conclude that larger principles do not influence the voting of senators; they certainly seem to do so for a few senators. Nevertheless, the overwhelming importance of the policy positions of senators for voting on reform suggests that, on the whole, senators' views about the rules are determined by the implications of those rules for the policy choices of the Senate.

The 1975 pattern warrants special notice. Senators' liberal-conservative policy positions were strongly related to the 1975 vote on reducing the threshold for cloture, although they miss statistical significance by a small margin. Indeed, the overall fit of the multivariate equation for 1975 is weaker than in most other years, which suggests that more senators than usual went beyond their political concerns to approve a change in the rule. This is the same conclusion reached by political scientist John Gilmour, who observes that "without becoming any more liberal, senators simply changed their attitude toward the filibuster and became more interested than before in being able to shut off debate."[40] But the declining centrality of civil rights legislation as a target of filibusters by 1975 (figure 4-1) is one key to understanding the successful reform effort. Filibusters on many other subjects had become common and senators who might have resisted reform earlier now had an interest in reducing the cloture threshold. Equally critical was the ruling of Vice President Nelson Rockefeller that a simple majority could close debate on a resolution concerning the Senate's rules at the start of a new Congress. The ruling, initially backed by a majority of the Senate, gave reformers a source of leverage with opponents to reform and produced a compromise reform that gained the support of some senators who otherwise appeared to be opposed to it. The vote on the compromise produced divisions that did not divide the parties or the supporters and opponents of civil rights legislation as cleanly as they did in reform-related votes in other years. Still, not all opponents to cloture reform—particularly southern Democrats led by James Allen (Democrat of Alabama)—accepted the compromise and voted against its adoption.[41]

Overall, the historical pattern of support and opposition to cloture reform challenges the view that senators' shared commitment to institutional values and interests underpins the very incremental changes that have been made to Rule 22 since 1917. Senators' commitment to the traditions of their institution surely are the most frequently cited reason, at least among senators, for supporting the Senate's rules. No doubt many senators genuinely believe that the Senate and the nation are best served by placing few limits on debate in their institution. But it may go without saying that principles are often devised in defense of positions taken for more political reasons. Even principles resonate more with some people than others because of differences in experience or political interest. In fact, most senators appear to view the Senate's rules in pragmatic terms: they support those rules they judge to be the best for them. Regrettably, this is not a claim that can be backed by direct evidence. Instead, the evidence shows that divisions among senators on cloture motions and on efforts to reform the Senate's rule on debate fall largely along the lines that political and partisan considerations would suggest.

Why Are There Not More (Trivial) Filibusters?

Complaints about the trivialization of the filibuster in recent decades raise an important question: Why don't opponents to bills filibuster all the time? As observed in chapter 1, a changing political environment—in the form of increased political benefits from championing a cause by leading a filibuster—has produced more obstructive behavior in recent decades. Yet even in recent years not every bill with opposition provoked a filibuster—not even every bill opposed by a cloture-preventing minority. Thus a few more speculative observations about the constraints on filibusters seem in order.

The tendency of senators to restrain themselves from fully exploiting their parliamentary rights likely stems from self-interest. Most of the time, the costs of filibustering are sufficiently high for nearly all senators to allow the Senate to proceed to act on measures without the threat of a filibuster. Costs are experienced in many ways, for both individual senators and parties.

For individual senators, opportunity costs, the loss of political capital, fear of retribution, and reputational effects may counterbalance the incentives to filibuster. Perhaps most important are opportunity costs. A filibuster takes senators and their staffs away from other valuable activities. And ultimately, senators want to get something out of the Senate, and having the Senate perpetually tied in knots reduces their chances of getting anything done. Moreover, a tough battle over cloture may cost a senator substantial political capital—legislative favors and other considerations that are in limited supply—that could be used for other purposes. Good relationships with colleagues also are a hard-earned form of political capital that a senator may put at risk by filibustering. Furthermore, tit-for-tat retribution against filibustering senators' bills may persuade senators that frequent filibustering is counterproductive.[42] Senators also may have reason to believe that frequent filibustering will hurt their reputation with their home electorate and with the media. Obstructionism on behalf of causes that are not salient to home constituencies is a good way to undermine one's reputation as a serious and effective legislator, which, opponents will surely argue, hurts a senator's ability to serve a state's interests in the Senate. And favorable treatment in the press has many possible benefits of its own. Plainly, there are many reasons why a colleague of Senator Orrin Hatch (Republican of Utah) reportedly once told him after he held up a State Department bill, "If you want to get anywhere in this place, you've got to stop this sort of nonsense."[43]

An example from the Senate's consideration of an omnibus trade bill in 1987 shows well how senators' self-interest restrains them at times from fully exploiting their procedural rights.[44] Trying to attach an amendment to the trade bill to limit the entry of ships into the United States that had previously docked in Cuba, Lawton Chiles (Democrat of Florida) ran up against a chamber more than ready to complete consideration of the bill after three weeks of debate. Chiles also ran up against Senator Lowell Weicker, who threatened to filibuster the bill if the Chiles amendment was adopted. If the Chiles amendment was defeated or dropped, the Senate would proceed under a unanimous consent agreement to close debate. Chiles backed down, knowing that he lacked the votes to prevail on his amendment and not wanting to provoke a filibuster by Weicker that might have prevented—or at least significantly delayed—passage of the trade bill. The trade bill subsequently passed 71-27, with Chiles's support. The desire to achieve a legislative outcome and to avoid the wrath of his colleagues appears to have compelled Chiles to give up his fight for an amendment of importance to his Florida constituents. "I got caught up in the maelstrom, the we-have-to-get-out-of-here rush," Chiles explained. "I think under the circumstances, I may lie down and lick my wounds and live to fight another day."[45]

The collective interest of a minority party or coalition also tempers the urge to filibuster. Quite commonly, avoiding blame for killing popular legislation leads the minority's leaders to allow legislation to go forward against the wishes of nearly every member of the party. In 1995, for example, it appeared that the reluctance of Senate Democrats to filibuster the Republican welfare reform bill reflected their hesitancy about obstructing a popular issue. From time to time, the minority has feared that Rule 22 and minority rights are at risk if the full range of parliamentary tools is used to obstruct popular legislation. And for good reason: Rule 22 itself was the by-product of the reaction of the president and general public to a filibuster in 1917.[46]

An alternative explanation is that adherence to Senate norms, rather than calculated self-interest, accounts for the absence of truly ubiquitous filibustering. And perhaps the norms are observed because they are recognized by senators as serving the public good or simply the good of the Senate as an institution. That is, as mentioned in chapter 1, senators may be taking into account the institution's collective interests. If so, it may indeed be that senators' procedural strategies are motivated by their calculations about the institution's general needs; or even that senators both support a rule that preserves individual and minority rights and avoid abuses of that rule in order to serve the larger public or institutional good.

Observing the Senate in the 1950s, political scientist Donald Matthews noted that a norm of reciprocity suffused senators' interactions with one another. One element of that norm was an understanding that senators would refrain from fully exploiting their procedural rights. Commenting on the power of senators to block action by objecting to unanimous consent agreements or by outright filibustering, Matthews observed that "while these and other similar powers always exist as a potential threat, the amazing thing is that they are rarely utilized. The spirit of reciprocity results in much, if not most, of the senators' actual power not being exercised."[47] Given the looseness of Senate rules, Matthews argued, adherence to reciprocity and other norms was critical to ensuring that the Senate could function. Socialization to these norms served the interest of the Senate as an institution. The individual sacrificed for the collective good.

That is not the Senate of the late twentieth century. The norms restraining behavior weakened markedly by the late 1960s. Maybe the restrictive norms in society at large influenced the decline of norms within the Senate; whatever the cause, it is clear that the institution's collective welfare did not have much staying power.[48] Perhaps the institution's collective needs, although articulated by many senators as the rationale for their behavior, were never very powerful influences. If so, linking senators' institutional choices to shared norms or principles is inadequate. Instead, a theory that accounts for the way that senators' personal interests were served by restrictive norms is required.

Mid–twentieth century congressional norms appear to have reinforced other factors that restrained senators from filibustering more often. The norms generally meant that senators were expected to defer to senior leaders, most of whom were conservative and who could count on fairly conservative majorities on the Senate floor to back them up. As prescriptions for acceptable behavior, the norms probably had some, but limited, effect on senators beyond the influence of the cost-benefit calculations of senators operating in that environment. As Matthews himself noted, nonconformists of the 1950s tended to be liberals and the election of more liberal and urban-oriented senators would likely undermine the norms. The norms restricting members' full participation in any or all debates quickly gave way when the balance of political forces changed in the Senate between 1958 and 1972, the endpoints of a period in which a large number of liberals were elected.[49]

The remaining collegial norms of restraint are grounded in senators' personal interest in maintaining a modicum of order and predictability in Senate floor action in order to pursue their goals. That is, the degree to which the collective goal of institutional predictability is served is a byproduct of individual senators' political interests, which must be pursued with the behavior and strategies of other senators in mind.[50] Plainly, self-interest can provide a basis for concern about the collective interests of the Senate, but a genuine commitment to the general welfare of the institution and the nation is more likely to secure such ends. At any one time, the rules and norms—as the product of inherited rules and the current balance of senatorial interests—are unlikely to robustly secure collective institutional or national interests.[51]

Nevertheless, the fact that senators do not filibuster every bill, even when they constitute a cloture-preventing minority, should temper claims about unrestrained filibustering in the modern Senate. It is true that the combination of old rules and today's political conditions often creates strong incentives for senators to engage in obstructive behavior. Still, filibustering entails costs for an obstructing senator, even when that senator simply places a hold on a bill or threatens to object to a unanimous consent agreement. These costs clearly restrain senators from filibustering every bill they oppose. Because senators generally value the respect of their colleagues and often need their support to pursue their own legislative goals, only with rare exceptions are they likely ever to engage in entirely unrestrained obstructionism.

Conclusion

The nature of the issues subject to filibusters—their policy substance and significance—is clearly quite different from what is suggested by the now conventional account of the recent trivialization of the filibuster. "Trivial" uses of the filibuster are not new to the late twentieth century. Moreover, the decades of the mid–twentieth century—with a few filibusters limited to civil rights measures—are no more of a norm for the Senate than are the patterns of the last two or three decades. And partisanship, which is decidedly a central feature of filibusters in recent years, is not new to Senate obstructionism. To the contrary, in the full scope of Senate history, partisanship is nearly as important as sectionalism to filibustering. In either case, political objectives, not a principled commitment to a procedural norm, appear to dictate senators' behavior on cloture and on cloture reform. When high principle underpins senators' actions, it appears to be in their choice of substantive public policies rather than in the means for obtaining their policy objectives. As a general rule, senators seem to use the rules to serve their goals (policy and otherwise), and they use those rules to protect rules that serve their goals.

Nevertheless, partisan and parochial uses of the filibuster have increased in recent decades. The filibuster has become far more than a procedural weapon of last resort; senators now must anticipate a filibuster on nearly every controversial measure. Thus, although trivial and partisan uses of the filibuster are not new, the frequency of such uses has surged in the late twentieth century, creating a decisionmaking environment within the Senate that is qualitatively different from what the Senate has previously experienced. Whether such filibustering has in the distant or recent past had a substantial effect on policy outcomes in the Senate is explored next.

Appendix 4-A

The votes noted in table 4-1 are listed and described below. In each case, we have listed the year and subject as in table 4-1, the vote number (variable number) as used by the Inter-university Consortium for Political and Social Research (ICPSR)(File #00004), the specific date, vote outcome, name of senator making the motion or sponsoring the bill, and the vote description in the ICPSR's roll-call data sets.

1841 appointment of Senate printers
Var 0117, 27th Congress, March 5, 1841
Y = 29 N = 22 Mangum, N.C.
To consider the resolution to dismiss Blair and Rives as printers of the Senate for the 27th Congress.

1841 creation of a U.S. bank
Var 0244, 27th Congress, July 28, 1841
Y = 26 N = 23 Clay, Ky.
To pass S. 5.

1846 Oregon statehood
Var 0123, 29th Congress, April 16, 1846
Y = 22 N = 32 Allen, Ohio
To amend the joint resolution H.J. res. 4 (9 stat 109, 4/27/1846), notifying Great Britain to annul and abrogate the convention of Aug. 6, 1827, relative to the Oregon territory, by eliminating the provision that it has now become desirable to abrogate this treaty by the mode prescribed in its second article, and inserting in its place the provision that it has become the duty of congress to consider what measures it may adopt for the security and protection of American citizens living in Oregon, and for the maintenance of our just title to that territory.

1863 habeas corpus indemnification
Var 0785, 37th Congress, March 3, 1863
Y = 13 N = 25 Bayard, Del.
To pass a resolution providing that the Senate send to the House of Representatives requesting the return of the conference committee report on H.R. 591.

1865 recognize Louisiana government
Var 0536, 38th Congress, February 25, 1865
Y = 12 N = 17 Wade, Ohio
To postpone until the first Monday in December any further consideration of S.J. Res. 117.

1879 army appropriation, election law
Var 0229, 46th Congress, June 20, 1879
Y = 15 N = 27 Conkling, N.Y.
To amend H.R. 2175 by declaring that nothing herein shall be construed to affect the right to use any part of the army to execute the laws authorized by Congress or the Constitution.

1881 nominations
Var 0117, 47th Congress, March 14, 1881
Y = 34 N = 37 Burnside, R.I.
To adjourn.

1881 officers of the Senate
Var 0133, 47th Congress, March 24, 1881
Y = 31 N = 33 Pendleton, Ohio
To table the resolution that the senate proceed to the election of its secretary, sergeant-at-arms, doorkeeper, chief clerk, principal executive clerk, and chaplain.

1890–91 force bill (federal elections)
Var 0411, 51st Congress, January 14, 1891
Y = 33 N = 33 Hoar, Mass.
To consider H.R. 11045. The vice president voted in the affirmative.

1893 silver purchase
Var 0066, 53d Congress, September 4, 1893
Y = 20 N = 31 Jones, Nev.
To adjourn, to postpone action on H.R. 1, a bill repealing part of an act approved July 14, 1890, directing purchase of silver bullion and the issue of treasury notes thereon.

1903 statehood bill
Var 0112, 57th Congress, January 21, 1903
Y = 27 N = 37 Cullom, Ill.
To proceed to executive session.

1907 ship subsidy
Var 0131, 59th Congress, March 2, 1907
Y = 23 N = 41 Rayner, Md.
To postpone consideration of bill S. 529, until 8:00 this evening instead of 4:00.

1908 emergency currency, banking
VAR 0023, 60th Congress, March 27, 1908
Y = 42 N = 16 Aldrich, R.I.
To pass S. 3023.

1911 Arizona, New Mexico statehood
Var 0277, 61st Congress, March 4, 1911
Y = 39 N = 45 Owen, Okla.
To amend H.J. Res. 295, relating to the formation of the territory of New Mexico constitution, and the entry into statehood of said territory, under the act of Congress approved 6/2/1910, and the ratification and adoption of said constitution as of 2/9/1911, by adding to the above resolution, as a new section, a provision that the state of Arizona be also admitted to statehood.

1913 public buildings
Var 0383, 62d Congress, February 26, 1913
Y = 35 N = 15 Swanson, Va.
To pass H.R. 28766.

1914 rivers and harbors
Var 0319, 63d Congress, July 1, 1914
Y = 38 N = 23 Simmons, N.C.
To proceed to the consideration of the river and harbor appropriation bill for 1915, H.R. 13811.

1914 Panama Canal tolls
Var 0297, 63d Congress, June 11, 1914
Y = 50 N = 35 O'Gorman, N.Y.
To pass H.R. 14385.

1914 Clayton Antitrust Act
Var 0418, 63d Congress, October 5, 1914
Y = 46 N = 16 Culberson, Tex.
To pass H.R. 15657.

Appendix 4-B. Weighted Least Squares Estimates for Votes on Cloture (corresponds to table 4-4)

In analyzing cloture votes by era, our dependent variable is the likelihood of voting for cloture. We have roll-call data on every cloture vote within an era of party control of the Senate. Given these data, we considered three possible data analysis strategies.

1. Analyze each cloture vote within an era separately, using logistic regression, then compare the estimated coefficients on our independent variables across votes. This would produce a separate equation for each of the more than 200 cloture votes. This strategy, however, would not allow for straightforward summaries of the effect of independent variables.

2. Analyze each cloture vote within an era simultaneously, again using logistic regression. This would produce a single set of results, but would create serious complications. By lumping together multiple votes by the same senator, we would expect correlated errors across senators. Current methods of estimating logistic regression would force us into a panel logit context, which would introduce both computational and modeling complexites without much gain in substantive insight.

3. For each senator, aggregate all the cloture votes within an era and calculate the propensity of each senator to vote for cloture. The cloture propensity is then used as the dependent variable. This strategy results in one regression equation per era. The aggregation of data by senator results in a loss of efficiency (and higher standard errors) relative to strategy (2), but we believe the gain in interpretability offsets the loss of efficiency. Because the number of cloture votes per era varies across senators, there will be unequal error variance across senators, violating the OLS assumption of homoskedastic errors. We correct for this by using a standard WLS transformation, weighting our data by $1/\sqrt{\text{number of votes/era}}$★ .5. The results are as follows:

Table 4B-1.

Variable	Majority party and years								
	1919–32 Republican	*1933–46 Democrat*	*1947–48 Republican*	*1949–52 Democrat*	*1953–54 Republican*	*1955–68 Democrat*	*1969–80 Democrat*	*1981–86 Republican*	*1987–94 Democrat*
Left-right policy position	−.07	**−.43**	[a]	[a]	[a]	−.28	−.14	**.33**	**−.35**
Civil rights policy position	**.56**	.20				**.97**	**.54**	−.14	.07
Party status	.21	−.04				.03	.16	.10	**.19**
Region	**−.20**	**−.72**				−.14	−.07	−.02	−.01
Small state	.08	**−.22**				−.08	−.04	−.03	.003
Seniority	**.01**	.01				**.02**	.003	.001	**−.01**
Extremism variables									
LR, Dem, Lib	.27	−.15				**−.50**	−.15	−.04	−.06
LR, Dem, Con	−.08	−.25				.07	−.11	−.03	.08
LR, Rep, Lib	**−.45**	−.13				−.04	**−.33**	−.07	**.15**
LR, Rep, Con	.10	—				—	.01	**−.22**	.01
CR, Dem, Pro	**−.45**	.07				**.37**	−.19	.19	.01
CR, Dem, Anti	.15	**−.30**				−.09	−.22	**−.36**	.07
CR, Rep, Pro	−.15	−.34				.01	−.09	**−.16**	−.02
CR, Rep, Anti	−.12	−.05				−.13	.11	.05	−.07
Constant	−.38	.27				**−1.26**	.26	**.56**	**1.16**
Adjusted R^2	.24	.44				.61	.35	.71	.90
F	**5.59**	**10.68**				**18.34**	**7.72**	**20.59**	**84.58**
Number of measures subject to cloture votes	11	7	0	1	1	12	53	36	93

a. Too few cases.

— Senators in the category (determined by location on the policy dimension) did not vote on cloture.

Bold: $p < .05$.

Note: Unstandardized coefficients. No estimates are provided for periods with a very small number of cloture votes. The dependent variable is the percentage of time a senator voted for cloture on measures during that period. Weighted least squares estimates are reported because the dependent variables are based on different numbers of cloture votes across senators. Ordinary least squares produces similar results but yields biased standard errors. Policy dimensions variables: the left-right dimension is the average of senators' scores on the first D-NOMINATE dimension for the Congresses included; the civil rights dimension is the average of senators' scores on second D-NOMINATE dimension for the Congresses included. Extremism variables: senators are extreme on each of the policy dimensions if they are located in the most extreme 5 percent at either end of the dimension within their party. LR refers to the left-right dimension; CR refers to the civil rights dimension; Dem refers to the Democrats; Rep refers to the Republicans. For the left-right dimension, Lib is the liberal end and Con is the conservative end. For the civil rights dimension, Pro is the pro–civil rights legislation end and Anti is the anti–civil rights legislation end.

Appendix 4-C. Logit Estimates for Votes on Cloture Reform (Corresponds to table 4-6)

In this analysis of individual cloture reform votes, the dependent variable is dichotomous. That is, it takes only two values, yea or nay. In this situation, OLS is inappropriate and a discrete choice model should be used. We elected to use logistic regression, often called logit. In logit, one estimates the B parameters, given the functional form $e^{XB}/(1 + e^{XB})$. Because this is a nonlinear functional form, the effects of the estimated coefficients do not have a simple linear interpretation. We are mainly interested in the direction of influence and statistical significance of the estimated coefficients.

Reform-related roll-call votes included in the analysis

The votes analyzed are listed and described below. In each case, we have listed the label used in the table, the vote number (variable number) as used by the Inter-university Consortium for Political and Social Research, the specific date, the vote outcome, and the vote description in the ICPSR's roll-call data sets (File #00004).

v286s65
Var = 0286 June 13, 1918
Y = 34 N = 41
To pass S. Res. 235.

v54s81
Var = 0054 March 17, 1949
Y = 63 N = 23
S. Res. 15. On Wherry substitute amendment providing for application of cloture to any measure, motion or other matter pending before the Senate on an affirmative Y-N vote by two-thirds of the entire membership, except that unlimited debate is permitted on a motion to proceed to the consideration of a motion, resolution, or proposal to change the Senate standing rules.

v33s83
Var = 0033 January 7, 1953
Y = 70 N = 21
Taft motion to table Anderson motion that the Senate consider the adoption of the rules of the 83d Congress.

v12s85
Var = 0012 January 4, 1957
Y = 55 N = 38
Motion to table motion to consider adoption of rules for Senate. Original motion was move to ease rules on limitation of debate, as prelude to civil rights legislation. Agreed to.

v13s86
Var = 0013 January 12, 1959
Y = 28 N = 67
S. Res. 5. Proposal to enable two-thirds of senators voting instead of two-thirds of the membership to shut off debate on an amendment to enable the majority to limit debate.

v11s87
Var = 0011 January 11, 1961
Y = 50 N = 46
S. Res. 4. Anderson proposal to revise rule 22, to enable three-fifths rather than two-thirds of senators voting to invoke cloture. Mansfield-Dirksen motion to refer to committee on rules and administration. Agreed to.

v13s88
Var = 0013 February 7, 1963
Y = 54 N = 42
S. Res. 9. Mansfield motion to invoke cloture on Anderson motion to take up the resolution. Two-thirds Senate majority required.

v11s90
Var = 0011 January 18, 1967
Y = 37 N = 61
To table a point of order, raised during debate on proceeding to consideration of S. Res. 6, which amends Senate rule 22. Senator McGovern moved to close debate on taking up S. Res. 6 by a simple majority, citing article I, section 5 of the constitution. Senator Dirksen made the point of order that this was not a constitutional question and McGovern was, in effect, moving the previous question by a simple rather than a two-thirds majority, as required by the rules.

v18s91
Var = 0018 January 28, 1969
Y = 50 N = 42
To impose cloture on the motion of Senator Hart to take up S. Res. 11, to amend Senate rule 22 so as to provide for the bringing of Senate debate to

a close under certain circumstances by a vote of three-fifths rather than two-thirds of the senators present and voting.

v19s92
Var = 0019 March 9, 1971
Y = 55 N = 39
To invoke cloture on the motion to consider S. Res. 9.

v65s94
Var = 0065 March 7, 1975
Y = 56 N = 27
To pass S. Res. 4, as amended.

v16s96
Var = 0016 February 22, 1979
Y = 78 N = 16
To agree to S. Res. 61. S. Res. 61 amends the standing rules of the Senate by restricting debate on an issue after cloture has been invoked (motion passed).

Table 4C-1.

Variable	*v286s65*	*v54s81*	*v33s83*	*v12s85*	*v13s86*	*v11s87*	*v13s88*	*v11s90*	*v18s91*	*v19s92*	*v65s94*	*v16s96*
Left-right policy position	**−4.46**	**−8.89**	−5.96	**−6.10**	**−14.08**	1.21	1.08	−4.92	**−11.04**	−.76	−6.47	**−33.38**
	(1.96)	(4.26)	(4.40)	(2.84)	(6.13)	(3.70)	(3.81)	(3.60)	(4.73)	(4.29)	(3.66)	(14.24)
Civil rights position	n.a.	**10.12**	**20.24**	**15.25**	**20.99**	**17.15**	**24.27**	**10.01**	**16.16**	**15.50**	−1.02	5.21
		(4.50)	(8.36)	(4.49)	(6.69)	(5.38)	(7.83)	(4.51)	(6.59)	(5.58)	(4.22)	(12.24)
Party status	−.49	−.02	−6.04	−.09	−3.83	3.26	2.71	1.13	−1.83	3.19	−.93	−8.41
	(1.58)	(2.94)	(3.92)	(1.91)	(3.19)	(2.88)	(2.94)	(2.29)	(2.83)	(2.89)	(2.28)	(6.21)
Region	−1.06	−10.81	−8.83	−9.62	−6.41	−7.64	1.17	−9.24	−3.70	−1.22	**−2.26**	−.26
	(.82)	(54.59)	(49.98)	(46.04)	(44.94)	(49.16)	(1.88)	(52.16)	(2.36)	(1.36)	(1.14)	(1.82)
Small state	−.93	−.41	1.00	−.22	−1.55	.07	−.47	−1.05	**−3.88**	−.94	**−2.14**	−.72
	(.83)	(1.16)	(1.39)	(1.09)	(1.04)	(.91)	(1.02)	(.71)	(1.54)	(.90)	(.90)	(2.60)
Seniority	.03	.22	−.23	−.19	.23	−.12	.13	.02	.36	.04	.07	.14
	(.11)	(.13)	(.19)	(.16)	(.13)	(.13)	(.15)	(.10)	(.19)	(.10)	(.08)	(.20)
Extremists												
LR, Maj, Lib	—	13.72	−2.84	15.54	**−4.40**	17.22	7.17	8.56	2.71	5.40	5.73	−11.25
		(164.65)	(246.12)	(144.79)	(2.19)	(140.94)	(111.44)	(151.84)	(116.12)	(110.29)	(67.66)	(115.54)
LR, Maj, Con	—	4.39	1.86	7.05	−1.03	4.06	.63	−7.68	1.24	−3.87	−7.11	12.18
		(196.32)	(185.19)	(956.23)	(129.26)	(271.60)	(164.30)	(127.60)	(85.05)	(115.43)	(99.64)	(116.17)
LR, Min, Lib	−.70	13.74	2.42	−8.82	−7.69	5.55	2.08	—	.18	3.86	4.73	−10.29
	(1.79)	(165.89)	(270.84)	(270.83)	(270.84)	(170.47)	(164.28)		(217.90)	(115.75)	(69.83)	(105.26)

LR, Min, Con	−1.99	−1.13	5.52	−5.30	5.12	−5.96	−4.68	−3.86	−3.43	−6.84	−8.15	−1.58
	(22.29)	(190.21)	(182.33)	(270.82)	(270.87)	(270.82)	(164.27)	(270.83)	(101.48)	(115.74)	(99.64)	(113.94)
CR, Maj, Pro	n.a.	5.67	3.45	5.14	18.29	4.96	1.62	5.29	.48	−2.32	—	−.86
	. . .	(151.12)	(183.98)	(956.23)	(136.91)	(271.24)	(197.89)	(153.99)	(105.80)	(115.56)	. . .	(201.20)
CR, Maj, Anti	n.a.	6.20	8.73	3.24	6.20	5.46	2.79	7.51	2.00	3.83	4.60	−9.98
	. . .	(155.35)	(186.75)	(191.29)	(181.35)	(156.22)	(92.44)	(155.78)	(112.87)	(115.94)	(57.41)	(114.67)
CR, Min, Pro	n.a.	**10.58**	9.82	−4.18	5.59	−5.61	−2.57	6.53	−1.20	−2.47	−8.03	5.41
	. . .	**(3.70)**	(197.47)	(190.89)	(270.87)	(270.82)	(164.28)	(275.81)	(108.26)	(113.98)	(99.65)	(7.25)
CR, Min, Anti	n.a.	9.14	3.12	6.38	4.99	3.94	.18	−14.10	−1.93	—	—	—
	. . .	(270.82)	(183.77)	(176.84)	(270.83)	(170.48)	(164.28)	(270.82)	(217.90)	. . .	. . .	. . .
Constant	.01	−.37	−1.53	−.71	**−5.81**	−3.73	−4.63	−3.03	−.96	−2.35	2.08	**9.81**
	(.92)	(2.27)	(1.68)	(1.77)	(2.61)	(2.53)	(2.90)	(2.05)	(2.13)	(2.00)	(1.67)	(4.98)
N	80	95	91	93	98	100	94	100	99	100	86	96
Chi-square	35.6	83.9	77.5	96.7	85.0	94.3	89.6	80.73	104.3	90.0	51.5	73.5
	(p = .00)	(p = .00)	(p = .00)	(p = .00)	(p = .00)	(p = .00)	(p = .00)	(p = .00)	(p = .00)	(p = .00)	(p = .00)	(p = .00)

Source: Senate roll-call votes (ICPSR File #00004).

—Senators in category did not vote.

n.a.: Not available. Standard error indicated in parentheses. **Bold:** $p < .05$.

Note: For the first vote, civil rights dimension scores are not available. LR refers to the left-right dimension; CR refers to the civil rights dimension; Maj refers to the majority party; Min refers to the minority party. For the left-right dimension, Lib is the liberal end and Con is the conservative end. For the civil rights dimension, Pro is the pro-civil rights legislation end and Anti is the anti-civil rights legislation end. Ns in each equation reflect the inclusion of paired and announced votes.

Round-the-clock filibustering: Richard Russell and Everett Dirksen take a break during an all-night civil rights filibuster.

5

The Filibuster and the Little-Harm Thesis

MANY SUPPORTERS of unrestricted debate argue that the use of the filibuster has done little harm to the public welfare and has sometimes done much good.[1] In 1926 political scientist Lindsay Rogers proclaimed, "the absence of closure has been justified by its results; no really meritorious measure has been defeated and some vicious proposals have been killed."[2] Perhaps the most fully developed exposition of the thesis that the filibuster has done little harm and much good was formulated by three senators as a dissenting view on the 1949 cloture reform proposal.[3] The senators—John Stennis (Democrat of Mississippi), Russell Long (Democrat of Louisiana), and Lester Hunt (Democrat of Wyoming)—observed:

> In the testimony favoring legislation on debate in the Senate presented to the committee, a great deal of theoretical handicaps and weaknesses of the present rules were presented, but the proponents of change failed to present one single example of any real injury to the American people caused by the delay on legislation due to extended debate. The opponents to change in the rules extend a challenge to the proponents to show such injury at any time since the free debate rule was instituted in the Senate in 1806. This challenge was made early during the hearings on this subject, and was unanswered throughout that period.[4]

Furthermore, they asserted, "Of the important measures which can be described as definitely defeated by filibusters, the list dwindles down to five": the force bill of 1890, the armed ship bill of 1917, the antilynching bills, the anti–poll tax bills, and the Fair Employment Practices Commission bill of 1946. The senators argued that the country was better off for the Senate's having killed the civil rights bills.

Arguments in favor of the little-harm thesis persist. In 1995 former congressman Bill Frenzel (Republican of Minnesota) claimed that "filibusters simply do not succeed *unless* they have popular support."[5] Senator Robert Byrd wrote in 1990 that the filibuster "never has been and never will be fatal to the overall public good."[6] In 1995 the senator insisted "the filibuster will not eternally kill something, kill legislation that the American people really want. It may slow it down for a while. It may stop it for a while. But in the process of education of the American people through unlimited debate, the American people often become more aware of what they are being asked to buy. . . . I have maintained that if the American people really understand a question, if they really understand it and they really want it, they will get it regardless of the filibuster."[7] Thus, if these defenders of extended debate are correct, little harm is done by the filibuster, while substantial good is done in the protection of minority interests, the maintenance of a deliberative process in the Senate, and the education of the public.

The little-harm thesis, at root, contends that senators prefer rules that protect the collective interests of the Senate. According to filibuster defenders, the country, or at least the Senate, has been better off by having the filibuster than it would have been without it. Some people or interests may have been disadvantaged, but the disadvantage is not large enough to prevent the larger good from being realized. If supported by the evidence, this argument undermines the alternative view that calculations about political advantage shape institutional development and props up the view that institutions evolve to serve the needs of the collectivity.

Conveniently for the defenders of Senate practice, the little-harm thesis is not easily challenged by hard evidence. To test the thesis directly, it would be necessary to distinguish meritorious from unmeritorious legislation, popular from unpopular legislation, or, as the Byrd test would have it, "really" wanted legislation from "not so really wanted" legislation. Needless to say, no one would be satisfied with any test of the proposition that good measures are not killed by filibuster, or that the bad bills killed outweigh the good bills killed, so we do not pursue one. Moreover, testing the proposition that filibusters do not kill popular or really wanted legislation would require measures of the breadth and intensity of public opinion. Unfortunately, data on public opinion are not available on the vast majority of matters that have been subject to filibusters. And if public opinion data were available on filibustered measures, a comparison with public opinion on other measures would be required to determine whether the patterns of public opinion on filibustered measures were distinctive.

In the absence of direct evidence, the little-harm thesis may be evaluated in several ways, starting with an analysis of how many times legislation has been killed or long delayed by a filibuster.

Measures Killed by Filibuster

It *almost* goes without saying that the cloture rule—and before 1917, the absence of a rule providing for an end to debate—sets a higher threshold for Senate approval of filibustered measures than for other measures and therefore makes it less likely that a filibustered measure will be approved by the Senate. On the face of it, then, cloture makes it more difficult to pass a controversial measure. Yet the little-harm thesis, if given a generous interpretation, suggests that few measures of significance (to senators, to the general public) are defeated because of the higher threshold. The natural place to begin an evaluation of the little-harm thesis is to determine how many measures, if any, have been supported by a Senate majority and yet killed by a filibuster, and, of those, how many were approved by the House and supported by the president. A measure that was supported by the House and president as well as by a less-than-required Senate majority—a majority smaller than required to invoke cloture—is one whose demise can be attributed to the Senate's rules. If many measures have been killed by filibusters, there will be some ground for questioning the little-harm thesis. Failure to find numerous measures killed by filibusters will lend credence to the thesis.

Obstacles to Testing the Little-Harm Thesis

Unfortunately, serious obstacles stand in the way of testing the little-harm thesis in this way. Perhaps most important is the usual problem of anticipated reactions—the possibility of a filibuster may discourage bill sponsors or floor leaders from bringing bills to the floor. Indeed, Senate history is littered with bills that were left for dead because their sponsors anticipated a filibuster.[8] Consequently, the filibuster may have killed far more measures in the Senate than would be shown by a count of measures defeated by manifest filibusters. Even detailed case studies would not reveal how many bills were set aside by bill sponsors or committee chairs who did not want to waste their time on legislation that was sure to die on the Senate floor. Perhaps one should be surprised when sponsors still bother to take measures to the floor only to be blocked by unlimited debate and dilatory motions on the part of a Senate minority.

A product liability bill brought to the Senate floor in 1986 is a good example of a Senate majority leader's anticipating a filibuster and allowing the bill to die. The Republican majority on the Senate Committee on Commerce, Science, and Transportation reported a bill that would limit certain court awards to victims of defective products and quickly gained a 97-1 vote to invoke cloture on the motion to proceed to the consideration of the bill. Thus it appeared that the bill had broad support, although a provision providing for a cap on awards for pain and suffering still divided Republicans and was opposed by most Democrats. An amendment to drop the cap was certain to engender a long debate and perhaps a successful filibuster. The majority leader, Robert Dole (Republican of Kansas), decided to pull the measure from the floor rather than risk a filibuster that would hold up other legislation in the waning days of the 1986 session.[9] In this case, the threatened filibuster combined with severe time constraints led the majority leader to set aside the measure. The November 1986 elections produced a new Democratic majority in the Senate and put Ernest Hollings (Democrat of South Carolina) in the chairmanship of the committee. Product liability reform was put off for several years.

House and presidential action also may reflect anticipation of Senate action. House leaders may not bother to act on a measure if it is likely to die in the Senate; the president may not have occasion to express support or opposition to a bill that is falling to a Senate filibuster. In 1903, for example, a threatened filibuster blocked Senate action on a currency reform bill pushed by Nelson W. Aldrich (Republican of Rhode Island), the leader of the majority party. Senator John T. Morgan (Democrat of Alabama), the leading filibusterer, saw through the Republican strategy, which provided for swift House action as soon as the Senate passed the bill. Morgan was quoted in the *New York Times*: "'There is evidently an arrangement made by which this bill is to be passed through the House under a rule for its consideration, and that there is nobody in that House, particularly a Democrat, who will be permitted to have a word to say about it.' It was an object lesson, he said, and shows the bill does not stand on the same footing as other legislation. The bill, he said, was a most dangerous measure. At this point Mr. Morgan remarked upon the fact that Mr. Aldrich was smiling."[10] The *Times*, siding with Aldrich on the substance of the legislation and operating under somewhat antiquated journalistic standards, observed in an editorial that a rumor was circulating in Washington that the filibustering senators would realize a windfall in their investments if the bill were killed. While the bill was debated briefly as the Congress was about to expire, a full-blown filibuster was not required to defeat the bill, and so the measure does not appear on lists of filibusters that appear in congressional publications.[11] The House leadership did not bring the bill to the floor, and journalistic accounts provide no clues about what might have happened in the House. No one has counted the bill as having been killed by a filibuster (and we do not either), although it almost certainly was.

Waiting for the Senate is still common in the House. In 1994 Congressman John Dingell (Democrat of Michigan), then chairman of the House Energy and Commerce Committee, chose to delay committee action on a product liability reform bill because it seemed likely that the bill would die under a Senate filibuster, as it did.[12] In the same year, House majority party leadership waited for the Senate to act on health care reform before finalizing its version and bringing the bill to the floor. The Senate bill died on the floor, so the House was never recorded on the matter. Neither bill, in the absence of strong indications about what the House would have done if the measure had been taken to the floor, is included in our list of bills killed by filibuster. Clearly, to require that the House and president are on record in favor of a measure before it is counted as having died because of a Senate filibuster is an inappropriately high standard, but there may be no other way to gauge House and presidential sentiment. As a consequence, requiring hard evidence of House support for a measure in order to count the measure as having been killed by filibuster will understate the number of measures delayed or killed by filibusters.

But that is not the end of the obstacles to testing the little-harm thesis. One additional difficulty is the *error of inferences drawn from roll-call votes*. Filibusters, of course, prevent the Senate from voting directly on the bill (or resolution, amendment, or motion) at issue and so make it difficult to determine how many senators supported the bill (or resolution, amendment, or motion). And when cloture votes are cast, not all senators who vote for cloture favor the affected bill, and not all senators who oppose cloture would vote against the bill. To be sure, the correspondence between voting on cloture and voting on the underlying measure is strong, but the exceptions to the rule are numerous. As observed in chapter 4, most southern Democrats opposed cloture motions during the mid–twentieth century regardless of the issue. Cases in which senators, particularly minority party senators, opposed cloture but eventually supported a bill are quite numerous.

And there are cases of senators who favor a measure voting against cloture when they see that the minority is sufficiently determined and large enough to prevent cloture. In 1938, for example, a majority of senators, but far less than the two-thirds majority required for cloture, appeared to favor an antilynching bill. Some of the senators favoring the bill voted against cloture to make it clear that they opposed spending more time on the bill; they feared that doing so would sidetrack the administration's program.[13] We can (and do) take this into account when contemporary observers offer credible evidence about the mismatch between policy preferences and voting on cloture, but we cannot be certain about how many cases we have missed.[14]

Another difficulty in counting measures killed by filibusters is in evaluating *collateral damage*. A count of the measures that were the immediate object of filibusters would ignore measures that died at the end of a Congress because delays created by filibusters on other measures made it impossible for the Senate to act on them. Minority senators might even pursue a filibuster on one measure in order to avoid having to openly conduct a filibuster against a popular measure that they oppose. In a few Congresses, in fact, the minority has employed a broad obstructionist strategy in order to prevent a number of bills from receiving action. This became the open strategy of the Republican minority at one point in the second decade of the twentieth century. In February 1917, after several years of aggressive filibustering, the Republicans decided to slow down or stop Senate business in order to force President Woodrow Wilson to call a special session after the mandatory March 4 adjournment. The Republicans believed that the necessity of a special session when the Democrats controlled both houses of Congress would be embarrassing to the Democrats and the president. The effort was by and large successful.[15] In that case, and others, estimating how many measures, if any, were caught up in end-of-session obstructionism is treacherous.

A close cousin to the problem of the collateral damage is ambiguity about the *target of the filibuster*. An amendment may be pending on the floor when debate becomes extended, but the underlying bill, not the amendment, may be the real target of the filibuster. In most cases, the real target of the filibustering senators is clear. More difficult is a situation in which a senator filibusters or threatens to filibuster one bill in order to gain or block action on another measure. In 1926, to cite one case, a sizable majority behind a bill on migratory bird refuges was unable to gain a vote on its measure because at least some senators were hoping to postpone action on other unrelated legislation. In this case, the bill had genuine opponents, who argued that the federal government should not be in the business of protecting bird refuges, but, not uncommonly, other senators seemed to have other political motives.[16] At a minimum, such strategic uses of the filibuster may camouflage its real target to both the contemporary audience and historical investigators. At the extreme, such strategies result in an inappropriate inference about whether a filibuster actually killed a bill.

Finally, senators' *tactical errors* sometimes lead to the demise of a bill, obscuring the role that the cloture rule played. Monday-morning quarterbacks are numerous in politics, of course, but they are sometimes right. Perhaps a measure would have fared better if its sponsor had pursued a better strategy; certainly senators do not always pursue their best strategies. In 1962, for example, Majority Leader Mike Mansfield was blamed for tactical errors that reduced the number of votes for cloture on a voting rights measure, a measure that observers claimed had the support of a majority of senators.[17] In this case, journalistic accounts indicate the level of support for the bill, but trustworthy accounts usually do not exist. Unfortunately, then, there is no practical way to evaluate the consequences of senators' tactics for an audit of successful and unsuccessful filibusters, even in the case of manifest filibusters.

In sum, the problems associated with anticipated reactions, inferences drawn from voting behavior, collateral damage, filibuster targets, and tactical errors bias assessments of the manifest historical record in favor of the little-harm thesis. Rules, or the absence thereof, shape senators' strategies in ways that cannot readily be measured. The threat of a filibuster and other obstructionist moves under Senate rules may be enough to prevent floor action on measures, or at least force the early withdrawal of proposals, that surely would be counted as having been killed or delayed by a filibuster had their sponsors chosen to push ahead anyway. Plainly, one should be highly suspicious of any empirical claims about the number and importance of measures killed by filibusters. Such claims will most certainly understate the number of measures killed by filibusters, manifest or anticipated.

Measures Killed by Filibusters

Although the problems involved in a count of measures killed by filibusters may seem daunting, claims about the number of measures killed by filibusters remain central to the arguments of defenders of extended debate in the Senate. For that reason, we have done our best to determine whether it is reasonable to attribute the demise of filibustered measures to the Senate filibuster.

To be counted as killed by a filibuster, a measure must be favored by a Senate majority, House majority, and the president and still have died (at least for that Congress) after debate on the Senate floor. This standard is applied to all measures through 1994 that appear to have been killed by filibusters, as reported in Franklin Burdette's 1940 book, *Filibustering in the Senate* and in a 1985 Senate committee print, or that were subject to cloture motions. In each case, contemporary newspaper or periodical accounts, the *Congressional Record* or its predecessors, and secondary sources were examined for evidence of the positions of the Senate, House, and president. The resulting list of measures killed by filibuster appears in table 5-1.[18]

The list looks remarkably short. In the period before 1917, only ten measures or sets of measures (the two filibusters in 1881 involved several presidential nominations) fell under filibusters. From 1917 through 1994, thirty-one measures died under filibusters. The list looks even shorter if items on the list are set aside that do not involve legislation that directly alters public law—Senate organization and rules changes, nominations, and the one sense-of-the-Senate resolution. Only twenty-six measures survive the cut. Thus, of the many thousands of bills that have been before the Senate, only twenty-six measures that would directly change public law were pushed to the floor and clearly killed because of the ability of a minority of senators to prevent action.

Beyond the so-called force bill, debated in 1890–91, perhaps the best known of the measures killed by filibuster before the adoption of Rule 22 is the 1917 bill to authorize the arming of American merchant ships. The administration requested the authority after a German declaration of unrestricted submarine warfare in the northern Atlantic Ocean and President Wilson's decision to sever diplomatic relations with Germany. Just as the Senate debate on the bill began, a publicly disclosed communication from the German foreign ministry aroused public indignation. The message suggested that, in the event of war between Germany and the United States, Germany would seek alliance with Mexico to help Mexico recover

Table 5-1. *Measures Killed by Filibusters, 1789–1994*

Before Rule 22 was adopted	
1881	Organization of Senate (3rd session)
1881	Presidential nominations
1881	Presidential nominations
1891	Force bill
1891	Cloture proposal
1901	Rivers and harbors appropriations bill
1903	Statehood bill
1907	Ship subsidy bill
1913	Presidential nomination
1915	Ship purchase bill
1917	Armed-ship bill
After Rule 22 was adopted	
1922	Antilynching bill
1935	Antilynching bill
1938	Antilynching bill
1946	Anti–poll tax bill
1946	Fair employment bill
1950	Fair employment bill
1963	Rule 22 reform
1966	Right-to-work bill
1966	Open housing bill
1967	Rule 22 reform
1968	Supreme Court nomination
1969	Rule 22 reform
1971	Rule 22 reform
1972	Consumer protection agency bill
1974	Genocide treaty
1975	New Hampshire Senate election contest resolution
1977	Draft-evaders' pardon sense of the Senate resolution
1977	Rule 22 reform
1978	Labor law reform bill
1980	Fair housing bill
1982	Televised Senate floor sessions
1984	Televised Senate floor sessions
1986	Antidrug, death penalty bill
1988	Great Smoky Mountains Wilderness bill
1989	Capital gains tax cut bill
1993	Supplemental appropriations bill
1994	Presidential nomination
1994	Striker replacement bill
1994	Campaign finance reform bill
1994	Lobbying disclosure bill

Source: See text.

former Mexican territory in the southwestern United States. Moreover, Japan would be asked to join in the alliance. The disclosure ensured popular support for President Wilson's modest request to arm merchant vessels. Nevertheless, in the waning days of the Sixty-Fourth Congress, a handful of antiwar senators—labeled "a little group of willful men" by Wilson—blocked action on the bill through extended debate. In fact, seventy-five senators signed a statement indicating their support for the bill. The firestorm generated by the death of the armed ship bill spurred the new Senate, meeting just a few days later, to adopt the first cloture rule as Rule 22.[19]

Table 5-1 makes plain that the filibuster became a more deadly weapon in recent decades. About two-thirds of the legislative deaths by filibuster occurred between 1962 and 1994, a period of just 33 years out of the 205-year history of the Senate before 1995. The measures killed by filibuster during that period span a very wide range of subjects: consumer protection, labor-management relations, the federal death penalty, taxation, an economic stimulus package, campaign finance reform, and lobbying reform. Thus it is easy to understand why many observers and senators before the mid–twentieth century observed that the filibuster had done little harm. It is equally plain that the rate of death-by-filibuster—even for manifest filibusters—has been increasing since that time.

Civil Rights Legislation and the Filibuster

Legislation related to civil rights issues is more common than legislation of any other kind. Nine of the twenty-six measures killed by filibuster and affecting public law concern civil rights issues. However, contrary to the impression created by the comments of Senators Stennis, Long, and Hunt in 1949, filibusters in 1901, 1903, 1907, and 1915 on non–civil rights measures, as well as the filibusters on presidential nominations, make the number of non–civil rights measures blocked by filibusters before that time about as large as the number of civil rights measures killed by filibuster. Still, by the mid–twentieth century it is clear that civil rights measures as a class were the dominant subject of measures that can reasonably be claimed to have been killed by filibuster. And the connection between civil rights and the cloture rule was plain to everyone. Not merely coincidentally, Senator Lyndon Johnson (Democrat of Texas), later Senate majority leader and president of the United States, used his first major speech in the Senate to oppose civil rights legislation and defend the right to unlimited debate.[20]

The extraordinary role of the filibuster in legislative battles over civil rights measures can be explained, no doubt, by the especially emotional, sectional, and lasting character of the issues. No issue in American politics has produced a voting electorate so polarized by region for so broad a time span as has the role of the federal government in race relations.[21] The Senate's high threshold for cloture—and, before cloture, the absence of a cloture or previous question motion—has often been defended on the ground that it prevented the enactment of legislation that would ignite racial violence and even rekindle intersectional warfare. Civil rights advocates charge that the welfare of millions of citizens over many decades has suffered immeasurably because of delays in federal civil rights creation and enforcement that were the product of the filibuster.

The defense of the filibuster as a means to prevent the enactment of civil rights legislation rests almost entirely on whether one supports or opposes the affected legislation. That certainly was true of Senators Stennis, Long, and Hunt in their minority views on the 1949 reform proposals. About the force bill of 1890, they wrote: "There is now general agreement among all schools of thought, no matter what the views about Federal supervision of election processes, that the famous force bill of 1890, with its provision for Federal control of elections in the south with the use of Federal troops, was unwise legislation. We now realize that it developed from the partisan feeling that remained following the War Between the States, and that its eventual defeat through the process of a filibuster has served the best interest of our Nation."[22] They had similar views of the antilynching, anti–poll tax, and fair employment measures.

> Each one . . . that has reached the floor of the Senate has been of gravely doubtful constitutionality. Even some of the present most ardent sponsors of an antilynching law agree that the early Dyer Act and the later versions of this bill contained unconstitutional provisions. The extent to which the constitutionality of an anti-poll-tax bill is doubted can be best demonstrated by the fact that 10 Democratic Senators have submitted a constitutional amendment dealing with that subject, believing that to be the manner in which Congress should take action on a suffrage question. The FEPC proposal of 1946 contained provisions which have been universally decried as violating the constitutional requirements of a fair and impartial trial.
>
> It would be superfluous to add that this type of legislation is conceded to be aimed at one section of the country, a type of action contradictory to the long-established American governmental principles first enunciated by President George Washington. Have the

American people suffered any injury through the defeat of these measures by the use of prolonged debate?[23]

Plainly, the three senators' answer to that rhetorical question is no. Equally plain, their answer is at odds with Senate majorities in many Congresses since the Civil War.[24] A brief review of the measures noted will make the point.

The 1890 federal elections bill was labeled the "force bill" by its opponents—mainly Democrats and southerners.[25] The demise of the bill in January 1891 marked the last time for three-quarters of a century that the Senate seriously debated a bill to guarantee fair elections by federal law. It came in the midst of rising physical intimidation of blacks by whites and the birth of a variety of legal barriers to the equality of rights in economic, social, and political life. Congressional efforts to create and protect civil rights by enacting and implementing the Thirteenth and Fourteenth Amendments to the Constitution were narrowed and often made ineffectual by Supreme Court rulings in the 1870s. The court ruled that the federal government could act on civil rights only in the narrow area of relations between the citizen and the national government and barred the federal government from applying the equal protection clause of the Fourteenth Amendment to private action.[26]

The 1890 bill represented an effort to protect voting rights in federal elections and, so it appeared to its proponents, was constitutional under the rulings of the Supreme Court. The bill provided for the appointment of election supervisors on a bipartisan basis and, in the event of a charge of election fraud or intimidation, empowered them to conduct investigations and determine the candidate to be certified as the winner. The election practices emerging in the South were the obvious target of the bill's chief proponents, but, contrary to the impression created by the bill's critics, the bill did not provide for the use of federal troops or apply to the conduct of state or local elections. The bill died after a long filibuster and an unsuccessful effort by Republican leaders to gain Senate action on a new cloture procedure. As a result, state efforts to raise obstacles to voting by African Americans continued apace.

The political alignment on the elections bill was indeed partisan. The Republican party platform of 1888 proclaimed the need for a federal law to guarantee honest elections.[27] The House had passed the bill in mid-1890 on a straight party-line vote after it was reported from a select committee created for the special purpose of getting the bill to the floor. In the Senate, Republicans were far from united about the priority that should be given to the bill, but the Republican caucus eventually agreed to keep the bill before the Senate until a vote was obtained during the short session at the end of the Fifty-First Congress that began in December 1889. Nevertheless, the partisanship on the elections bill was hardly distinctive, at least not in the Fifty-First Congress. In fact, party-line votes were more common in that Congress than in most others in Senate history.[28] It seems fair to infer that attitudes about race, southern society, and states' rights combined with partisanship to produce particularly strong emotions about the elections bill on both sides of the issue, in the country as well as in the Senate.[29]

In the 1920s and 1930s civil rights advocates shifted their legislative efforts to the enactment of legislation that would empower federal authorities to investigate and prosecute lynchings. Lynchings, which were often investigated and documented by the National Association for the Advancement of Colored People (NAACP), numbered at least ninety per year in the 1890s and had been declining, but still averaged about sixty per year in the 1910s.[30] By the turn of the century, most lynchings occurred in the rural South and often involved accusations of sexual relations between a black man and white woman. But, as politicians, political activists, and sociologists have argued convincingly, the goal of lynchings was intimidation and compliance with a racial caste system. The threat of federal action against lynching is thought to have helped to reduce official tolerance of lynching in the South, but the frequent recurrence of lynchings into the 1930s kept federal involvement a live issue until midcentury.[31]

Three bills designed to create federal authority to investigate lynchings died by filibuster in the Senate in 1922, 1935, and 1938.[32] The bills were supported by large majorities in the House. If passed, the bills were likely to be signed by the president at the time—Republican Warren G. Harding in 1922, Democrat Franklin D. Roosevelt later, both of whom probably preferred that the issue not arise but did not oppose the legislation and varied from indifferent to favorable in personal views about the measures. And although one cannot be confident about the extent of support for the measures among senators, the filibusters appear to have been required because a Senate majority favored the bills. Thus the Senate filibuster delayed federal action against lynching and no doubt extended the life of the practice, particularly in the rural South.

In the 1940s attention moved to the enactment of legislation banning poll taxes—fees that otherwise eligible citizens were required to pay before voting. Civil rights advocates believed that removing this obstacle to voting would allow African Americans, as well as poor whites, to exercise greater influence on local and federal elections and gain changes in public policy that would improve their economic, political, and social condition. Their opponents insisted that federal action would unconstitutionally infringe on states' rights to regulate elections. A more partisan overlay on the issue was the implication of new African-American voters for the parties. Some Democrats feared or threatened that the new voters would be Republican in the context of southern politics; some Republicans feared that the new voters would be New Deal Democrats.

The poll tax fights illustrate the difficulty of interpreting votes on cloture. Bills banning poll taxes died under filibusters in 1942, 1944, and 1946. Only in 1946 did the cloture motion related to the bill garner majority support, so it is the only one of the three bills listed in table 5-1. But in both 1942 and 1944 at least some contemporary observers believed that a Senate majority would have voted for the bill if a direct vote on the bill had occurred. In 1942, the *New York Times* reported that some Democrats hid behind the filibuster—they would vote for the bill if a vote occurred but preferred not to "deliver the Democratic South into the hands of the Republican Party" by reducing barriers to voting by African Americans.[33] A reasonable inference is that a procedure that could have guaranteed a direct vote on the bill would have produced a majority for the bill. Instead, at least a few senators who would have voted for the bill if confronted with a roll-call vote were able to defend their behavior by noting their commitment to unrestricted debate.[34] Because we cannot be sure that even a previous question motion would have received a majority vote, the 1942 and 1944 cases are not included in table 5-1.

After 1946, civil rights measures on employment and housing were blocked by filibusters. The 1949 change in Rule 22—which applied cloture to any pending matter but also set the threshold at two-thirds of the entire membership, up from two-thirds of those voting—ensured that the civil rights program of the Truman administration would have no chance in the Senate. Indeed, civil rights legislation stood little chance until after the 1964 elections, when the addition of liberal Democrats shifted the balance of forces enough to create a two-thirds majority for cloture on the Civil Rights Act.

A 1962 bill intended to ban arbitrary literacy tests as a condition for voting might well be added to the list of measures killed by filibusters. The bill, according to some accounts, had majority support but was blocked when two cloture votes failed to produce even a majority for ending debate. In fact, after the first cloture motion failed by a 43-53 vote, sixty-three senators voted against a motion to table the bill, presumably because they wanted the Senate to eventually act on it.[35] As in the 1940s, some senators expressed support for the bill and yet voted against cloture. One such senator was Norris Cotton (Republican of New Hampshire), who explained, "As a Senator from a small state, who may some day find the welfare of his own people threatened by combinations representing the more powerful and populous states of this nation, I do not intend to surrender this (filibuster) weapon. Unless it be a very extreme case when the will of the Senate is obviously being thwarted, I do not intend by my vote to establish a precedent."[36] With conflicting evidence about the views of a majority of senators on the bill, the 1962 literacy bill is excluded from table 5-1.

By 1964 the Senate had voted eleven times to invoke cloture on civil rights measures, each time without the necessary two-thirds majority.[37] After the Civil Rights Act of 1964 and Voting Rights Act of 1965 were enacted, however, only a 1980 fair housing bill, among several civil rights measures considered, was killed outright by a filibuster. Other civil rights legislation was amended under threat of a filibuster, but compromises managed to salvage the bills. When viewed over the history of civil rights legislation in the Senate, there is little doubt that the filibuster was a powerful and often decisive procedural weapon.

Beyond Measures Killed by Filibusters

The preceding discussion pertains only to whole bills that were killed by filibusters, and not to measures affected by manifest or threatened filibusters. In 1968, to note one example, a filibuster forced open-housing advocates to reduce the coverage of their antidiscrimination bill and to drop key enforcement provisions—greatly changing the import of the bill—in order to gain cloture on an amendment and pass the bill. (Curiously, Senator Cotton managed to vote in favor of cloture on all but the first of the four cloture votes on the open housing bill.)[38] In 1976 a filibuster forced significant changes in an antitrust bill. The 1976 bill was especially significant because the filibustering senators took advantage of loopholes in the 1975 cloture rule to hold up action indefinitely *after* cloture was invoked (see box). It was also noteworthy because a southern senator, James Allen (Democrat of Alabama), led the filibuster on a matter that had nothing to do with civil rights; in fact, Allen opposed provisions in the bill that would have empowered states' attorneys general to bring certain suits to federal courts for the first time. In 1995, to take another example, proponents of a broad reform of the civil litigation system were forced to accept modest and circumventable limits on jury awards in product liabil-

Post-Cloture Filibustering

In the spring of 1976, Senators James Allen (Democrat of Alabama) and Roman Hruska (Republican of Nebraska) exploited loopholes in Rule 22 to gain leverage over the Senate majority on an antitrust bill. In the end, Allen and Hruska managed to get the Senate to limit government powers and penalties in antitrust actions by federal and state governments.

The bill's sponsors easily obtained cloture on the antitrust bill (67–22, with 60 votes required for cloture) and faced, they thought, a few additional hours of debate before bringing the bill to a final vote. Under Rule 22, each senator had one hour to debate after cloture is invoked, but proponents of the bill clearly would not use their time. Rule 22 also allowed germane amendments pending at the time cloture is invoked to be considered, which gave Allen, Hruska, and their allies an opportunity to demand roll-call votes to reconsider votes, to table amendments, to demand the presence of absent senators, and so on. In all, seventy roll-call votes, each taking fifteen minutes or more, were cast, the time for which was not counted against any senator's one-hour limit. With no end to the post-cloture delays in sight, the bill's sponsors agreed to support an amendment demanded by Allen and Hruska.

During the post-cloture debate, Majority Leader Mike Mansfield and Majority Whip Robert Byrd charged Allen and Hruska with undermining the viability of the cloture rule. Mansfield said, "I warn those who will return for the 95th Congress and those who would preserve the tradition of unlimited debate in the Senate that the actions of the minority on this bill will inevitably lead next year to a major attempt in the Senate to alter Rule 22 to provide for majority cloture."[a] The rule was not changed until 1979, by which time the Senate had experienced additional episodes of post-cloture filibusters, as they came to be known. The 1979 rule reduced post-cloture debate to 100 hours and included votes on procedural motions within the time limit.

a. Quoted in "Senate Passes Compromise Antitrust Bill," *Congressional Quarterly Weekly Report*, June 19, 1976, p. 1591.

ity cases under threat of filibuster. Such casualties of the filibuster are almost always ignored by its defenders.

Plainly, filibusters, or the threat thereof, shape legislative outcomes in ways beyond the killing of bills, notably through changes in legislation that they stimulate and their influence on the political setting beyond the outcome of the legislation directly affected by them. These political consequences have obvious and significant implications for public policy. The question is, does the Senate's rule actually moderate public policy, by requiring larger majorities to overcome filibusters, as some would argue? The irony of this argument is of course that it is not entirely consistent with the view that the Senate's rule has little policy significance. In fact, unlimited debate has a pervasive effect on the Senate, an effect that goes well beyond its measurable consequences for public policy.

Filibusters and the Content of Legislation

Accounting for the frequency and importance of changes made to bills that were caused by a filibuster or threatened filibuster is just as difficult as counting whole bills killed by filibuster. The senators and staff members responsible for drafting, introducing, or modifying legislation usually leave little retrievable documentation that could be used to attribute to them the motivation of overcoming a filibuster. Even for the modern Senate, an exhaustive search of journalistic accounts and official congressional documents is likely to miss many cases of legislation influenced by the threat of defeat by filibuster.

Nevertheless, we have surveyed *Congressional Quarterly Weekly Report*, *National Journal*, the *New York Times*, and the *Washington Post* for the 1985–95 period to uncover legislation on which the Senate outcome is attributed, at least in part, to a filibuster or threatened filibuster. The legislation is listed in table 5-2. The list includes only measures that eventually passed the Senate and only measures for which a majority of senators appeared to have preferred a somewhat different outcome.[39] And the list includes only measures and parts of measures for which the connection to a filibuster or threatened filibuster is direct and credible. The mere mention of a possible filibuster or the high threshold that a bill might have to pass in the Senate did not put the bill on the list. In many cases among the items on the list the Senate refused to invoke cloture for an amendment that appeared to be supported by a majority and so the amendment was dropped. In other cases, part of the text of the bill or committee substitute was modified or deleted. And, in a couple of cases, the threat of a Senate

Table 5-2. *Senate Actions Influenced by a Filibuster or the Threat of a Filibuster, 1985–95*

1985	Farm relief legislation: presidential nomination filibustered to get this legislation considered
1985	South Africa sanctions bill: filibuster threat forced House to compromise
1986	Defense appropriations bill: compromise on T46 jet trainer funding
1986	Antidrug bill: dropped death penalty provisions
1987	Supplemental appropriations bill: dropped SALT II compliance provisions
1987	Trade bill: dropped amendments on ships visiting Cuba and Kuwaiti ship reflagging
1987	Defense authorization bill: dropped SALT II compliance and SDI testing ban provisions
1988	AIDS bill: dropped provisions for confidentiality of AIDS testing results
1990	Defense authorization bill: dropped amendment on abortion at U.S. military facilities abroad
1990	Clean air act: dropped provisions for protection of visibility in national parks
1990	Immigration reform bill: changed family preference quotas
1990	Foreign aid appropriations bill: dropped amendment on organizations that counsel abortions
1991	Crime bill: changed handgun purchase waiting period provisions
1991	VA/HUD appropriations bill: dropped amendments on savings and loan audits
1991	Foreign aid authorization bill: dropped amendment setting El Salvador aid conditions
1991	Defense authorization bill: dropped amendment on abortion at U.S. military facilities abroad
1991	Interior appropriations bill: dropped amendment on TVA–North Carolina county settlement
1992	Energy bill: dropped Alaska drilling provisions and compromised on coal miners' benefits
1993	Motor voter bill: changed provisions on registration at welfare and unemployment offices
1993	Campaign finance reform bill: changed public funding and political action committee contributions provisions
1993	National service bill: changed program size and participants benefits
1993	Crime bill: added provisions limiting federal benefits for illegal aliens
1993	Handgun regulation bill: changed waiting period provisions
1993	Hatch Act: changed provisions limiting political activities of top civil servants
1993	Interior appropriations bill: dropped provisions increasing grazing and mining fees
1994	Crime bill: dropped racial justice provisions
1994	Competitiveness bill: authorized level of funding for program cut
1995	Supplemental appropriations bill: dropped striker replacement amendment
1995	Second supplemental appropriations bill: restored funding for many programs
1995	Line-item veto: changed Republican plan
1995	Product liability reform: abandoned broad reform of civil litigation system
1995	Defense authorization bill: dropped provisions for a new missile defense system
1995	Cuba sanctions bill: dropped lawsuits provision
1995	Foreign policy reorganization bill: changed provisions on reorganization of agencies; concessions on other legislation

Source: See text.

filibuster forced the House to back down from its position on an issue. Because journalistic accounts generally do not address the possibility of a filibuster until a bill emerges from committee, the list includes no measures that were written or modified during initial committee action with a floor filibuster in mind.[40]

The list of measures in table 5-2 whose content was influenced by the filibuster looks long. The list includes on average more than three measures per year for the eleven years in the search. Thus the number of bills whose Senate outcome was influenced by the filibuster in that eleven-year period is larger than the twenty-six policy-related bills killed by the filibuster between 1789 and 1994 (table 5-1). Gauging the significance of the measures and provisions affected by the filibuster is a subjective matter, but most of the items made end-of-session reviews of congressional action and most reflected important issues of the day. And the issues range across domestic and foreign policy: antiapartheid sanctions against South Africa, weapon systems and arms control, AIDS, abortion, immigration, crime and gun control, aid to El Salvador, energy and Alaska oil drilling, and product liability and the cost of litigation. The list extends well beyond the confines of civil rights legislation. Plainly, legislation of at least moderate policy significance has been influenced by filibusters or threatened filibusters with regularity in recent years.

One condition of the use of the filibuster as a procedural weapon—the constraint of time—is common to several of the measures on the list. Sometimes time is a constraint because of events external to Congress, as was the case when growing violence in South Africa in 1986 played a role in gaining House and Senate acceptance of less severe sanctions on South Africa in order to overcome a Senate filibuster threat and speed action on the bill.[41] In other cases, deadlines set in statute, such as the beginning of the federal fiscal year for appropriations bills, give filibusters added bite. More frequently, senators' eagerness to adjourn at the end of a session, particularly at the end of the second session with an election looming a few days or weeks in the future, motivates concessions to the senators who are filibustering or threatening to filibuster. In some cases, the filibustering senators are few in number: in October 1990 Senator Alan Simpson (Republican of Wyoming) successfully extracted concessions from a conference committee on immigration reform. It appears that senators can sometimes be enticed to make policy concessions in exchange for two or three days at home to campaign in an approaching election.

Time is exploited for political advantage in numerous ways beyond end-of-session tactics. At times partisans seek to give lobbying efforts an opportunity to influence a few senators' votes. At other times partisans hope to stimulate favorable public opinion, or perhaps to let interest in an issue fade, before proceeding to floor votes. And the ability to delay Senate action on a measure increases the viability of hostage-taking strategies; delay may give the obstructionists an opportunity to tie their support on one measure to concessions on another matter. Indeed, one oft-cited defender of the filibuster, political scientist Lindsay Rogers, went so far as to applaud the use of threatened filibusters as a means to gain action on unrelated measures.[42] Deliberative delay often is combined with public proclamations that more time is required to devise detailed alternatives or to conduct negotiations. In each case, substantive changes in legislation may be achieved that are very difficult to quantify after the fact.

Still, perhaps contrary to a common conception about filibusters, time was not a major factor in Senate action on a majority of the measures listed in table 5-2. In most cases opposition in the form of a filibuster or threatened filibuster occurred before the end of a session and without some other impending deadline. The substance or politics of the issue appeared to dictate the obstructionism quite apart from the timing of Senate action or bargaining leverage that may have been gained on other matters. This may be testimony to the strong political incentives to exploit the rules in the modern Senate.

Of course, the Senate's experience in 1985–95, as reflected in table 5-2, probably is not typical of Senate experience over its entire history. To the contrary, the list is consistent with the observation that the filibuster is used or threatened more frequently in recent years than in the past. The list also confirms that the increase in cloture votes observed for recent years is not merely the result of unprovoked procedural uses of cloture by impatient majority leaders. Many bills were modified as a direct response to filibusters, manifest or threatened. Moreover, the fact that several of the items on the list were not subject to a cloture vote indicates how dangerous it is to rely on cloture votes to identify instances of leverage gained under Rule 22. The circumstantial evidence is fairly strong that the number of filibusters or threatened filibusters with meaningful consequences was substantial in the late twentieth century.

Other Legislative and Political Consequences of the Senate Rule

The instances of bills killed by filibuster or modified under the threat of filibuster do not exhaust the consequences of the filibuster. Many of the effects are more indirect than those discussed so far. It should not be surprising that the indirect effects are more difficult to document, so they are only briefly illustrated here, without a comprehensive survey, even for a limited period.

SHORT-SESSION OBSTRUCTIONISM. Before the implementation of the Twentieth Amendment to the Constitution in 1933, Congress often met for a third session—often referred to as the "short session"—from the December immediately following an election through March 3, the day before the new Congress was sworn into office. Short-session obstructionism occurred in the nineteenth century but intensified after the turn of the century. In 1903 the *New York Times* observed that Senate Democrats pursued such a strategy: "The unblushing frankness with which Senators declared that there would be no vote on any contested bill was unusual and unprecedented. There have been many periods when partisan feeling has produced a bitter and revengeful situation in the Senate, but it is almost beyond recollection that there has been such an avowed condition of deadlock."[43] The certainty of the adjournment date contributed to the effectiveness and frequency of obstructionism during the short sessions. At least that is what many observers believed. Indeed, before 1933 many opponents to filibuster reform argued that rescheduling sessions so that the ending dates were uncertain was all that was required to end the pettiness of short-session obstructionism.[44] And an election that produced a change in party control of the Senate was sure to motivate the winning party to obstruct the agenda of the outgoing majority. Short-session obstructionism often targeted specific bills (those that make the list in table 5-1), but it had unmeasurable consequences for other legislation on which a Congress could not act before it expired as March 4 arrived. In some cases, action on appropriations bills was delayed until the new Congress, with a different alignment of preferences, convened. But, as already mentioned, end-of-session filibustering remains a common tactic in the Senate.

GENERAL SLOWDOWN STRATEGIES. The Twentieth Amendment did not end general slowdown strategies on the part of Senate minorities. On several occasions since that time, it appears that a minority party has deliberately slowed Senate action throughout a session of Congress in order to reduce the productivity of the majority, to contribute to the impression that the majority party cannot govern, or to create a backlog of legislation at the end of a Congress, thereby making filibusters more effective. In 1987 and 1994, for example, newspapers reported that Senate Republicans, a minority in both cases, pursued a deliberate strategy of slowing Senate action.

In both cases the effect of the strategy on individual pieces of legislation is debatable, but in both cases an argument can be made that the slowdown strategies tarnished the reputation of the majority party and may have had more important long-term consequences than the immediate targets of the obstructionism might indicate.

In the early months of 1987, a new Democratic majority showed remarkable cohesiveness in its effort to challenge President Ronald Reagan, whose popularity had slipped and who, in the last two years of his administration, had little legislative agenda of his own. The new Speaker of the House, Jim Wright (Democrat of Texas), was driving a large agenda of his own and Senate Democratic leader Robert Byrd was eager to reestablish himself as an effective leader. Having just fallen to minority status after six years in the majority, Senate Republicans soon became frustrated by their inability to influence policy and decided to exploit more fully their parliamentary prerogatives.[45] Byrd charged that the Republicans were pursuing a "'scorched-earth' strategy," and the Republicans could hardly deny that they were being obstructionist. According to the *Washington Post*, Republican strategy was aimed at "preventing the Democrats from using Congress as a platform for mounting a campaign focusing on their ability to produce results, especially when those results undermine the legacy of President Reagan and the Republican-led Senate of the last six years."[46]

Republican strategy at the end of the second session of the 103d Congress in 1994 appeared to have a similar motivation. Senator Carl Levin (Democrat of Michigan) claimed that the Republicans were seeking to "deny a reform success to Congress" so that they could build a case against Democratic control of Congress in the fall campaigns.[47] Republicans responded that Democrats controlled the House, Senate, and the White House and could not avoid the blame for inaction on numerous measures.[48] Health care reform, telecommunications reform, lobbying reform, and other measures were affected by Republican obstructionism, but, the Republicans believed, the Democrats and President Bill Clinton would be blamed for their failure to fashion legislation that could survive the legislative process even if Republican tactics were the immediate cause for the death of the measures. As it turned out, the ineffectual Democrats did seem to be blamed for the "mess in Washington" in the 1994 elections, in which they lost control of both houses.[49]

In both cases, then, the real target of the Republicans seemed to be as much the majority party's reputation as its legislation. If a party's reputation affects its electoral fortunes, as it seems to, then the consequences of the general slowdown extend far beyond that Congress.[50] As Senator

Joseph Lieberman (Democrat of Connecticut) observed in 1995: "It is hard for a majority to be held accountable fairly to the public if a minority, a party, for instance, can block the majority from attempting to work its will, from attempting to pass its program, and then, unfairly in some cases, the majority may be held accountable for that failure even though it was the minority who blocked action by filibustering that resulted in the failure to produce."[51] If the composition of the next Congress or control of the White House turns on party reputation, at least in part, the consequences of obstructionism may be substantial.

How can the majority be blamed for inaction in the face of minority obstructionism? There is no simple or tested answer, but several factors seem to contribute to the success of the minority. Minority party efforts to demonstrate it had alternative proposals that the majority refused to give serious consideration may succeed at times. Republican efforts to generate their own health care proposals and to criticize the Clinton administration's unwillingness to pursue bipartisan negotiations probably contributed to their success in shifting blame to the Democrats in 1994. Differences within the majority party may add credibility to the minority's inevitable claim that the majority is incapable of governing, even if a cohesive majority would still lack the votes to invoke cloture. And, when the majority forces the minority to follow through on its threat to filibuster, the minority can charge that the majority is responsible for delaying action on other legislation of importance.[52] Perhaps most significant, the public may give greater weight to majority control of the Senate, along with the other institutions, than to the niceties of Senate procedure in attributing blame for gridlock. If so, then blocking the majority's measures, even popular ones, may redound to the minority's advantage, particularly when the minority can do so without a direct vote on the measure.[53] Partisan bickering and legislative gridlock, whatever their source, seem to affect the majority party more than the minority party.

PROTECTING THE PRESIDENT. From time to time, the president seems to prefer seeing a bill killed by a filibuster rather than having the measure make it to his desk for signature or veto and thus force him to take a stand on the issue. Aware of the president's interests, his Senate supporters filibuster a bill that could more easily be killed by a veto (which can be overridden only with a two-thirds vote in both houses) or, in other circumstances, do not work as hard as they might to overcome the obstructionism. The effect is to spare the president the political fallout of making a choice. If that fallout has electoral consequences, as is sometimes claimed, then the longer-term policy consequences may be substantial. Some examples illustrate the point.

Perhaps the more common use of the filibuster is to relieve the president of the burden of vetoing a bill. An end-of-session filibuster against a river-and-harbor bill spared President William McKinley the necessity of vetoing that popular bill in 1901. The lead filibusterer, Senator Thomas H. Carter (Republican of Montana), had been defeated for reelection in November 1900, in his state's legislature, and was rewarded with a salaried appointment with the St. Louis Exposition.[54] In 1992 Senate Republicans successfully blocked action on an anticrime bill that the Democrats may have loved to have Republican President George Bush veto. The successful filibuster of the conference report spared President Bush the difficulty of explaining a veto in the midst of a presidential election campaign. The same might be said of an education bill conference report that Republicans refused to allow to come to a vote at the same time.[55]

The filibuster also may save the president the burden of supporting a controversial measure and reduce his accountability for the outcome. In 1938, as noted above, the Senate considered legislation to authorize federal authorities to conduct criminal investigations and prosecutions when state and local authorities failed to do so in the case of lynchings. Eleanor Roosevelt, the president's wife, was a strong advocate of the legislation; the president remained silent. Everyone assumed that he would sign the legislation if forced to choose between signing or vetoing it (thus there was reason for southerners to filibuster the measure), but he probably preferred to have the issue disappear from the national agenda without taking a public position on the matter. To take a position would worsen the divide between northern and southern Democrats and, in the view of some observers, would lead some southerners to desert to the Republican party. Not surprisingly, the Republican leader urged the majority party leadership to fight for the bill until the bitter end. In response, the Democratic leadership allowed the issue to come to the floor but quickly pulled the bill from the floor after cloture failed. If not for the successful filibuster, President Roosevelt would have been compelled by congressional majorities to take a public position on the matter.[56] No one doubts that the combination of race relations and states' rights reflected in attitudes about the measure represented a volatile mix for Roosevelt and the Democrats.

SENATORS' POWER AND HOLDS. As noted in chapter 3, Senate majority leaders pursue unanimous consent agreements whenever possible to lend order to Senate floor proceedings.[57] Unanimous consent is required because of the absence of general limits on debate and amending activity, the absence of majority cloture or a previous question motion, and the pressure to use floor time efficiently. The necessity of obtaining unanimous consent has led floor leaders to seek advance warning of potential objections to their scheduling plans. They do so by consulting widely, using a "hot line" phone system to notify senators of hour-to-hour developments and entertaining special requests from individual senators to notify them in advance of floor action, to be sure to protect their prerogatives, or to simply object to any action on a measure. Registered objections to requests to take up a measure are known as holds. Holds delay action when the leader does not want to risk an objection to his request for unanimous consent that the Senate proceed to a bill, particularly when the objection would upset his plans and lead to a time-consuming parliamentary move and perhaps an embarrassing squabble on the Senate floor. Holds gain their bite from the heavy burden of business, the majority leader's dependence on the cooperation of his colleagues and the goodwill of the minority leader, and the evolved expectations of senators about the observance of holds.[58]

Holds are sometimes placed on measures for purposes other than obstructing floor action. In some cases, the hold is no more than a request to be notified in advance so that a senator can be prepared when the bill comes to the floor. In other cases, the senator wants to be sure that his or her opportunity to offer an amendment is protected in any unanimous consent agreement. But in other cases, the hold is intended to be obstructive. The purpose of the obstructionism ranges from a minor change in the bill at hand to gaining a concession from a committee chair, the leader, or even the administration on an entirely unrelated matter.

This pyramid of rules and practices—the difficulty of limiting debates and amendments under cloture, reliance on unanimous consent agreements, and holds—empowers individual senators to delay action on matters of moderate importance. At a minimum, individual senators can demand that floor action be scheduled to their convenience. More seriously, individual senators often can extract concessions from bill sponsors and managers even when they lack the support to carry on a filibuster for long. They can even block floor action on legislation altogether when the price of overcoming their objections is too high for an overburdened floor leader. From time to time, in fact, holds have become a serious problem for floor leaders of both parties. One senator noted, "You have to think of the Senate as if it were 100 different nations and each one had the atomic bomb and at any moment any one of you could blow up the place. So that no matter how long you've been here or how short you've been here, you always know you have the capacity to go to the leader and threaten to blow up the entire institution. And, naturally, he'll deal with you.''[59]

Holds—which come down to threatened objections to taking up measures—do not prevent the majority leaders from gaining floor consideration of the most important legislation. Some bills, such as budget-related matters, are highly privileged and cannot be blocked by a single senator. Other legislation is simply too important to many senators of both parties for a single senator to risk being blamed for inconveniencing his or her colleagues by forcing them to endure unnecessary delays so that parliamentary procedures can be pursued to overcome the obstacle. But for many other measures, the policy or political consequences of the leverage gained through holds are meaningful. Unfortunately, the extent to which legislation is influenced by the obstructionism of individual senators is not easily measured.

Not surprisingly, holds became more of a problem for floor leaders as filibusters became more common and post-cloture filibusters broke out in the late 1970s.[60] In the Ninety-Fifth Congress (1977–78), then Senate majority leader Robert Byrd proved reluctant to bring to the floor measures on which holds had been placed. The heavy burden of the Carter administration's program and frequent filibusters put a premium on gaining unanimous consent for action whenever possible and on avoiding delays for legislation of only moderate significance and on which holds had been placed. Byrd's successors, Republicans Howard Baker (of Tennessee) and Robert Dole, suffered under the burden of holds as well. They sometimes had to contend with Republican colleagues who would take turns placing holds on a measure, in tag-team fashion, to tie up a measure for weeks or months.[61] Despite their efforts to proceed with legislation even when members of their own party registered holds, they could do little about a minority leader who dutifully objected to unanimous consent requests whenever a hold was placed on a measure by a member of the minority party.[62] Subsequent floor leaders have been equally frustrated by minority holds and appear to have responded by filing cloture petitions more frequently.

A Pervasive Effect

Without a doubt, Rule 22 has pervasive effects on policymaking in the Senate. This is a point on which many, although not all, defenders and reformers agree. For the defenders, the rule ensures that minority views are heard by making it easy for even a single senator to slow floor action on a measure or amendment. For reformers, the rule undermines accountability by allowing senators and even presidents to hide behind a procedural device whose consequences are difficult to gauge. Whether these effects are harmful remains a debatable question; whether the effects are substantial does not, as explained in chapter 7.

The Filibuster and the Moderation of Legislation

The little-harm thesis has several rhetorical siblings:

—The filibuster has killed bad legislation more often than good legislation.

—The filibuster has occasionally prevented a Senate majority from passing legislation that was opposed by popular majorities.

—The filibuster has not prevented a Senate majority from acting on measures favored by a popular majority of the country.

—The extraordinary majority requirement for cloture forces compromises.

One might even infer from this line of argument, as some do, that the filibuster has a moderating influence on public policy. That is, by making it more likely that Senate action on a House-passed or president-backed bill will be slowed or blocked, Senate procedures increase the probability that radical or divisive measures will not become law before substantial revisions are made to moderate their policy consequences.

There is little to be gained by arguing about whether more bad than good legislation has been killed by the filibuster, since there is no sound basis for making such a judgment in this context. But the other arguments, leading to the inference that the Senate's rule has a moderating effect, warrant closer inspection. Indeed, two related but distinct arguments are made about popular majorities and the filibuster. The first argument is that the filibuster occasionally prevents a Senate majority from passing legislation that is opposed by a majority of Americans.[63] As Senator Orrin Hatch put it, "The filibuster rule is the only way the majority of the people, who are represented by a minority of the Senate, can be heard."[64] The second and more common argument is that the filibuster has not prevented Senate action on legislation favored by a popular majority of Americans. The usual argument is that at least some senators will succumb to public pressure eventually if the public has clear preferences about an issue.

The arguments are strange twists of logic for defenders of the filibuster who otherwise give high priority to the preservation of minority rights. Oddly, defenders of the filibuster feel compelled to argue an empirical case

Figure 5-1. *Hypothetical Alignment of Senators along a Single Dimension*

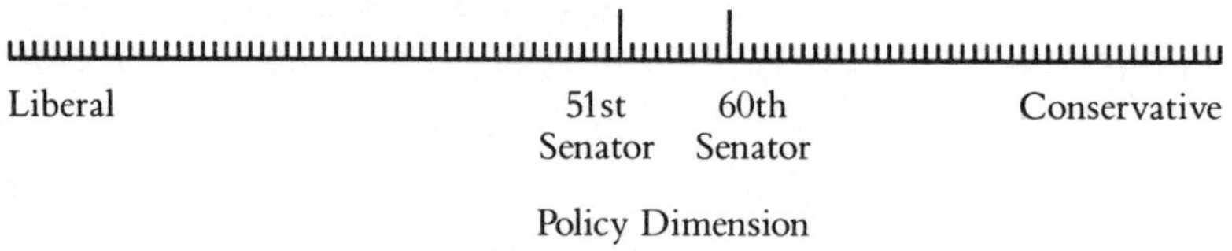

that the preservation of minority rights in the Senate serves the will of the popular majority. This observation need not be pushed any farther. But it is important to note that the arguments are not backed by systematic analysis of Senate action and public opinion. As noted at the beginning of the chapter, marshaling evidence about majority opinion in the general public and the Senate for or against these arguments is not feasible. Not surprisingly, no one has made more than a token effort to identify more than a few cases that seem to support or undermine the arguments.

The basic logic of the filibuster and popular will is not too complicated. In a single dimension (see figure 5-1) and a one-hundred-member Senate, the fifty-first senator is pivotal to the outcome.[65] Both ends of the spectrum must appeal to that median senator in order to have a majority. The supermajority requirement for cloture under the current rule makes the sixtieth senator pivotal. The question of popular will therefore comes down to whether the fifty-first or the sixtieth senator is closer to the preference of the median voter in the general public, the person who determines the popular majority's view. There is no necessary correspondence between the Senate's decision rule and the fit of the Senate outcome to popular will. It is certainly reasonable to assume that the fifty-first senator is as likely as the sixtieth senator to hold a policy position near the median position of the general public. The citation of isolated, or even numerous, cases in which the filibuster seemed to pull the outcome closer to the position of a popular majority does not prove that the popular majority is generally better off with the filibuster than without it.

In any event, the proposition that the public serves as an effective watchdog on the many filibusters, threatened filibusters, and holds that are employed each year is wildly unrealistic. Most civil rights legislation considered during the twentieth century appears to have been supported by popular majorities and yet was successfully bottled up by filibusters, actual and potential. To be sure, public opinion on civil rights legislation was sectionally divided, and therefore southern minorities in the Senate were able to withstand the pressures of national public opinion. And yet in more recent decades the sheer frequency of filibusters and their deployment on legislation of just moderate significance has greatly reduced the chances that public opinion will discipline the behavior of minority factions in the Senate. Information overload, conflicting claims, divided party control of government, and other factors make it nearly impossible for the public to assess responsibility for the lack of Senate action on a matter and then to express disapproval of the minority's behavior with sufficient force to be registered in the Senate.

The claim that the compromises forced by Senate minorities are desirable is equally dubious. True, satisfying sixty senators certainly entails more extensive compromise than satisfying just fifty-one. And many people might agree with defenders of the filibuster that there have been cases of legislation's being "improved" under threat of a filibuster. Moreover, all things being equal, the perceived legitimacy of a public policy surely is enhanced when the policy has broad, bipartisan, support. However, the implication that the general public will be more satisfied, or that more of the public will be satisfied, with legislation considered under the protection of a filibuster is unwarranted. In some cases, the higher threshold prevents legislation favored by a popular majority from being enacted at all. And when legislation is adopted after substantial concessions are made to gain the support of at least sixty senators, the loss of satisfaction among some elements of the public may exceed the gain in satisfaction experienced by other elements by virtue of the additional compromises. Such a judgment requires an interpersonal comparison of utility that analysts and politicians cannot make with confidence.

Finally, and perhaps most important, appealing to the sixtieth senator may or may not require the moderation of legislation. Whether a more moderate outcome is produced by satisfying the sixtieth, as opposed to just the fifty-first, senator depends on many factors.

First, different meanings can be attached to the phrase "moderating influence." It may be that the fifty-first senator, sitting at the median position within the Senate, is the moderate senator by definition, or at least is more moderate than the sixtieth senator, in which case the filibuster hardly has a moderating influence. Or, as some defenders of the filibuster argue, it may be that filibusters are "moderating" by encouraging "less drastic change" in current public policy. But then one must allow that a more moderate change, forced by the sixtieth senator, could yield a policy that is quite immoderate in its effects if changing economic, physical, political, or social conditions require a more dramatic change in policy. In sum, the claim that the Senate's rule has a "moderating influence" may confuse as much as it clarifies the issue.

Second, the moderating influence depends on the particular distribution of preferences among senators. Many observers often intuitively consider senators' preferences to be evenly distributed across the policy spectrum, or perhaps to be normally distributed in the form of a bell-shaped curve (figure 5-2, top). In that case, the fifty-first senator is in the middle of the spectrum while the sixtieth senator is a small distance to the left or right of that senator. The fifty-first senator might still be the more moderate of the two senators, but the concessions required to attract the support of the sixtieth senator would not be too great. In contrast, if the distribution of preferences is highly polarized (figure 5-2, bottom), the distance between the fifty-first and sixtieth senators may be great, so that the influence of the sixtieth senator is to bring the outcome far from the middle range of the policy spectrum. Polarized distributions are not uncommon. Highly partisan Congresses, and debates over civil rights, abortion, and other matters, occur with some frequency and produce polarized distributions that make the cloture rule a quite immoderate instrument of the minority.

Third, the moderating influence of the filibuster depends on the consequences of killing a measure. It is usually assumed that a successful filibuster means that existing policy, the status quo ante, is retained. If conditions have not changed much recently, the status quo ante may be a quite moderate outcome, in that it may have been the result of years of an incremental process of give and take about the shape of policy in that area. In recent decades, sunset provisions have transformed many permanent authorizations into periodic authorizations and required new legislation to be enacted for even the status quo ante to be retained. To defeat an authorization bill by filibuster in such cases is to radically change policy. So, for a reauthorization bill, the sixtieth senator enjoys tremendous leverage because the failure to act on the legislation has major consequences. The leverage may be so great that the majority accepts an immoderate outcome in order to avoid the even more immoderate outcome of not passing the bill.

Finally, even as some defenders of the filibuster emphasize, the Senate may be more conservative or liberal than the public. As the defenders argue, this *may* mean that the sixtieth senator is closer to the middle of the spectrum, as measured by the distribution of preferences in the general public, but it could just as easily mean that the sixtieth senator is even more distant from the middle of the spectrum than is the fifty-first senator.

Figure 5-2. *Hypothetical Distribution of Senators' Preferences*

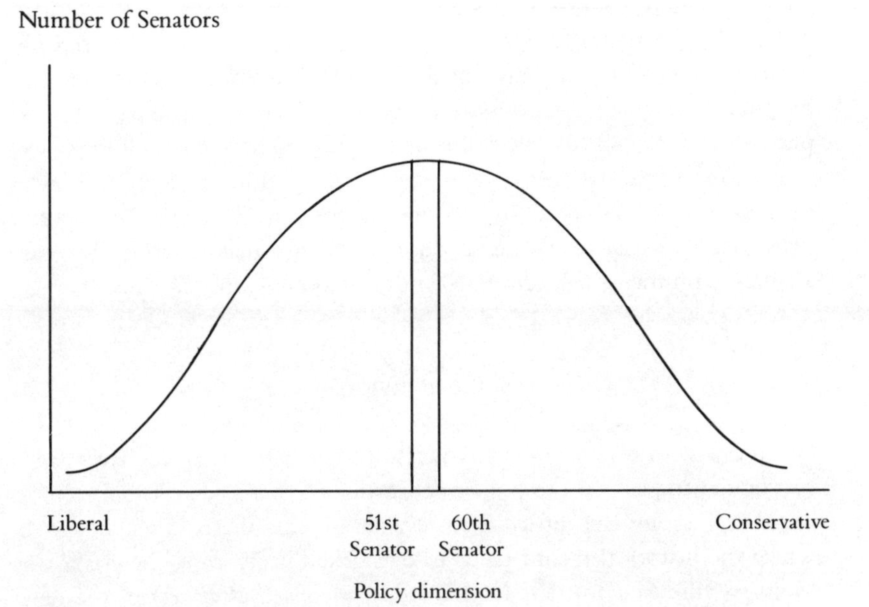

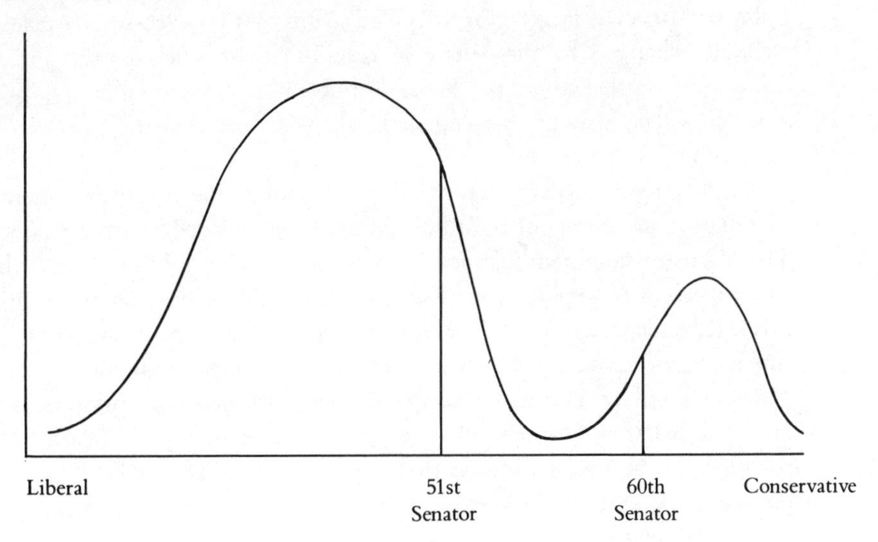

No defender or critic of the filibuster is in a position to reliably determine which situation is more common.

Clearly, the rhetorical siblings of the little-harm thesis—that the filibuster often produces an outcome that is more moderate or more preferred by popular majorities—are weak arguments. There is little basis for expecting, as a general rule, that filibuster-produced outcomes will represent a more moderate outcome (as judged by the alignment of preferences in the Senate) or an outcome closer to the one preferred by a popular majority than outcomes that would be produced by simple majority rule. The case for these arguments rests entirely on the citation of isolated cases.

Conclusion

Contrary to the little-harm thesis, filibusters appear to have had a substantial impact on the policy choices of the Senate, at least in recent decades. Despite the difficulty of evaluating this thesis and the way in which the historical record tends to be stacked in its favor, there is a way to assess filibuster impact. In this study, a conservative test of the decisiveness of the Senate rule uncovered numerous measures, particularly in more recent Congresses, that can fairly be said to have been killed by filibuster. An even larger number of bills in recent Congresses were substantially changed by the Senate in response to manifest or threatened filibusters. Furthermore, the Senate's rule influences the larger political game in which senators are engaged. The inference that the Senate rule matters seems inescapable.

As the foregoing discussion has shown, many of the arguments offered by senators in defense of the filibuster stand on decidedly weak ground. The filibuster cannot simultaneously secure minority rights and serve the preferences of a popular majority. The historical record, so frequently invoked by defenders of the Senate's rule (whatever it is at any point in time), cannot both exhibit only a small effect of filibusters on public policy and illustrate how essential extended debate is to the preservation of minority rights. The Senate's rule *does* affect policy outcomes, frequently at the margins, and sometimes at the core. The rule may still be desirable, but not because it has little effect or is generally used in the interests of a popular majority.

The weakness of the evidence for the little-harm thesis and its variants also has implications for the dynamics of institutional change in the Senate. The filibuster has proved to be far more than a necessary means for forcing the Senate to set aside legislation that would harm the nation. It is, and has been seen by senators to be, an all-purpose tool for influencing the distribution of winners and losers in national politics. The filibuster is used in ways that are hardly relevant to the nation's welfare, in ways that most people would argue are contrary to the nation's welfare, in ways that undermine Senate effectiveness on legislative measures unrelated to the targeted measures, and in ways that prevent moderate positions from receiving Senate approval. The fit between a policy outcome on a filibustered measure and the popular will is often merely coincidental. Consequently, the record does not lend support to the view that the filibuster is used, on the whole, to protect the larger good of the Senate or of society. If so, there is no viable case that the Senate's rule has evolved to enhance the collective well-being of the Senate or the nation. Rather, the development of the filibuster is better viewed as a by-product of strategic competition for advantage in the policymaking process.

Past Democratic party leaders Mike Mansfield and Robert C. Byrd

6

Senate Support for Limits on Debate

THE KILLER ARGUMENT in defense of the right to conduct extended debate is that a majority of senators support a continuation of the practice. Such an argument was made in an influential study authored by political scientist Raymond Wolfinger in 1971. Wolfinger, after reviewing efforts to reform Rule 22 between 1946 and 1969, concluded that "most senators consistently have opposed carrying the principle of majority rule so far as to weaken or abolish a minority's power to prevent the Senate from voting on a bill." Many senators, he believed, value the filibuster even if it frustrates their policy objectives from time to time. Their position was understandable, Wolfinger continued, because they viewed filibusters as a problem limited to civil rights bills. It was not a widespread problem that would motivate a majority of senators to sacrifice their commitment to freedom of speech and minority rights.[1]

The proposition that the filibuster has been reserved historically for the large sectional conflict over slavery and later civil rights was examined in chapter 4. As explained there, the proposition does not fit the periods before and after the mid–twentieth century decades that Wolfinger studied. Here the discussion turns to Wolfinger's more important point about majority support for Rule 22. If he is right, then the reasonable claim that more radical reform of Rule 22 has been delayed or blocked by filibustering minorities loses much of its force. It is conceivable that senators value so highly the special character of the Senate that a majority of them have favored few limits on debate, even if many of them resent some uses of unrestricted debate.

As also noted in Chapter 4, senators' votes on motions related to cloture reform tend to be structured by their policy positions and party interests. This pattern provides strong circumstantial evidence that short-term political considerations play a major role in shaping the Senate's procedural history. But if it is true that no majority of senators has favored tighter restrictions on debate, even for the three decades Wolfinger reviewed, then the pattern of voting among individual senators would not be very important, at least for that period. After all, if a majority of senators have not favored strict limits on debate, then it remains possible that collective interests—the general welfare of the Senate or the nation—remains a pivotal consideration for at least some senators whose views have determined the fate of reform proposals. Thus, if Wolfinger is correct, the case for viewing Senate development as a product of the pursuit of collective interests would be strengthened.

The claim that a majority of the Senate has favored, and still favors, few restrictions on debate is best tested in two steps. First, it is important to examine the expression of sentiment in roll-call votes about creating *standing rules* that make it easier to limit debate. This analysis leads to the conclusion that minorities have, on several occasions, prevented majorities from adopting rules that would make it easier to limit debate. Moreover, some cases of apparent majority opposition to tightened debate limits cannot be taken as evidence that Senate majorities actually prefer cloture by supermajorities. A variety of legitimate, practical political considerations—minority party status, sectional interests, small-state interests, and others—have combined to produce minorities of sufficient size to prevent the adoption of simple-majority cloture in the Senate. That is, concerns about how political advantages and disadvantages would be redistributed in the chamber—more than the well-being of the Senate—appear to have been critical in shaping procedural choices in these particular cases. The history of Senate action on reform proposals suggests that there may never have been a majority for simple-majority cloture, but that majorities have been prevented from adopting much tighter rules on many occasions because of inherited rules and precedents dating back to 1806.

Second, it is useful to consider the more than three dozen instances in recent decades in which the Senate has placed into *statute* strict limits on debate and amendments for specific purposes. Starting with the Executive Reorganization Act of 1939 and continuing into many policy areas such as budget and trade matters during the last three decades, the Senate has supported limits on debate and amendments for specific types of legislation. A close perusal of this practice indicates that senators have supported these limits when practical political trade-offs dictate that senators give up their freedom to filibuster. Senators have been quite willing to limit their prerogatives when it suits their policy interests. No overriding commitment to unlimited debate as a means of protecting the deliberative character of the Senate—or even the interests of the minority, sections of the country, or small states—seemed to exist among a majority of senators when these provisions were enacted.

Placing Limits on Debate in the Standing Rules

Inasmuch as Rule 22 was adopted in 1917 and later modified by Senate majorities, it is obvious that majorities have been marshaled for reform from time to time. In fact, fifty-one senators sponsored a reform proposal in 1971, the year that Wolfinger's essay was published.[2] Their resolution died when, for the fourth time in eight years, only a majority, but not the required two-thirds majority, voted for cloture on the resolution. In retrospect, it seems clear in each case that Senate majorities were prevented from gaining a vote on a reform proposal that would have reduced the threshold for cloture from two-thirds of senators present and voting. That certainly is how contemporary reformers saw it. Then, in 1975, a majority of fifty-six senators passed a resolution providing for a three-fifths constitutional majority for cloture on measures other than those to amend Senate rules. The rule was tightened in 1979 to make the 100-hour limit on post-cloture debate effective. And post-cloture debate limit was reduced to 30 hours in 1986. That remains the Senate rule. Plainly, and contrary to Wolfinger's inference, a majority of senators in the 1960s and 1970s approved of a rule that reduced the threshold for cloture from the one first established in 1917.

At other times, it is not easy to determine the views of senators on reform proposals. Table 6-1 lists the votes that have been cast on propositions related to limits on debate in the standing rules of the Senate. A large share of those votes occurred at the few times that reforms were adopted. Before 1917 few roll-call votes were cast on reform proposals because filibusters and threatened filibusters easily prevented votes. In the period before 1917, only five votes were cast on resolutions providing debate limits, or on procedural motions related to those resolutions. Senate majorities appear to have been blocked from adopting a previous question

Table 6-1. *Votes Related to Proposals to Change the Standing Rules in Order to Limit Debate, 1851–1995*

1851	To adopt a resolution making the motion to proceed nondebatable. ***Rejected, 22-27.***
1872	To adopt a resolution providing "that during the remainder of the session it should be in order, in the consideration of appropriations bills, to move to confine the debate by any Senator, on the pending motion to five minutes." ***Adopted, 33-13.***
1873	To consider a resolution providing that the Committee on Rules "be instructed to look into the propriety of so amending the rules" so that debate is required to be relevant to the subject matter before the Senate, that the previous question may be demanded by a majority vote or in some modified form, and that bills be considered in the regular order. ***Rejected, 25-30.***
1891	Concerning a resolution providing that "when any bill, resolution, or other question shall have been under consideration for a considerable time, it shall be in order for any Senator to demand that debate thereon be closed. On such demand no debate shall be in order, and pending such demand no other motion, except on motion to adjourn, shall be made."
	To table the resolution. ***Rejected, 33-36.***
	To adopt the motion to proceed to the consideration of the resolution. ***Adopted, 36-22.***
1917	To adopt a resolution providing a substitute for Rule 22. The new rule provided for cloture "by a two-thirds vote of those voting" and provided a one-hour limit on speech for each senator. ***Adopted, 76-3.***
1918	Concerning a resolution providing "during the period of the present war the rules of the Senate be amended by adding thereto the following: 'That no Member shall occupy more than 1 hour in debate, unless by unanimous consent, on any bill or resolution and not over 20 minutes on each amendment proposed thereto.' "
	To amend the resolution to limit the application of the new rule to calendar 1918. ***Rejected, 29-41.***
	To amend an amendment to the resolution to provide that "this rule limiting debate shall not apply, except by unanimous consent, to any bill, measure, or question which has been determined upon or agreed to by or in a party caucus or conference of the Senators of the majority party." ***Adopted, 40-35.***
	To amend the resolution to provide that "no Member shall occupy more than 1 hour and 30 minutes in debate on any bill or resolution and not over 20 minutes on each amendment proposed thereto; Provided, that the Senate upon request may enlarge the time by a majority vote, the question to be decided without debate; Provided further, That when an amendment is pending a Senator may use all or any part of his time allowed for debate upon the bill or resolution. And provided further, That this rule limiting debate shall not apply, except by unanimous consent, to any bill, measure, or question which has been determined upon or agreed to by or in a party caucus or conference of the Senators of the majority party." ***Adopted, 73-3.***
	To adopt a resolution, as amended. ***Rejected, 34-41.***

1949 Concerning a resolution providing for the application of cloture to any measure, motion, or other matter upon a vote "of two-thirds of those voting."

To table an appeal of a ruling of the vice president that Rule 22 applied to debate on a motion to proceed. ***Rejected, 41-46.***

To proceed to consider an alternative resolution providing for cloture to any measure, motion, or other matter by vote of "two-thirds of Senators duly chosen and sworn," but to exclude measures that would change the Senate's rules. ***Adopted, 78-0.***

To amend a substitute amendment to provide that cloture may apply to a motion to approve or amend the *Journal*. ***Rejected, 14-72.***

To amend a substitute amendment to provide for cloture by two-thirds of those voting, except for a motion, resolution, or proposal to change the rules, which would require two-thirds of Senators duly chosen and sworn. ***Rejected, 29-57.***

To adopt an amendment (to a substitute amendment) providing for cloture by a vote of a simple majority. ***Rejected, 17-69.***

To adopt an amendment (to a substitute amendment) providing for cloture by a vote of a simple majority of those voting. ***Rejected, 7-80.***

To adopt a substitute amendment providing for the application of cloture to any measure, motion, or other matter by a vote of "two-thirds of Senators duly chosen and sworn." ***Adopted, 63-23.***

1953 To table a motion that the Senate proceed to the consideration of the adoption of its rules. ***Adopted, 70-21.***

1957 To table a motion that the Senate proceed to the consideration of the adoption of its rules. ***Adopted, 55-38.***

1959 To table a substitute for the Johnson resolution. The substitute provided for the adoption of the old rules of the Senate and then proceeded to consider a new Rule 22. ***Adopted, 60-36.***

To amend the Johnson resolution to provide that a simple constitutional majority of the Senate was required for cloture after fifteen days of debate. ***Rejected, 28-67.***

To adopt the Johnson resolution to provide for cloture by three-fifths of senators voting. ***Rejected, 36-58.***

To amend the Johnson resolution providing for cloture by a vote of "two-thirds of Senators present and voting," as well as providing that Rule 22 apply to changes in the Senate rules and that "the rules of the Senate shall continue from one Congress to the next Congress unless they are changed as provided in these rules." ***Adopted, 72-22.***

1961 To adopt a motion to refer to committee a resolution providing for cloture by a vote of three-fifths of senators present and voting. ***Adopted, 50-46.***

To invoke cloture on the motion to proceed to the consideration of the resolution providing for cloture by three-fifths of senators present and voting. ***Rejected, 37-43*** (two-thirds of senators voting required).[a]

1963 To invoke cloture on a resolution providing for cloture by a vote of three-fifths of senators present and voting. ***Rejected, 54-42*** (two-thirds of senators voting required).

Table 6-1. *Votes Related to Proposals to Change the Standing Rules in Order to Limit Debate, 1851–1995 (Continued)*

Year	Vote
1967	Concerning a resolution providing for cloture by a vote of three-fifths of senators present and voting.
	To table a point of order against a motion to end debate on the resolution. ***Rejected, 37-61.***
	To sustain a point of order against a motion to end debate on the resolution. ***Adopted, 59-37.***
	To invoke cloture on the resolution. ***Rejected, 53-46*** (two-thirds of senators voting required).
1969	Concerning a resolution providing for cloture by a vote of three-fifths of senators present and voting.
	To invoke cloture on the resolution under a ruling of the vice president that only a simple majority was required. ***Adopted, 51-47.***
	Appeal of the ruling of the vice president that only a simple majority was required (to reverse the effect of the previous vote). ***Adopted, 53-45.***
	To invoke cloture on the resolution. ***Rejected, 50-42*** (two-thirds of senators voting required).
1971	Concerning a resolution providing for cloture by a vote of three-fifths of senators present and voting.
	To invoke cloture on the resolution. ***Rejected, 48-37*** (two-thirds of senators voting required).
	To invoke cloture on the resolution. ***Rejected, 50-36*** (two-thirds of senators voting required).
	To invoke cloture on the resolution. ***Rejected, 48-36*** (two-thirds of senators voting required).
	To invoke cloture on the resolution. ***Rejected, 55-39*** (two-thirds of senators voting required).
	To table an appeal of the ruling of the chair that a two-thirds vote is required to invoke cloture. ***Adopted, 55-37.***
1975	Concerning a resolution providing for cloture by a vote of three-fifths of senators present and voting.
	To table a point of order against a motion that would have allowed a majority to invoke cloture on the resolution. ***Adopted, 51-42.***
	To adopt a motion to reconsider the vote by which the Senate tabled the point of order. ***Adopted, 53-38.***
	To table the point of order. ***Rejected, 40-51.***
	To sustain the point of order. ***Adopted, 53-43.***
	To invoke cloture on the motion to proceed to the consideration of the resolution. ***Adopted, 73-21*** (two-thirds of senators voting required).
	To proceed to the consideration of the resolution. ***Adopted, 69-26.***
	To invoke cloture on the resolution, as amended. The resolution had been amended to provide for cloture by a vote of "three-fifths of the Senators present and sworn," except for cloture on a measure or motion to change Senate rules, which would require a vote of two-thirds of "Senators present and voting." ***Adopted, 73-21*** (two-thirds of senators voting required).
	To adopt the resolution, as amended. ***Adopted, 56-27.***

1977 To table an appeal of the vice president's ruling that an amendment not directed at that subject under consideration after cloture was invoked is dilatory and that "when the Senate is operating under the cloture, the Chair is required to take the initiative . . . to rule out of order all amendments which are dilatory or which on their face are out of order." ***Adopted, 79-14.***

To sustain a point of order that a senator has the right to recall his own amendments, qualified and pending under cloture, prior to being called up. ***Adopted, 59-34.***

To sustain a point of order that actions ruled dilatory do not constitute the transaction of business for the purposes of demanding a subsequent quorum call. ***Adopted, 74-21.***

1979 Concerning a resolution providing for a limit of 100 hours' actual time for post-cloture debate, a nondebatable motion (requiring a three-fifths majority vote) to further limit debate (but not to less than 30 hours) that is in order once each day, and a nondebatable motion (requiring a three-fifths majority vote) to increase the limit beyond 100 hours.

To table a substitute amendment providing for a limit of one hour of debate for each senator, charging a quorum call or roll-call vote against the senator requesting one, and allowing a senator to be yielded time by other senators up to a limit of ten hours. ***Adopted, 51-38.***

To table an amendment that would limit post-cloture debate to no more than eight hours each calendar day. ***Adopted, 52-39.***

To adopt an amendment that deleted the provision for further limits on debate. ***Adopted, 92-2.***

To table an amendment that allowed a senator to be yielded time by other senators up to a limit of three hours. ***Adopted, 51-43.***

To table an amendment that exempts time required for roll-call votes from the 100-hour limit on debate after cloture. ***Adopted, 55-37.***

To adopt the resolution, as amended. ***Adopted, 78-16.***

1986 Concerning a compromise resolution providing for a trial period of broadcast coverage of the Senate and for certain changes in floor procedure (limiting debate on a motion to proceed to two hours, requiring amendments to be germane by a three-fifths vote, raising the number of votes required for cloture to two-thirds of senators voting, and setting a twenty-hour limit on post-cloture debate, all of which were eventually dropped or defeated). An amendment, limiting post-cloture debate to thirty hours, was adopted by voice vote.

To amend the resolution by deleting the provision requiring amendments to be germane by a three-fifths vote. ***Adopted, 60-37.***

To adopt the resolution, as amended. ***Adopted, 67-21.***

To adopt a resolution making permanent broadcast coverage and the thirty-hour limit for post-cloture debate. ***Adopted, 78-21.***

1995 To table a resolution providing for a stepwise reduction of the number required to vote for cloture over a period of days, eventually to a simple majority of senators voting. ***Adopted, 76-19.***

Source: Senate roll-coll votes (ICPSR File #00004).

a. The resolution was then tabled on a 46-35 vote.

motion in 1841 (when no relevant vote was cast) and a majority cloture rule in 1891 (see chapter 3). Between 1917 and 1996 the existence of cloture made additional reforms more (but not highly) likely, so there have been more roll-call votes cast related to efforts to debate limitation proposals. In that period, thirty-one votes were cast on cloture, motions to table, points of order, or appeals with regard to cloture reform. Many of these votes are likely to have involved at least some strategic voting, which makes it difficult to infer genuine preferences for reform.[3]

Even the votes that occur directly on reform proposals are not easy to interpret. Most of the votes on reform proposals concern a proposal for supermajority cloture, so they cannot be taken as a measure of the strength of support or opposition to simple-majority cloture. Votes on simple-majority cloture, it is reasonable to assume, are uncommon because either the proposal is successfully filibustered or the reformers focus on modest supermajority cloture reforms in order to avoid or overcome a filibuster.

Clearly, the roll-call record provides a weak basis for judging senators' support for simple-majority cloture. It is for that reason that Senate tradition was explored in chapters 2 and 3 without emphasizing the voting record. Nevertheless, previous Senate action on reform proposals has been a regular subject of discussion in past debates about reform and is likely to be again in the future. One must confront the Senate's voting record on reform proposals in order to understand the development of the Senate rule and to avoid unwarranted inferences about Senate support and opposition for limits on debate.

Several votes require scrutiny, which are discussed here in roughly chronological order.

—On three occasions—1873, 1918, and 1949—a majority of senators appear to have rejected substantially tighter limits on debate. Only the 1918 episode withstands close scrutiny as a case of majority opposition to tighter limits on debate. In 1959, the Senate made it somewhat easier to invoke cloture but also rejected more substantial reforms.

—Significant votes also occurred in 1963, 1967, 1969, 1971, and 1975. On the first four of these attempts to reform Rule 22, a simple majority, but not the required two-thirds majority, voted to invoke cloture on a reform proposal. The outcomes in 1967 and 1969 suggest that senators' views about cloture thresholds can be separated from their views about the Senate as a continuing body.[4] Once that is recognized, the 1967 and 1969 reform efforts appear to be cases of minority obstructionism to a reform desired by a majority of senators. A reform resolution was adopted in 1975.

—In the 1995 vote all majority party Republicans voted to table a proposal that would have allowed simple-majority cloture.

In each case, enough background is available to describe the choices made and to offer a tentative explanation of the outcome. The obvious conclusion from these attempted reforms is that simple-majority cloture has seldom, perhaps never, been supported by a majority of the Senate. Nevertheless, on many occasions Senate majorities seeking tighter limits on debate have been thwarted by minorities using the inherited rules.

Majority Votes against Simple-Majority Rule

Only two times, in 1873 and 1949, has the Senate voted on a proposal to allow a simple majority to close debate and bring a matter to a vote.[5] In 1873 the Senate refused, by a 25-30 vote, to consider a resolution instructing the Rules Committee to study the reinstatement of the previous question. In 1949, the Senate rejected two similar proposals for simple-majority cloture, both by large margins. In a third case, in 1918, the Senate rejected, 34-41, a resolution providing for a specific limit on debate by individual senators on a measure or amendment. Thus a Senate majority has never voted in favor of simple-majority cloture when that proposition was close to being put to a direct vote, and it turned down a debate limit on individual members the only time it voted on such a standing rule. Moreover, in 1957 and 1959, when the Senate was presented with a motion to consider new rules, a majority of senators voted to table the motion.

These observations, combined with the observation that the Senate has supported supermajority cloture, might suggest that the Senate opposes simple-majority cloture and individual debate limits but supports supermajority cloture. Unfortunately, the world of Senate rule making is not so simple. In two of the three cases, one cannot simply infer that a majority of senators opposed tightened debate limits. In the third case, the 1918 fight over individual debate limits, the outcome is more clearly a case of a majority rejecting tighter limits on debate.

THE 1873 REFORM EFFORT. On the surface, the 1873 vote appears to be the first vote taken by the Senate on a rule that would allow a simple majority to close debate. The Senate actually did not vote directly on the issue of closing debate by majority vote. Instead, the Senate voted down a motion to proceed to the consideration of a "resolution of inquiry." The resolution provided

> that the Committee on the Revision of the Rules be instructed to inquire into the propriety of so amending the rules as to provide—
>
> First. That the debate shall be confined and be relevant to the subject-matter before the Senate.
>
> Second. That the previous question may be demanded either by a majority vote, or in some modified form.
>
> Third. For taking up bills in their regular order on the calendar; for their disposition in such order; prohibiting special orders, and requiring that bills not finally disposed of when thus called shall go to the foot of the calendar, unless otherwise directed.[6]

If it had been adopted, the resolution would only have required that the Rules Committee report its views on the reform proposals. The use of a resolution of inquiry for such a purpose was unusual. Resolutions of inquiry had been used to direct a committee to conduct an investigation of events outside of Congress, such as a scandal in the executive branch.

The resolution's author, Senator George Wright (Republican of Iowa), plainly hoped to start a discussion of his reform proposals without stimulating a filibuster against them. In fact, Wright asked for consideration of his resolution by downplaying its significance: "If there is any objection to taking up the resolution at this time I shall not press it; but I supposed there would be no objection, as it is a mere resolution of inquiry. I do not propose to discuss it at all."[7] Wright's hopes were dashed immediately by minority party Democrats who strongly opposed a change in the rules. Senator Thomas Bayard Sr. (Democrat of Delaware) proclaimed, "I shall at all stages oppose any proposition that undertakes to limit debate beyond the just discretion of members here."[8] Equally threatening comments were made by Bayard's party colleague, Allen Thurman (Democrat of Ohio). Perhaps most disheartening was the observation of a Republican, first-term senator Matthew Carpenter (Republican of Wisconsin), who argued that "the rule of free debate . . . has never been abused" and indicated that he would "vote every time I can get a chance not to change it."[9] After some discussion, sixteen majority party Republicans joined the Democrats to defeat Wright's motion. All twenty-five votes for the motion were cast by Republicans, including the de facto Republican leader, Roscoe Conkling (Republican of New York).[10]

The temptation is to count the 1873 vote as an instance of a Senate majority voting against granting simple majorities the power to close debate. The position of the minority party Democrats is not surprising; they benefit from being able to obstruct the majority. But did other Republicans voting against consideration of the resolution share Carpenter's views of unlimited debate? Perhaps not.

The inevitable lengthy debate on the resolution may have led some Republicans to fear that the chamber's other business would be delayed indefinitely by the discussion of the resolution. Two days later, when Wright offered his reform proposal as a regular resolution and sought referral to committee, Oliver Morton (Republican of Indiana) observed that "there are some members of this body who are so much opposed to any resolution of this character that they are unwilling even to countenance it by a reference. The Senator has had some evidence of that already."[11] Morton had voted against Wright's initial motion. Another Republican, John Scott (of Pennsylvania), concluded that "whatever may be our opinions as to the propriety of adopting these rules, it is perfectly obvious that no action can be had upon them at this session, and I rise in the interest of the dispatch of business, intending to make a motion, if it be in order, which will test the sense of the Senate upon the propriety of taking up further time in discussing this question about the rules."[12] Scott, who had voted in favor of Wright's initial motion, then moved to table the Wright resolution.[13] Clearly, the Republican votes against Wright's initial motion cannot be assumed to represent sincere opposition to a previous question motion. At least some of Wright's majority party colleagues saw his effort as hopeless and unnecessarily time-consuming and so moved to set it aside as quickly as possible.

THE 1918 REFORM EFFORT. In June 1918 a majority of the Senate appeared to oppose a resolution to tighten limits on debate. The 1918 discussion is particularly interesting because it concerned limits on debate that applied directly to individual senators, although it applied only for the period of the world war. The resolution voted on, which was an amended version of the original resolution authored by Oscar Underwood (Democrat of Alabama), provided that "during the period of the present war the rules of the Senate be amended by adding thereto the following: 'That no Member shall occupy more than 1 hour in debate, unless by unanimous consent, on any bill or resolution and not over 20 minutes on each amendment proposed thereto.'"[14] Underwood argued that the national interest dictated that some limit on debate was required to expedite consideration of Senate business.

The Underwood proposal generated a firestorm of opposition.[15] Many senators did not understand why debate limits for individual senators were necessary. After all, they observed, the cloture procedure was adopted less than a year earlier and no filibuster had occurred since that time. In fact, under cross-examination, Underwood admitted the Senate had acted responsibly on war-related legislation until that time. But the ever-suspicious Lawrence Sherman (Republican of Illinois) noted: "I have found that these movements to regulate the Senate, coming unheralded and without apparent reason, always have some concealed foundation. I state it as my own judgment . . . that the proposed new rule is urged in preparation of the presentation to the Senate of a treaty, which will come possibly sooner than many Senators expect, and it is desired to thrust it upon the Senate and ratify it without discussion other than that allowed under the limitations of the proposed rule."[16] Sherman had in mind the peace treaty, which some senators were anticipating at the time and did not trust President Woodrow Wilson to negotiate on terms acceptable to them. James E. Watson (Republican of Indiana) even charged that the president originated the reform proposal and was seeking to manipulate Senate rules for his own purposes.[17] Still, most critics—Republicans and southern Democrats—objected on the more traditional grounds of minority and individual rights. Although the new rule would apply only for the period of the war, opponents were leery about setting a precedent. Several opponents predicted that the new rule would lead to proposals for even tighter limits.

Underwood and other proponents responded by observing that the Senate confronted a heavy workload of war-related measures, that Rule 22 was difficult to use, and that the senators concerned about the Senate's interests, not the president, originated the proposal. However, Underwood confessed his hope that the rule would outlast the war: "I believe that the Senate will find, if it tries it, that a reasonable limitation on debate will be beneficial to the transaction of the business of the Senate without depriving a Senator of any material right that he possesses in the body now. . . . If my own view of the question is sustained by the trial, then I take it that the Senate at the end of the war will adopt the rule as a permanent part of the machinery of this body."[18]

Underwood's response to the critics was inadequate. In fact, as the Senate was wrapping up its debate on the resolution, Senator Reed Smoot (Republican of Utah) said, smugly, one may suppose, "I think the Senator [Underwood] will concede that the majority of the Senate are opposed to this resolution." Smoot was right. On a 40-35 vote, the Senate adopted a gutting amendment to Underwood's resolution that exempted measures that had been subject to action by the majority party caucus. Then, after adopting an amendment that liberalized the debate limits, the Senate defeated the resolution itself on a 34-41 vote.[19] Most Republicans and southern Democrats voted for the key amendment and against the resolution.

THE 1949 REFORM EFFORT. Since 1918, the Senate has not seriously considered limits on speech for individual senators, except for the period after cloture is invoked. The 1917 rule went unchanged, and largely unchallenged, until 1949, when Senate liberals, backed by the Truman administration, sought to make the rule easier to use. Liberals and the administration recognized that civil rights measures and other administration-backed legislation would be killed by filibusters if a recent interpretation of the rule were not overturned. In August 1948 Senator Arthur Vandenberg (Republican of Michigan), when presiding over the Senate, ruled that a motion to proceed was not a pending measure and so was not subject to Rule 22.[20] The ruling made Rule 22 useless as a means for gaining Senate action on a measure because a small group of senators could easily prevent a vote on a motion to proceed. An earlier interpretation of the rule also made approval or amendment of the Senate's *Journal* subject to unrestricted debate. Reformers sought to close these loopholes.

A resolution reported from the Committee on Rules and Administration, under threat of discharge, provided that cloture applied to "motions and other pending matters" as well as to the "pending measure." Reformers, led by Majority Leader Scott Lucas (Democrat of Illinois), were unable to overcome a filibuster conducted by southern Democrats. They had hoped to do so by gaining majority support to table an appeal of the ruling by Vice-President Alben Barkley that Rule 22 applied to a motion to proceed (in this case, a motion to proceed to the consideration of the reform resolution). By tabling the appeal, the Barkley ruling would stand, and the Senate could proceed to consider the reform resolution. The reformers failed, 41-46, on the motion to table the appeal. Critically, some Republicans who favored closing the loopholes in Rule 22 also opposed the motion to table. Vandenberg, most notably, argued that to endorse Barkley's ruling would be to allow "the transient, unregulated wishes of a majority of whatever quorum is temporarily in control of the Senate" to interpret the rules as they desire.[21] Democratic leaders charged that the Republicans voted against the motion to table in order to block civil rights legislation. A newspaper reporter seemed to second that judgment: "The question of rules changes rather than that of civil rights provides Republican senators with safe ground on which to oppose Administration moves."[22]

Upon the rejection of the tabling motion, the initiative shifted to the leaders of the southern Democrats and the Republicans. Southern Democrats appeared to oppose any change in the rule, even to close loopholes, but saw an opportunity to join with Republicans, who appeared to favor closing the loopholes, in order to foreclose future changes in the rule. The two groups agreed to support a substitute amendment that closed the loopholes, raised the threshold for cloture from a two-thirds majority of senators present and voting to two-thirds of the entire Senate, and explicitly excluded changes in Senate rules from cloture. Republicans claimed that by providing for cloture on a motion to proceed they were making action on civil rights legislation possible. Neither southern nor northern Democrats seemed to see it that way.[23] In any event, fifty-two senators—thirty Democrats, mostly southerners, and twenty-two Republicans—cosponsored the substitute. The motion to consider the alternative resolution was adopted unanimously. Reformers realized that offering amendments to the alternative was the only way to get votes on their proposals. They also knew that the narrowly crafted committee proposal had no chance of passing; raising it as an amendment to the new alternative would only stimulate another filibuster.

While the substitute was being considered on the floor, the coalition of southern Democrats and Republicans remained cohesive and defeated all amendments to their substitute. The Senate rejected, 29-57, a proposal that retained the cloture threshold of two-thirds of senators voting, except for measures that change the Senate's rules, in which case a two-thirds constitutional majority would be required. Majority Leader Lucas endorsed this proposal as the best feasible outcome, although he had been advocating a threshold of a simple constitutional majority for some time. The Senate also rejected two amendments, one providing for simple-majority cloture and one providing for a simple constitutional majority, by lopsided margins, 7-80 and 17-69, respectively.

Obviously, a majority for simple-majority cloture did not exist in 1949. To be sure, the proposals for simple-majority cloture came to a vote only after the ultimate outcome was a foregone conclusion. Just how many senators favored simple-majority cloture as their first preference cannot be determined with certainty. But Majority Leader Lucas observed that only "six or eight" Democrats favored some form of simple-majority cloture, as Lucas did.[24] It is unlikely that more than a handful of minority party Republicans would have supported simple-majority cloture if it had been a viable alternative.

It is also likely that a majority of senators would have preferred not to raise the threshold from two-thirds of those voting to two-thirds of all senators, but, given the successful filibuster of the southerners, accepted the change as the best available alternative. Unfortunately, this is not a testable proposition, in large part because of the gamesmanship in which the Republicans engaged. At early points in the events of 1949, Republicans enthusiastically supported the committee resolution that simply extended the old rule, with its threshold of two-thirds of those voting, to all motions.[25] Indeed, the Republicans' threat to pursue a motion to discharge the committee of the reform resolution prompted quick action by the committee. Only after considerable discussion within their party did a majority of Republicans oppose the vice president's ruling. Some of them seemed to relish the opportunity to intensify the deep division between southern and northern Democrats. Once the vice president's ruling was overturned, the only way to get Senate action was to avoid any objection to the consideration of a reform measure, which, in turn, meant gaining the support of southern Democrats. At that point, some Republicans may have reasoned that raising the cloture threshold and exempting measures affecting Senate rules were acceptable costs for having cloture apply to all motions.

More difficult to explain is the behavior of liberal Democrats. Some liberal Democrats argued that the substitute was worse than the old rule with its loopholes, so we might have expected them to filibuster the substitute.[26] They did not. Instead, they permitted the Senate to proceed to the consideration of the resolution and the substitute, suffered defeat on their amendments, and finally allowed the substitute to come to a vote. Perhaps, upon reflection, they thought the new rule was a small improvement on the old rule, given the Senate's judgment that the old rule did not apply to a motion to proceed. More likely, they did not want to commit the same parliamentary crime that they were seeking to prevent.

THE 1959 REFORM EFFORT. The 1959 reform may seem surprising in light of the ease with which the reform could have been blocked by a small group of senators operating under the 1949 rule. The adopted resolution, authored by Majority Leader Lyndon Johnson, provided for cloture by two-thirds of senators voting, applied Rule 22 to measures changing the Senate's rules, and stipulated that the Senate's rules continue from one Congress to the next.

Two events combined to produce the change. The first event was a 1957 ruling by Vice President Richard Nixon that a majority can vote to approve a motion to consider the adoption of new rules at the beginning of a Congress.[27] Under the ruling, if the motion is adopted, perhaps after considering a nondebatable motion to table it, the Senate can consider new rules. In 1957 the motion to table carried, 55-38, so the Senate did not consider new rules. The ruling would have made it possible for a majority to gain action on a reform resolution, although the resolution itself might be subject to obstructionism. The second event was the 1958 election, which brought nine new liberal Democrats to the Senate. By January 2, 1959, as the new Congress was about to be sworn into office, *Congressional Quarterly* found fifty senators who had voted against the tabling motion in 1957 or who were willing to say that they would support the motion to proceed to the consideration of new rules. Forty-six reported that they would oppose the move; two were undecided.[28]

Southern Democrats and Republicans were persuaded by Majority Leader Lyndon Johnson that they faced a reform of Rule 22 written by liberals unless they rallied behind his proposal. With their support, and after substantial arm twisting on the part of the majority leader, Johnson's coalition succeeded in tabling the motion to consider new rules and defeating a substitute that provided for cloture by three-fifths of senators voting. An amendment providing for cloture by a simple constitutional majority after fifteen days of debate was rejected 28-67. Thus, although a large majority favored the Johnson resolution, the same majority was able to fend off all other reform proposals.

Debate Limitations and the Senate as a Continuing Body

As the Senate moved into the 1960s, the conservative coalition of Republicans and southern Democrats that had been able to block substantial reforms of Rule 22 in 1959 began to dissolve. In 1963, 1967, 1969, and 1971, a majority (but not the required two-thirds majority) voted to invoke cloture on a reform proposal. In each case, the outcome of the cloture vote prevented the Senate from voting on a resolution that provided for cloture by three-fifths of senators present and voting. At first glance, it seems that majorities were prevented from gaining a vote on a reform proposal, in each case to reduce the threshold for cloture from two-thirds of senators present and voting. But in 1975 a sufficiently large majority managed to invoke cloture on a reform resolution that was eventually approved, after amendment, by a majority of fifty-six senators.

The first four votes were frustrating to reformers because the votes indicated that there might have been enough votes to adopt their reform resolutions if only they could have brought the matter to a vote. In that respect, the votes demonstrated the self-perpetuating tendency of a rule that requires an extraordinary majority to close debate.[29] Two of the votes, the 1967 and 1969 votes, are of special interest here because they were accompanied by majority votes against the proposition that a simple majority can close debate on Senate rules at the beginning of a Congress. So in those two years a majority favored cloture on the reform proposal and a majority opposed simple-majority cloture on the rules. The votes against the special interpretation of the rules at the beginning of a Congress prevented action on the reform proposals. This outcome led Professor Wolfinger to his conclusion that most senators actually liked Rule 22 and were unwilling to take the steps necessary to change it.

An alternative inference—that some senators favored reform but opposed the procedure under which the reformers wanted the Senate to consider their proposal—may be more appropriate. This alternative explanation keeps alive the possibility that a majority existed for a three-fifths cloture rule in the 1960s and, consequently, leads to the conclusion that reform of the two-thirds rule was delayed by more than a decade. This was a serious matter for the reformers. Between early 1973 and early 1975, it turns out, four cloture motions—concerning voter registration, the boycott of Rhodesian chrome, legal services, and campaign finance reform—failed, with votes in favor of cloture numbering fewer than two-thirds of senators voting and more than three-fifths of senators present and sworn (the standard adopted in 1975). And in several other cases in the 1960s and 1970s—concerning open housing legislation, electoral college reform, the loan to Lockheed, the powers of the Equal Employment Opportunity Commission, the creation of a consumer protection agency, the Genocide Treaty, and the Import-Export Bank—a cloture motion was defeated that would have met the threshold of three-fifths of senators present and voting, the standard proposed by the reformers in the 1960s.[30]

Direct evidence for either the Wolfinger or the alternative explanation is difficult to find. But the floor debate in 1967 indicates that concern about the procedure pursued by the sponsors of the reform proposal led at least three senators to support a point of order and contributed to the majority that compelled the reformers to overcome the existing two-thirds hurdle to get cloture on their resolution (rather than adopting new rules by majority vote at the start of the Congress). The story of the 1967 effort is worth detailing because it indicates that Senate attitudes about Rule 22 were not perfectly coincident with attitudes about the continuing nature of the Senate.

THE 1967 REFORM EFFORT. Senators George McGovern (Democrat of South Dakota) and Thruston Morton (Republican of Kentucky) introduced Senate Resolution 6 that provided for cloture by a vote of three-fifths of senators present and voting. Expecting to be blocked by a filibuster whenever they moved that the Senate proceed to consider the resolution, McGovern, Morton, and others argued that the Senate could, by a majority vote, get a vote on a change in the rules at the beginning of a Congress. They submitted a brief justifying their position to Vice President Hubert Humphrey, whom they expected to be cooperative and hoped would rule in their favor. Their position was that the Senate's constitutional power to make its own rules applied to each new Congress and that traditional parliamentary law, not the Senate's rules in the last Congress, governed until new rules were adopted. Traditional parliamentary law provided for deciding questions by simple majority votes.[31]

McGovern offered a complicated motion that he hoped would pave the way for a limit on debate for his resolution. The motion provided that the Senate vote immediately to end debate on his motion to proceed to the consideration of Senate Resolution 6; and that after the motion was adopted by a simple majority of senators present and voting, the Senate would debate the motion to proceed for two hours and then vote on the motion to proceed. The motion, if adopted, would have limited debate only on the motion to proceed but would have set a precedent for a similar motion that McGovern might offer once the Senate was debating the resolution itself. Senate Minority Leader Everett Dirksen (Republican of Illinois) raised a point of order against the McGovern motion on the grounds that it violated Rule 22.

Humphrey did not rule on the point of order but rather submitted the issue to the Senate. In doing so, he said, he was taking the traditional position of the Senate's presiding officer and allowing the Senate to determine constitutional questions. He submitted the question, "Shall the point of order made by the Senator from Illinois be sustained?" He also noted that the question was debatable but ruled that it could be subjected to a motion to table. Because a motion to table is not debatable, McGovern and his allies had the opportunity to set aside the point of order by a majority vote. And Humphrey aided McGovern by ruling that a majority vote on the motion to table the point of order would immediately lead to a vote on the motion.[32] In effect, Humphrey was allowing the vote on the motion to table to determine the constitutional question of the power of a Senate majority to limit debate on the rules at the beginning of a Congress.

McGovern must have known that his motion to table was in trouble when Senators Albert Gore (Democrat of Tennessee) and Mike Mansfield (Democrat of Montana) each raised objections to the way he was proceeding. Gore and Mansfield supported McGovern's three-fifths cloture proposal and later voted to invoke cloture on the motion to proceed to the consideration of McGovern's resolution. Without their support, the motion to table was likely to fail. Mansfield, as the majority leader, probably was the most critical.

Gore objected to Humphrey's view that a successful motion to table the point of order would bring an immediate vote on the McGovern motion to limit debate on the motion to proceed. In his view, McGovern's motion would remain debatable and subject to a yet unchanged Rule 22. Gore asked, "Does not the presiding officer put himself in the position of holding that because a point of order against a proposed motion has failed, the terms of that motion, without further action by the Senate, ipso facto, become instructions to the Senate?"[33] Senator Gordon Allott (Republican of Colorado) joined Gore by objecting to his inability to offer an amendment to the McGovern motion under Humphrey's ruling.

Mansfield more directly opposed the implications of McGovern's actions for the treatment of the Senate as a continuing body. After explaining his support for cloture by a three-fifths majority of senators present and voting, Mansfield complained:

> The urgency or even wisdom of adopting the three-fifths resolution does not justify the path of destruction to the Senate as an institution and its vital importance in our scheme of government. And this, in my opinion, is what the present motion to invoke cloture by simple majority would do. The proponents would disregard the rules which have governed the Senate over the years simply by stating that the rules do not exist; that until the rules are changed to their liking and in the manner they choose, the Senate is consigned to oblivion. . . .
>
> This biennial dispute for a change in the rules has brought to issue the question of the Senate as a continuing body. The concept is really symbolic of the notion of the Senate in our scheme of government.[34]

Mansfield offered no additional reasoning for his position, but it may be that Mansfield, as majority leader, had more reason than most senators to fear an open season on Senate rules at the start of each new Congress.[35]

To the great frustration of the reformers, the motion to table the point of order was defeated, 37-61. Fourteen senators, five Democrats (including Gore, Allott, and Mansfield) and nine Republicans, voted with Dirksen against the motion to table the point of order but later voted with

McGovern to invoke cloture on the motion to proceed to the consideration of Senate Resolution 6. Some of the nine Republicans (none of whom addressed the Senate on the issue) may not have been willing to desert their leader on a procedural matter. But it appears, as the Gore and Mansfield comments suggest, that at least some of the fourteen senators were genuine supporters of a lower threshold for closing debate. They simply did not like the other implications of McGovern's approach.

THE 1969 REFORM EFFORT. In 1969, a somewhat different sequence of events produced the same result as the 1967 reform effort.[36] The chief sponsor of the 1969 reform resolution, Senator Frank Church (Democrat of Idaho), asked Humphrey to rule that only a simple majority was required to invoke cloture on his motion to proceed to the consideration of his resolution. Humphrey agreed to make such a ruling. After so ruling, Humphrey noted that any senator could appeal his ruling to the Senate and the appeal could be decided by a simple majority vote, which would allow the Senate to once again determine a constitutional question about the validity of Rule 22. Critically, Humphrey added that the appeal could not be debated under Rule 22.[37]

A majority voted in favor of cloture—the vote was 51-47—and Humphrey ruled that the cloture motion was adopted.[38] His ruling was appealed and reversed on a 45-53 vote, so the cloture motion failed. Six senators, including Gore and Mansfield, voted in favor of cloture but against Humphrey's ruling. The four senators joining Gore and Mansfield on both votes were Republicans. Mansfield and Gore offered arguments very similar to those they made in 1967.

The 1967 and 1969 episodes indicate that senators' views about three-fifths cloture were not fully coincident with their views about the continuing nature of the Senate. It certainly is inappropriate to infer from the events of 1967 and 1969 that most senators preferred to leave Rule 22 unchanged. It is more likely that the majority of senators who voted for cloture in 1967 and 1969 genuinely favored a new rule. If so, it is plain that the requirement of cloture by supermajority delayed reform of the cloture rule from a point early in the 1960s to the mid-1970s.

Nevertheless, something less than a majority supported simple-majority cloture during the 1960s. Mansfield made it clear to his colleagues that he preferred a supermajority rule, although he thought that a three-fifths rule achieved a more appropriate balance between the need to close debate and minority rights than did the two-thirds rule.[39] It appears that Gore fit the same category. Other senators of the 1960s and 1970s probably did as well, but, unfortunately, their number cannot be determined with any confidence. The leading reformers recognized that they lacked majority support for simple-majority cloture and so agreed to pursue a three-fifths rule that could attract majority support.[40] Consequently, the Senate of the 1960s and 1970s did not vote on simple-majority cloture (or even on procedural motions related to such a proposal).

THE 1975 REFORM EFFORT. The 1975 reform effort paralleled the 1969 effort in several respects. The vice president—in this case, Republican Nelson Rockefeller—ruled in order a motion offered by Senator James Pearson (Republican of Kansas) that a simple majority be able to close debate on a reform resolution sponsored by Pearson and Walter Mondale (Democrat of Minnesota). A point of order was raised against the motion by Majority Leader Mansfield, who again supported reform and opposed establishing the ruling that a simple majority can close debate on new rules at the beginning of a Congress. But Rockefeller ruled that a simple majority may close debate on a resolution providing for new rules at the beginning of a Congress. The vice president's ruling was upheld when the Senate voted 51-42 to table the point of order. For the first time, a Senate majority endorsed Pearson's interpretation of the Constitution that the Senate's standing rules cannot prevent a simple majority from acting on new rules at the beginning of a Congress. The Senate reinforced the precedent on a 46-43 vote to table another point of order raised by Mansfield against a motion to consider the reform resolution that was offered by Mondale.[41] The vice president's ruling opened the possibility of more radical reform in the future and gave reformers a strong hand in bargaining with their opponents.[42]

Opponents of reform still had the means for delaying action on the reform resolution. After the motion to table was adopted, Democratic Senator James Allen successfully demanded that the Pearson motion be divided so that the Senate would be required to vote on each part. He then proceeded to use quorum calls, motions to postpone action on the reform resolution, motions to adjourn, amendments, points of order, and other dilatory motions to delay action on the resolution for nearly two weeks. A few other southerners, led by Democrat Russell Long, seemed willing to accept some modification of Rule 22, but they did not like the Pearson-Mondale plan, which set a cloture threshold of three-fifths of senators voting, and were upset that Rockefeller's ruling would pave the way for simple-majority cloture in the future. They appeared to be willing to assist

Allen in his dilatory tactics unless a compromise plan acceptable to them was devised.[43]

A number of reformers became convinced that concessions to the southerners were required to gain Senate action on a reform proposal. They agreed to reconsider and reverse the motion to table Mansfield's second point of order, to support a cloture threshold of three-fifths of all senators, and to exempt changes in the rules from the new threshold (the old threshold—two-thirds of senators voting—applied to rules changes). Reformers who agreed to this approach were careful to note that their views about simple-majority cloture on new rules had not changed; they switched their votes in order to facilitate action on the new threshold.[44] Once the Senate reversed itself on the point of order (thereby resurrecting the notion of the Senate as a continuing body), cloture was invoked on the motion to proceed and on the reform resolution itself. The new threshold was adopted in an anticlimactic vote, 56-27. No vote was cast on any proposal providing for a lower threshold.

Again in 1975 a Senate majority struggled against a stubborn minority using the inherited rules. Clearly, a majority of senators favored an interpretation of the Constitution and Senate rules that would have permitted a simple majority to close debate on new rules at the beginning of a Congress. But the difficulty of overcoming the obstructionist tactics of Allen and his collaborators appeared to require that the precedent remain ambiguous and that the standing rule maintain the two-thirds majority threshold for closing debate on measures that would change the rules. The muddied precedent and the standing rule for cloture on rules changes have not been touched since 1975.

A Majority Party against Debate Limitations

Since 1975 the Senate has established precedents that reduce the use of dilatory tactics after cloture is invoked, reinforced the limit on post-cloture debate by specifying that the time limit includes the time consumed by quorum calls and other actions, and reduced the length of the period of post-cloture debate from 100 to 30 hours. All of these developments have reduced the ability of a senator or a group of senators to pursue amendments, motions, and appeals after cloture is invoked as means to further delay Senate action on the pending measure. In each case, most majority party senators favored the new rulings or rules.

In 1995, however, the majority party Republicans unanimously opposed a proposal sponsored by Tom Harkin (Democrat of Iowa) and Joseph

Lieberman (Democrat of Connecticut). The proposal provided that the "vote required to bring to a close debate upon that measure, motion, or other matter, or unfinished business (other than a measure or motion to amend Senate rules) shall be reduced by three votes on the second such motion, and by three additional votes on each succeeding motion, until the affirmative vote is reduced to a number equal to, or less than, an affirmative vote of a majority of the Senators duly chosen and sworn. The required vote shall then be an affirmative vote of a majority of the Senators duly chosen and sworn."[45] Thus the proposal would ratchet down the cloture threshold from sixty votes to fifty-seven, then to fifty-four, and finally to fifty-one. A cloture petition could not be filed until after the vote on a previous cloture petition, creating a spacing of votes on cloture of a minimum of two days.[46] No alternative plans were considered at the time, although Republicans indicated that they hoped that a proposal to limit debate on a motion to proceed would be considered later in the year.

Relatively little debate took place on the Harkin-Lieberman proposal before the nondebatable motion to table the proposal was offered. Democratic Senator Robert Byrd led the opponents by making the traditional case for few limits on debate. He was joined by Harry Reid (Democrat of Nevada), who made an unusually strong defense of the role of Rule 22 in preserving small-state interests. Only nineteen senators, all Democrats, opposed the motion to table the Harkin-Lieberman proposal. Curiously, all majority party members voted to table the proposal, as did more than half of the minority party. According to Senate staff members working on the issue, Republicans did not want an extended debate over reform of Rule 22 to delay action on the large legislative agenda that the new Senate and House majorities had before them. Republicans seemed particularly suspicious of Harkin's motivations, who as a strong liberal might have had reason to disrupt their plans for quick action on the Republican program. To be sure, some Republicans made the case against reform on other grounds. Senator Ted Stevens (Republican of Alaska), for example, opposed reform because he wanted to preserve the influence of small-state senators. Minority party Democrats opposing Harkin did so for the obvious reason that the filibuster might be a useful tool in opposing the majority party's legislation. But some liberal Democrats were free to vote with Harkin and Lieberman in favor of reform with the knowledge that the Republicans had the votes to table the proposal.

Some Republicans, of course, may have later regretted their decision to set aside reform on Rule 22. Throughout the 104th Congress, Democrats used filibusters and threatened filibusters to block action on the Republican program, including elements of the House Republicans' Contract with America. The initial eagerness of the Republicans to move on the Contract items seems to have produced remarkable shortsightedness about what it would take for their program to survive Senate floor debate. Still, not every Republican favored the House-passed version of the Republican agenda—with Republican moderates, for example, joining with Democrats to block action on regulatory reform in 1995. Thus some Republicans likely voted against reform knowing that their political interests required retaining their power to force changes in or to block conservative legislation passed by the new Republican majority in the House.

Summary

Two features of Senate rules and practice combine to make the Senate's rules more difficult to change than the rules of most legislatures. First, Rule 22 makes it possible for a sizable minority to block changes in the Senate's rules. Before Rule 22 was adopted in 1917, just a few committed senators could block changes. Second, the Senate has long considered itself to be a continuing body that does not reconstitute itself at the start of each Congress. The Senate need not reaffirm its rules every two years, as the House does. Consequently, the burden of change rests squarely on the shoulders of proponents of reforming Rule 22. They must interrupt Senate action on substantive policy problems and muster an extraordinary majority to bring their proposal to a vote. In the nineteenth century, even a consensus in favor of reform was not enough as long as a number of senators coordinated the efforts to block change. The high cost and low probability of success has, historically, discouraged attempts to change the Senate's rules.

Reformers, not surprisingly, have attacked both features that have reinforced the right to extended debate. From the mid–nineteenth century until the 1940s, reformers focused on debate limits themselves. During that period, Senate majorities reduced, in increments, the barriers to majority action on measures. In most instances when reform was adopted, the ability of a minority to obstruct action under the inherited rules forced a Senate majority to accept a more modest reform than the majority often appeared ready to support.

Nevertheless, the history of Senate action on floor procedure yields no evidence that a majority of senators favored simple-majority cloture. A majority may have existed in 1873 for reinstatement of a previous-question motion, but the obvious ability of the minority to obstruct the reformers made the effort pointless and appeared to lead some reformers to agree to set aside the reform resolution. At this writing there is little doubt that a majority of senators oppose simple-majority cloture.

Starting in the late 1940s, reformers also worked to gain rulings that would undercut the interpretation of the Senate as a continuing body at least to the extent that simple majorities could change the rules at the beginning of a Congress. Only in 1975 did a majority, which also favored reducing the threshold for cloture, clearly express itself in favor of that interpretation of the Constitution and Senate rules. That interpretation of the status of Senate rules has not been important to subsequent efforts to modify Rule 22 (to reduce the length of post-cloture debate), but may again become critical to a Senate majority whose reform proposal is blocked by a sizable minority.

Placing Limits on Debate in Statutes

On many occasions, numbering well over thirty, the Senate has accepted limits on debate to ensure that a resolution approving or disapproving an action proposed by the president or other executive officer will receive a vote.[47] Most of these episodes involve a congressional effort to check the exercise of authority that has been delegated to the executive branch. Without debate limits, a sizable minority that opposes a resolution of approval or disapproval could block Senate action by extended debate. If a resolution of approval must be passed before an executive branch initiative can be implemented, a filibuster would kill the initiative. If a resolution of disapproval must be adopted to prevent an executive branch initiative from being implemented, a filibuster would secure implementation of the initiative. Debate limits commit the Senate to voting on the proposed exercise of delegated authority.

As far as we can determine, the first provision for a resolution of approval or disapproval of an executive action was included in the Executive Reorganization Act of 1939. In passing the 1939 act, Congress gave President Franklin Roosevelt the authority for two years to reorganize most federal agencies, subject to a sixty-day waiting period during which Congress could block implementation of the plan by adopting a concurrent resolution of disapproval. If either house of Congress failed to adopt the resolution of disapproval, the president was authorized to implement his reorganization plan. The 1939 act also provided for a limit on Senate debate in order to guarantee that a simple majority of the Senate could act as it desired on such a resolution.[48] The 1939 act, with its combination of a waiting period, a resolution of approval or disapproval, and limited debate served as a blueprint for subsequent reorganization acts and many other measures that delegated authority to the president or executive agencies. Senators eventually came to refer to the blueprint as "expedited consideration" or the "fast-track procedure." The provision for a resolution of disapproval became known as a "legislative veto."

The debate on the 1939 act illustrates the pattern that would develop in subsequent debates. Most debate concerned the delegation of power to the executive branch, but only a little debate and no votes concerned the limitations on debate for a resolution of disapproval. The trend-setting debate on the bill deserves a brief review.

The Reorganization Act of 1939

By the late 1930s, Congress seemed eager to restructure the accumulated clutter in executive branch agencies and departments. But previous congressional efforts to pass significant reorganization legislation were unsuccessful. Senator Francis Maloney (Democrat of Connecticut) offered an explanation:

> Much as I dislike to be the one to admit it on the floor, Mr. President, Congress finds itself unable to cope successfully with the matter of reorganization. This is . . . because of the wide difference of interests over the land, because of sectionalism, or because one Senator or another has a favorite bureau, institution, commission, or organization.
>
> Mr. President, I have concluded that the only way reorganization can come is by delegating the power to the Chief Executive, and at the same time retaining, as best we can, the influence and the power of Congress.[49]

Congress had experimented in the early 1930s with granting reorganization authority to the president without explicit provision for a check by Congress, and most members seemed unwilling to do so again.[50] An effort to pass a reorganization measure in 1938 died in the House, in large part because the bill failed to include a guarantee that the House would be able to vote on a reorganization plan proposed by the president before the plan was implemented.

The 1939 bill reflected a concerted effort by its proponents, working with the parliamentarians of the two houses, to devise procedures that would guarantee to opponents of a reorganization plan that a resolution of disapproval would receive a vote.[51] The bill, as introduced and passed, provided

—that any member could introduce a concurrent resolution of disapproval;

—for referral of the resolution to committee;

—for a nondebatable discharge motion if the committee failed to report in a certain number of days;

—for a highly privileged motion to consider the resolution on the floor;

—for ten hours of floor debate;

—that no motion to reconsider the vote on the motion to proceed and no amendment is in order; and

—that other motions and appeals are not debatable.

The measure specified that these rules superseded any conflicting standing rules of either house. The measure also preserved "the constitutional right of either house to change such rules (so far as relating to the procedure in such house) at any time, in the same manner and to the same extent as in the case of any other rule of such house."[52]

The Senate manager of the bill, James Byrnes (Democrat of South Carolina), observed that the limit on debate was the only controversial part of the bill.[53] He was too optimistic. Many Republicans and some Democrats objected to the delegation of reorganization responsibility to the president. In fact, the decisive vote occurred on an amendment that would have required Congress to adopt a joint resolution of approval—that is, a measure approved by both houses—in advance of the implementation of a reorganization plan. The amendment would have limited debate to ten days on a resolution of approval.[54] Nevertheless, objections to debate limits were registered in rhetoric similar to that heard in defense of unlimited debate for decades. It was a southerner, Senator Josiah Bailey (Democrat of North Carolina), who made the most impassioned attack: "When this body ceases to have the utmost freedom of motion, of resolution, of discussion, and of debate, it has ceased to be a Senate, has become merely a legislative mill, under the control of any majority that may be in possession of it. And that is the destruction of the greatest and the last of the free parliamentary bodies on the face of the globe."[55]

After the amendment providing for a joint resolution of approval was defeated, no further amendments were offered that affected Senate procedure. No filibuster occurred, and only a couple of additional amendments concerning the agencies to be exempt from presidential reorganization plans were considered. The 63-23 vote on final passage broke nearly perfectly on party lines, with both southern and northern Democrats voting to give the Democratic president a year's opportunity to reorganize executive agencies under the terms of the act.

The absence of a no-holds-barred defense of Rule 22 may be surprising. The narrow purpose and limited duration of the delegation of power and the debate limits probably reduced fears among those senators, southern Democrats, who might have been most concerned about the precedent being set. The popularity of government reorganization and the president's support for the bill contributed, no doubt, to the urgency of acting on the bill. And, perhaps, the large number of senators favoring the bill discouraged a filibuster.

Other Statutory Limits on Debate

Table 6-2 presents selected laws that provide for debate limits, beginning with the Reorganization Act of 1939. For most of the laws listed, the legislative procedures and debate limits follow the template provided by the 1939 act. Two-year extensions of reorganization authority were granted to presidents, subject to resolutions of disapproval considered under debate limits, on several occasions until 1984. The table makes plain that the Congress of the 1970s frequently combined provisions for a resolution of approval or disapproval with provisions for expedited Senate action on such a resolution. Congress's interest in reasserting its influence over the executive branch motivated many of these measures. The table also demonstrates that the Senate extended debate limits for resolutions of approval or disapproval into a wide range of policy areas: energy and environmental regulations, foreign assistance, arms trade, arms control agreements, retirement benefits, and others. The laws setting Senate rules for action on trade agreements and budget measures warrant closer scrutiny because of the obvious importance of the legislation that they affect and the nature of the Senate debate about the debate limits they include.

TRADE MEASURES. In successive trade measures during the 1934–62 period, Congress granted the president authority to negotiate and implement, without additional legislation, international agreements providing for mutual reductions in tariffs.[56] Implementation required the modification of U.S. law on tariffs and duties. Similar authority was not granted for agreements concerning nontariff trade barriers, which became more important in the 1960s and 1970s. The situation changed with the enactment of the Trade Act of 1974.

Table 6-2. *Selected Laws Providing for a Limit on Debate in the Senate*

Executive Reorganization, 1939 and later
War Powers Act
Budget Act of 1974 and subsequent budget enforcement acts
National Emergencies Act
International Emergency Economic Powers Act
District of Columbia Home Rule Act
Foreign Spent Nuclear Fuel Provisions, Department of Energy Act of 1978
Pension Reform Act of 1976
Employee Retirement Income Security Act of 1974
Nuclear Non-Proliferation Provisions, Atomic Energy Act of 1978
Trade Act of 1974
Child Support Standards, Social Security Act of 1975
Arms Control and Disarmament Act
Federal Salary Act of 1967
Energy Policy and Conservation Act
Extensions of Emergency Authorities (42 U.S.C. 8374)
Nuclear Waste Fund Fees Act
Arms Export Control Act
Foreign Assistance Act of 1961
Federal Election Commission
Alaska Natural Gas Transportation Act of 1976
Crude Oil Transportation Systems
Alaska National Lands and Conservation Act
Federal Land Policy and Management Act of 1976
Marine Fisheries Conservation Act of 1976
Outer Continental Shelf Lands Act
Defense Production Act
Nuclear Waste Policy Act of 1982
Marine Protection, Research, and Sanctuaries Act of 1972
Comprehensive Anti-Apartheid Act of 1986
Foreign Assistance Act of 1961 and subsequent authorizations
Military Base Closings, National Defense Authorization Act of 1991

The Nixon administration sought renewed executive authority, which had expired in 1967 under legislation passed in 1962, to pursue trade negotiations. It sought authority to implement agreements on nontariff trade barriers, subject to notification of Congress and a simple resolution of disapproval (one-house legislative veto) that was to be considered under procedures modeled after the reorganization acts and adopted within ninety days. The administration argued that it could negotiate effectively only if it could assure trading partners that Congress would not amend an agreement and that definitive congressional action would take place by a certain date. In addition, it is reasonable to speculate, the administration may have realized that shortening the period of congressional consideration of a trade agreement would reduce the time available for affected interests to mobilize opposition to the agreement.

The House approved the proposal, but some senators balked. While the bill was under consideration in the Senate Finance Committee, Senator Herman Talmadge (Democrat of Georgia) objected that the procedure might be appropriate for government reorganization but was inappropriate for substantive policy changes. Repeating some arguments made in 1939, Talmadge insisted that such an open-ended delegation of power to the executive branch was unconstitutional. Nevertheless, Talmadge accepted an alternative approach to an agreement on nontariff trade barriers. The new approach guaranteed congressional action on a joint resolution of *approval* within a period of sixty days. The guarantee came in the same form as in the reorganization acts: a privileged resolution, effective debate limits, and a ban on amendments. The act also provided for other concurrent and simple resolutions of approval and disapproval, with corresponding debate limits, for certain kinds of trade agreements that previously were not subject to congressional review. The most important ones, which were added to the bill by 88-0 vote on a large and complicated amendment, concerned the president's ability to grant most favored nation trading status to the Soviet Union.[57]

Nevertheless, fast-track procedures have been controversial. In 1993, for example, the Senate approved an extension of the president's negotiating authority and fast-track procedures for considering the General Agreement on Tariffs and Trade. Senator Jay Rockefeller (Democrat of West Virginia) recounted the history of fast-track procedures for trade agreements and made the case in favor of such procedures:

> The so-called fast-track process for considering trade agreement implementing legislation was initially developed in the Trade Act of 1974 in response to complaints from our trading partners, as well as our own executive branch, that the United States could not credibly negotiate in a situation where Congress could unravel a completed agreement by rejecting or amending any specific provision of it. This concern was prompted in part by Congress' rejection of the Antidumping Code that was negotiated in 1967.

The process devised was a specific, time-limited grant of negotiating authority to the President with the proviso that an agreement concluded and submitted within the time period would be considered by Congress without amendment. This procedure was followed with respect to the Tokyo round in 1979 and the United States-Canada and United States-Israel Free-Trade Agreements in the 1980's, and a method of operation evolved in which the two committees of primary jurisdiction, Ways and Means and Finance, in consultation with the other committees and with the administration, would informally draft an implementing bill and give it to the President with the recommendation that he submit it as his legislation. Once formally submitted, of course, it could not be amended, either in committee or on the floor. . . .

Over the years, Congress and the executive have developed mechanisms for close consultation and coordination during the pendency of the negotiations and in the preparation of implementing legislation in order to provide assurance to Members of Congress that their concerns are being heard and taken into account by our negotiators.

On the whole, this has been a successful process, and I think it is fair to say that our current negotiators, Ambassador Kantor and his staff, have taken it to heart and have been exceptionally thorough and responsive in their consultation with Congress. In saying that, I do not refer only to the Finance and Ways and Means Committees. Ambassador Kantor has been available to virtually everyone here who wanted to talk to him, and he or his top aides have provided frequent briefings and consultations to anyone interested.

Given that history, Mr. President, and the clear intent of the current negotiators to continue the tradition of cooperation, I think it is entirely appropriate to renew fast-track authority. That judgment is also made easier by the fact that it is for a limited period—the talks will have to conclude in less than 6 months—and that all parties are indicating this will be the last renewal. The round will either be finished on December 15, or it will be abandoned.

Under those circumstances, I think it is entirely appropriate to give our new President a chance to conclude the round under the same rules and procedures as his predecessors.[58]

Opponents to the extension of presidential authority and the fast-track procedures made the predictable argument that these procedures prevented the Senate from exercising its will.[59] It is noteworthy, however, that opponents' objections to the process concerned their inability to offer amendments to the changes in public law that would be proposed in the implementing legislation. Time limits for debate were scarcely mentioned as a significant problem. Only sixteen senators voted against the extension.[60]

BUDGET MEASURES. Beginning in 1974 the Senate approved restrictions on debate and amendments as a part of the procedures governing budget measures (budget resolution and reconciliation bills) and resolutions of approval or disapproval for presidential impoundments (rescissions and deferrals). The debate limits in the budget process reforms ensured that the Senate would vote on measures that provided for, and implemented, a congressional budget plan. Budget resolutions are subject to a fifty-hour limit on debate, while a twenty-hour limit applies to reconciliation bills and narrow limits are specified for amendments, motions, and appeals.[61] A ten-hour limit applies to conference reports on budget measures. Debate limits on rescission and deferral resolutions were an essential part of the effort to clarify the role of the president and Congress in decisions to delay or withhold appropriated funds. As Congress struggled to reduce the federal deficit in the 1980s and 1990s, debate limits were continued as a vital part of mechanisms designed to enforce spending and deficit limits. Fast-track procedures were added to provide for rapid congressional action on a presidential recommendation to suspend budget enforcement provisions in the event of war or low economic growth and to provide for a rapid Senate vote on a bill that responds to a sequestration order (that is, an across-the-board cut in spending). Budget measures incorporate language, which dates to the Reorganization Act of 1939, that protects the right of each chamber to determine its own rules.[62]

The debate limits established in 1974 were not controversial. Senator Talmadge, who objected to the debate limits in the Trade Act of 1974, raised no objection to debate limits when he endorsed the budget process reforms earlier in the same year.[63] The limits were the handiwork of Senator Robert Byrd, who has been the Senate's leading champion of minority rights under Rule 22 in recent decades. Byrd chaired the Rules and Administration subcommittee that wrote the parts of the bill affecting Senate procedure. When the bill reached the floor, he showed just pride in his work. He observed, "I wanted to be sure that the bill would be workable and that it would not too greatly disturb the existing methods of doing business in the Senate." His comments, backed by his recognized parliamentary expertise and long-standing support for preserving Rule 22, probably eased acceptance of the bill and helped it gain unanimous approval in committee. But Byrd also noted that he "wanted to be sure that a majority of the Senate would be able to work its will in all of the important decisions to be made in this new budgetary process." That meant closing loopholes that might be exploited by obstructionists. The result was a lasting set of limits on debate for budget measures, even for complex reconciliation bills that extend to hundreds of pages in length and affect the full scope of the federal government.[64]

The severity of the Budget Act debate limits became controversial in 1995 when budget reconciliation measures became the vehicle for a massive effort by Republicans to alter the policy priorities of the federal government and to provide for a balanced budget in seven years. Senator Byrd raised the issue when the 1,949-page reconciliation bill was debated on the Senate floor: "The fast-track reconciliation procedures that were established in the Congressional Budget Act of 1974 were never intended to be used as a method to enact omnibus legislative changes under expedited, non-filibusterable procedures. I know, because I helped to write the Congressional Budget Act in 1974, and it was never in my contemplation that the reconciliation legislation would be used in this fashion and for these purposes—never! I would not have supported it; I would have voted against it."[65] Same rules, changed circumstances, different consequences. Byrd's amendment to extend debate limits on reconciliation bills to fifty hours and on reconciliation conference reports to twenty hours was defeated on a party-line vote.[66] Majority party Republicans took little interest in a rules change that would slow down consideration of reconciliation legislation.

Use of expedited procedures for budget matters continued to provoke controversy in 1996. When majority party Republicans outlined a budget resolution calling for three separate reconciliation bills (including one for a package of tax cuts), minority Democrats charged that such extension of expedited procedures was an abuse of a reconciliation process intended to enforce deficit reduction: "We will be giving more and more power to the Budget Committee," argued minority leader Tom Daschle (Democrat of South Dakota), "power cloaked in the fast-track protection of the budget process itself. We will be granting immense power to the majority."[67] Indeed, the implication of the Republicans' expansion to three reconciliation bills was not lost on the Democrats: "I cannot see any reason why Democrats—once back in the majority—cannot conveniently begin to use reconciliation packages for all kinds of legislative agendas." Moreover, Daschle continued, "We will change the very character of this institution in a very permanent way. . . . If we are going to bend and change the rules so dramatically to serve the political needs of the moment, we are not living up to our responsibilities to the institution of the Senate."[68] Democrats appealed a ruling of the chair that the use of three reconciliation bills was permissible under the budget act but lost on a strictly party-line vote.[69] Such debate over expedited procedures suggests again that senators are well aware of the consequences of Senate rules for their own political and legislative interests—sometimes protecting collective congressional interests against the executive branch, but other times putting a party's or coalition's political interests at risk.

DEBATE LIMITS REMAIN A COMMON SOLUTION. Debate limits continue to be integral to proposals that involve the delegation of power to the executive branch. In late 1987 the Senate adopted for the remainder of that Congress a resolution that would give procedural precedence to, and limit debate on, a resolution to invoke the War Powers Act. The rule was a critical feature of a compromise designed to fend off a more direct challenge to President Ronald Reagan's decision to flag Kuwaiti ships facing threats from Iran.[70] In 1994 both Democratic and Republican (failed) efforts to find compromises on health care reform produced proposals to create an independent commission that would formulate and recommend to Congress certain policies if universal health care coverage was not achieved. The commission's proposals would be given fast-track status. In the spring of 1995, a bipartisan Senate majority approved a measure providing for an expedited procedure for resolutions of disapproval for new regulations issued by federal agencies.[71] Using fast-track procedures to protect policy compromises continues to be a favored solution for taming the unpredictability of the Senate fostered by the right of nearly unlimited debate.

Conclusion

Senate majorities have never endorsed simple-majority cloture but have endorsed both the principle of simple-majority cloture for adopting new rules at the beginning of a Congress and strict debate limits for certain single-purpose measures. Support for and opposition to limits on debate appear to turn on pragmatic (and legitimate) political considerations. Only a few senators, it seems safe to say, have opposed debate limits because of a principled commitment to minority rights and quality deliberation. With no exceptions that we can find, defenders of extended debate in the modern era have supported very strict limits for certain kinds of measures, including measures with significant policy consequences.

This record suggests that a theory of institutional development that takes account of senators' calculations about parliamentary advantage—rather than the collective interests of the Senate—can well account for the Senate's history of action on debate limits. To be sure, there have been times, as in 1917, when a large majority of senators appeared to take a position consistent with both their personal interest and the larger interest of the Senate. In such cases, distinguishing political from principled motivations is difficult. But the general pattern is one in which contested positions reflect the likely short-term consequences of changes in the rule for the policy or political objectives of the senators, their factions, or their parties. With considerable frequency in recent decades, senators even have taken opposite positions on limits on debate as the implications of those limits changed from context to context.

The U.S. Senate in session, 1894

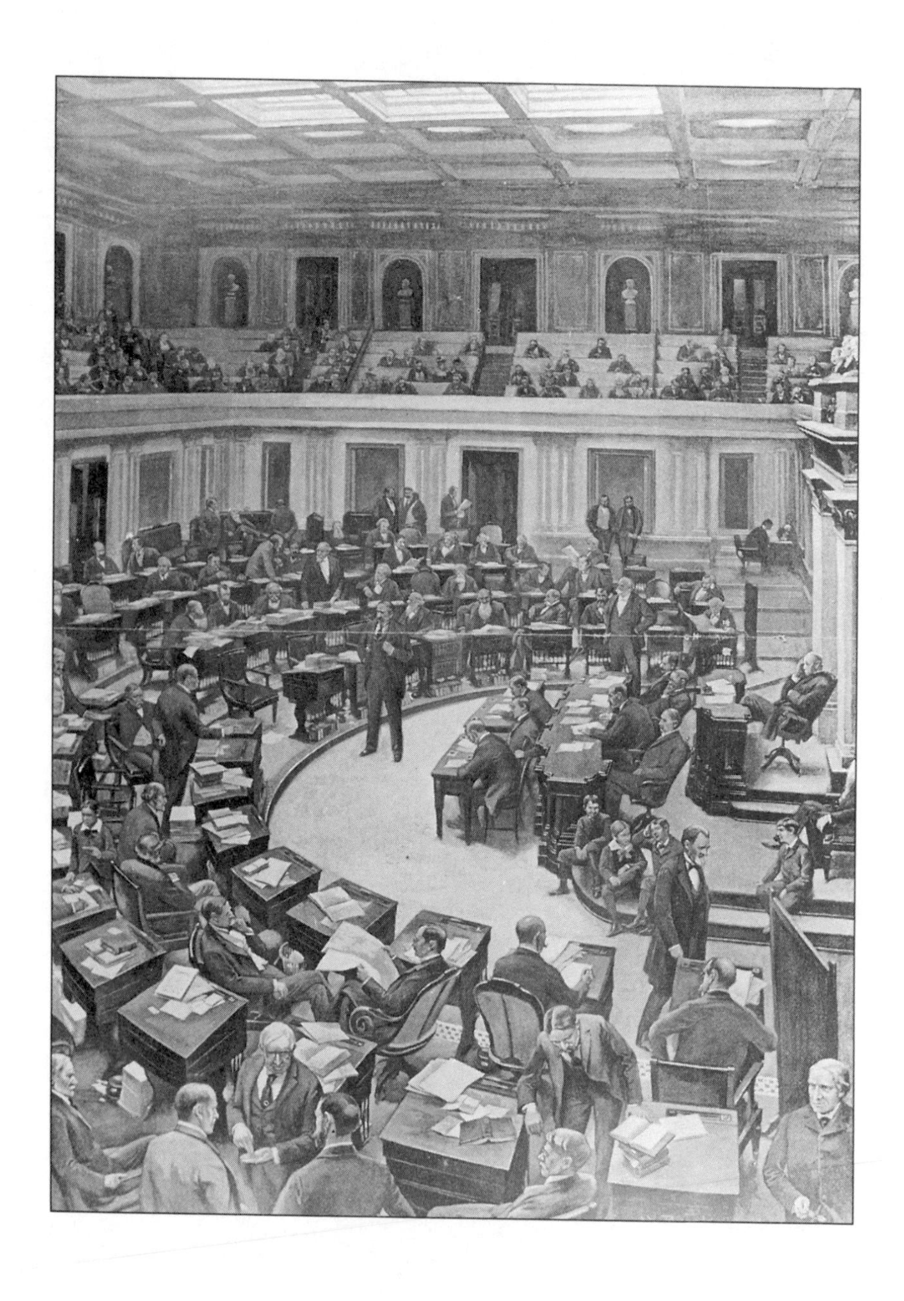

7

The Past and Future of the Senate

COMMENTING ON the development of the Senate, Robert Byrd once observed that "the current rules are the result of experience and trial and testing over the period going back to the beginning of this republic."[1] Byrd's view, and that of many defenders of the filibuster, is that senators have designed their institution on the basis of a conception of the general welfare or collective interests of the Senate and the nation. Senators' commitment to free speech and deliberation, the defenders imply, has produced a legislative body in which rules shield the interests of political and partisan minorities. We have argued to the contrary that no single institutional vision of the Senate has been responsible for producing the Senate as it exists today. In fact, the Senate—like most political institutions—has evolved out of choices made by its members over the course of its history, choices more often than not shaped by senators' policy and political objectives and constrained by the effects of inherited rules.

This chapter reviews the evidence that casts into doubt the conventional wisdom about the filibuster and outlines the conditions most likely to foster change in the rules of the Senate. The discussion concludes with proposals for reforming Senate rules, proposals based on conclusions about the pervasive effects of filibusters and threatened filibusters on the character of the Senate. Procedural features of the Senate affect how and when senators spend time with each other, how outside pressures are channeled in the chamber, and how senators respond to these and other demands as they attempt to forge public policy together. It seems that a rapidly changing political environment has rendered the Senate's inherited procedures incapable of serving the needs of the modern Senate. Focusing on the politics of Senate procedure, in other words, is a necessary step to reinvigorating policymaking in the Senate. Our goal is a future Senate that retains and improves its capacity for deliberation and yet rebuilds its faculty for addressing the nation's problems.

Lessons Learned: The Political Past of the Filibuster

Much of the received wisdom about extended debate in the Senate is not supported by the historical record. In testing propositions about the choice and exploitation of rules permitting nearly unlimited debate, we have found very little empirical evidence that supports important conventional beliefs about the Senate filibuster. Even when sophisticated observers of the Senate assess the practice of extended debate, they quite often rely on too limited a period of Senate history from which to draw their conclusions. Most commonly, characteristics of the filibuster during the period dominated by the conservative coalition from the late 1930s into the 1960s have been used to generalize about the Senate's experience with extended debate. Had the period dominated by the conservative coalition been representative of the Senate's history before the 1930s, that narrow period would in fact provide firm ground for generalizing about the filibuster. Instead, much of what is known about the Senate and extended debate from that period turns out to be atypical of the Senate both before and after. A summary of the received wisdom—some, but not all, drawn from the period of the conservative coalition—and our alternative findings follow.

Designing the Senate

Conventional wisdom: Supermajority requirements and unlimited debate were features of the Senate envisioned and preferred by the framers of the Constitution and the first senators.

Revised wisdom: Neither supermajority requirements nor extended debate were necessary features of the original Senate. The framers, in fact, considered supermajority requirements a recipe for minority vetoes and preferred a system of simple majority rule.

The framers of the Constitution did indeed desire a Senate that would act as a brake on the more popular and populous House (see chapter 2).

But it was the composition of the Senate—not its rules or practices—that most concerned the framers. By creating a body with older and fewer members, staggering their elections by state legislatures, lengthening their terms, and granting equal power to large and small states alike, the framers believed they had designed an upper chamber of superior wisdom that would be capable of refining legislation approved by the House. So little were they concerned with procedural protections for Senate minorities that they gave no direction to the first senators over what rules to choose for the new upper chamber. Had they specified any procedural rules, they doubtless would have cautioned against supermajority requirements: the experience of the Continental Congress—mired in gridlock owing in large part to its several supermajority thresholds—gave the delegates little reason to prefer more than a simple majority on most legislative votes. Minority interests, Madison made clear in the Federalist Papers, would be secured by the system of checks and balances and separation of powers in which the bicameral Congress was embedded. Empowering the minority over the majority could only produce an unwanted system of minority rule. The filibuster, as suggested by Senator Joseph Lieberman (Democrat of Connecticut), "turned the intention of the Framers . . . on its head."[2]

Not only did the original institutional vision for the Senate preclude special procedural protections for Senate minorities, but early senators seem to have had little need to exploit the rules of debate to block legislative action. To be sure, senators were not beyond manipulating the rules for political advantage, as is clear from their use of the Senate's original previous question rule. Still, few of the factors leading later senators to filibuster were present in the early congresses. Workload remained low, partisan differences muted, and there was little public audience for the chamber's work. As a result, there is no record of filibusters before the 1830s—undoubtedly because early senators were able to secure their legislative goals without exploiting the laxity of Senate rules.

These findings suggest there is little evidence that a principled commitment to free speech and minority rights shaped the adoption of early Senate rules. Had the first senators explicitly sought to protect the collective interests of the states by creating parliamentary rules protecting minority rights, they might at least have selected rules that differed significantly from those of the House. Instead, early senators followed procedural precedents inherited from colonial legislatures and the British parliament. Nor was the decision to drop the Senate's previous question rule shaped by any concerns about the protection of minority rights and unlimited debate: cleaning up the rule book to purge the rarely invoked rule, senators in 1806 were little motivated by their beliefs about the unique features of the Senate. Instead, they expected debate to be exhausted within a period acceptable to nearly all senators, and simple majorities were sufficient to handle the unusual circumstances when that did not happen. In retrospect, it appears that early senators were able to secure their policy interests without significantly trying to change chamber rules. Facing a small workload, lacking partisan acrimony, and finding themselves for the most part happily shielded from public view, Senate coalitions had little incentive to try to alter institutional arrangements to better serve their political objectives. Such complacency, of course, disappeared as the nineteenth century wore on.

The Golden Age of the Senate

Conventional wisdom: Senators' institutional commitments to free speech best account for the resilience of rules protecting extended debate in the nineteenth-century Senate.

Revised wisdom: A majority of great Senate leaders of the nineteenth century favored rules that made it easier to limit debate. Senators seeking rules changes were periodically thwarted when Senate minorities exploited inherited rules to block reform.

By the 1830s the reputation of the Senate had begun to outstrip that of the House of Representatives as the more deliberative and powerful legislative body. There is no doubt that the Senate in the few decades before the Civil War enjoyed a "golden age": an era in which the Senate fulfilled what one historian has termed "the Whig ideal of a great deliberative body, at once solid and brilliant, dedicated to preserving liberty and self-government from tyrannical executive power."[3] Indeed, it is from this period that much of the conventional wisdom about Senate tradition stems—yielding a historical portrait of a chamber committed to protecting minority rights and opposed to any restrictions on the freedom of debate.

Popular images of the Senate's golden age provide a partial and at times distorted portrait of Senate tradition (see chapter 3). To be sure, senators valued the freedom of debate they found in the chamber, and many of them opposed changes in Senate rules that would have limited their right of unrestricted debate precisely on those grounds. But there is more to Senate tradition. First, the practice of protecting Senate minorities was given its most robust theoretical justification (and empirical workout) by the southerner John C. Calhoun, a defender of the southern institution of slavery, who cared more about protecting economic interests of the South than about preserving the right of minorities to dissent in the Senate.

Second, a survey of great Senate leaders in the nineteenth century—presumably those most committed to the inherited traditions of the Senate—found a majority in favor of stricter limits on the right of unlimited debate. Third, efforts to alter Senate rules several times failed not for the lack of a majority but in the face of a determined minority using inherited rules to block reform. Finally, portraits of the Senate's antebellum golden age leave untouched the rest of the nineteenth-century Senate. Although senators surely valued the freedom of debate, they eventually proved quite adept at manipulating the rules to serve their political and partisan interests. An increasing workload and intensifying partisanship—along with other changes in the policymaking environment—created a legislative world in which senators quite often failed to exhibit the restraint and civility assumed to be characteristic of the Senate. Not surprisingly, many Senate leaders reacted not by defending the tradition of unlimited debate, but by pressing for reforms to empower a Senate majority to act.

Once again, although chamber rules had the effect of protecting minority rights, there is little evidence that senators were exclusively motivated by collective institutional interests in making choices about their procedural rights. Because of the power of Senate individuals and minorities to block majorities from altering chamber rules, the resilience of rules protecting debate cannot be attributed simply to senators' principles and values. Instead, senators throughout the nineteenth century appear to have made choices about the structure of the Senate primarily on the basis of their respective political goals. The Whig majority in 1841 proposed strict limits on the right of debate in order to secure its policy agenda; the Republican majority in 1891 advocated majority cloture when it found its electoral reforms blocked by the Democratic minority. The Senate refused to reform itself not because it was wholly committed to free speech, but because a minority of the Senate was able to block change by exploiting the rules. When ideas of free speech and minority rights were invoked, they were usually put to the service of senators' political and policy interests. Parliamentary advantage, not collective interests or values, best seem to characterize procedural choices in the Senate's golden age.

Issues, Partisanship, and the Trivialization of the Filibuster

Conventional wisdom: The filibuster has historically been reserved for the large sectional conflicts over slavery and civil rights; today it has been trivialized and newly used for purely partisan purposes. Procedural principles, not policy positions, best account for senators' votes on cloture and cloture reform.

Revised wisdom: Before and after the mid–twentieth century, trivial and partisan filibusters flourished, although an increase in both is evident today. Senators' votes on cloture and cloture reform follow predictably from partisan and policy interests, although the relative importance of each has shifted over time.

The use of the filibuster for trivial and partisan purposes in the late twentieth century has led reformers to conclude that further restrictions on debate are required. They often accept at face value the conventional wisdom that the filibuster was once reserved for the great issues of nationhood, such as the extension of slavery to the West, and then decry the lack of self-restraint exercised by senators operating in the lobbyist-infested, media-oriented, campaign-driven environment of modern Washington. Indeed, there is a great deal of truth to the claims that the use of the filibuster has changed since the late 1960s and that the changes appear to be the product of new incentives for senators to fully exploit their procedural prerogatives (see chapter 1).

But trivial and partisan filibusters are not new (see chapter 4). Such use of the filibuster was common in the late nineteenth and early twentieth centuries, before seeming to fade (along with the filibuster itself) in the mid–twentieth century. It seems that a conservative majority, which dominated the Senate at midcentury, had a small agenda that would not stimulate liberal filibusters and that the filibuster, as a tool of obstructionism, was not of much use to the liberal minority, which had a sizable agenda. Only when civil rights proposals had a chance of attracting enough Republican votes to generate a majority did the filibuster become a tool of southern conservatives. After a more liberal majority materialized and passed civil rights legislation, the filibuster once again emerged as an all-purpose weapon.

Having placed trivial and partisan uses of the filibuster in proper context, we have shown that the strongest correlates of voting on cloture and cloture reform are senators' positions on the major policy dimensions. Very few senators exhibit a purist view of cloture. Most senators vote on cloture as their policy goals would suggest. If there is principled behavior, and there certainly is, the principles concern policy goals and not Senate procedure. In fact, several of the considerations often mentioned in debates about Rule 22—small-state interests, the voice of ideological outliers in Senate deliberations, and the appreciation for Senate tradition gained with experience—have little systematic influence on senators' votes on cloture and cloture reform.

The Little-Harm Thesis and Related Corollaries

Conventional wisdom: Few measures supported by a majority of the House, Senate, and the president have ever been killed by a filibuster. Supermajority requirements ensure the moderation of public policy in the interests of popular majorities.

Revised wisdom: The filibuster has been responsible for killing or delaying enactment of a considerable body of legislation otherwise headed for enactment into law. The filibuster also has political consequences for legislative outcomes and strategies. And there is no necessary theoretical connection between supermajority requirements and policy moderation.

Senators value the filibuster because it protects their right to influence legislative deliberation when they are in the minority—either a partisan minority or a numerical minority of the chamber. But more is often claimed for the filibuster than its power to protect the minority. In fact, defenders of the filibuster often argue that the filibuster poses little threat to majority interests and quite often ensures that policy outcomes are consistent with the preferences of a popular majority. A minority within the chamber, it is often said, may represent a majority outside. There is, however, little empirical or theoretical support for the little-harm thesis and its corollaries (see chapter 5).

A conservative test of the effect of the filibuster on policy outcomes demonstrates that the filibuster over time has had a substantial impact on the policy choices of the Senate. Particularly in recent decades, there is ample evidence to undermine the little-harm thesis. Increasingly, filibusters have prevented passage of bills that otherwise appeared headed for enactment into law. Even bills that have not been killed outright by a filibuster show the effects of both manifest and threatened filibusters. A review of the number of bills in the past decade altered by threatened or actual filibusters shows that substantial modification of Senate bills seems to have been the result of supermajority thresholds for cloture. Such modification of legislation, however, does not necessarily mean that the resulting policy outcomes were more moderate or closer to those preferred by popular majorities. There is little theoretical basis or sustained empirical support for the proposition that supermajority requirements produce policy outcomes more likely to reflect the interests of congressional and popular majorities.

Once the effects and political consequences of the filibuster have been scrutinized closely, it is even more difficult to maintain that senators chose rules based on their consequences for the collective interests of the chamber and nation. First, it seems difficult to argue that the general welfare is protected by the filibuster. If the filibuster ensured that policy outcomes supported by the president and a majority of the House and Senate were enacted, the welfare of the polity would be maximized by the filibuster. But if the filibuster has been responsible for killing legislation even in light of such support, there are few grounds for maintaining that collective interests are secured by the institution of the filibuster. Second, it is not clear that the filibuster ensures Pareto superior results. If supermajority requirements ensure that policy outcomes reflect the interests of a popular majority and more moderate outcomes generally, then it makes sense to connect the filibuster with Pareto superiority: everyone is better off and no one worse off under Senate rules. But if there is no necessary connection between the filibuster and the moderation of legislation—as shown to be the case in this book—it is difficult to argue that Senate rules will necessarily promote the public good. Senate rules instead protect some interests at the expense of others. Finally, does the filibuster ensure political stability? Refuting the little-harm thesis raises questions about the stability of outcomes under the filibuster. The pattern of violence that followed obstruction of civil rights legislation in the twentieth century, for example, casts doubt on such claims about the power of the filibuster to promote stability.

Senate Majorities and Extended Debate

Conventional wisdom: A majority of the Senate has consistently opposed rules changes weakening the right of extended debate.

Revised wisdom: Senate minorities at times have prevented majorities from adopting rules changes limiting debate; majorities at times have strategic reasons to oppose strong restrictions on debate despite their preference for reform; Senate majorities often successfully impose statutory debate limits when it serves their policy interests.

Marshaling any amount of empirical evidence in support of reforming the filibuster means little if a majority of the Senate has always preferred inherited Senate rules that empower the minority to block Senate action. The roll-call record yields only limited evidence to support such a proposition about Senate majorities and extended debate (see chapter 6). First, a minority of the Senate on several occasions has blocked the majority from passing rules changes that would have made it easier to limit debate. Second, even when a majority has failed to vote in favor of rules changes limiting debate, there has at times been evidence that strategic considerations persuaded a majority to give up its effort for significant reform. Oftentimes, settling for half a loaf of reform has been preferable for majorities seeking ways to limit chamber debate: compromising with an obstructive minority at times yields more desirable outcomes than holding out for a full loaf, especially if the risk is great that the minority would otherwise choose to block any reform at all.

Senators' efforts to make it easier to restrict debate have not been limited to the pursuit of changes in the Senate's standing rules. In more than three dozen instances in recent decades, Senate majorities have placed firm limits on debate and amendments into statutes, writing laws that prohibit or severely cramp the minority's right to filibuster on particular policy matters. The filibuster is banned on certain important budget and trade matters, as well as on much less visible international and domestic legislation. Senators from both the minority and majority have been willing to foreclose their right of extended debate when it promises to serve both immediate and future policy interests. Senators' increased willingness to place such debate and amending restrictions into statutes reflects their recognition that the right to filibuster will not necessarily preserve their most preferred outcomes: guaranteeing final votes and presidential signatures quite often better serves senators' political goals. There is no better evidence that most senators seek practical, rather than highly principled, outcomes in designing their institution than their recent tendency to use statutory debate limits to govern the floor. In resorting to such alternative procedures, senators place the highest priority on rules that protect some interests at the expense of others. The general welfare, if it matters at all, plays only a secondary role in shaping most senators' preferences about special rules governing debate in the Senate.

When Is Reform Expected?

Institutional change, as mentioned at the outset of this volume, may have effects that enhance the collective welfare of the Senate or the nation, that redistribute parliamentary advantage among senators, factions, or parties, or that have both collective and redistributive implications. Arguments about Senate rules are usually conducted in terms of collective interests. For more than a century, southerners argued in favor of weak limits on debate on the grounds that social peace would be threatened if the northern majority in the House and Senate could impose civil rights legislation on one section of the country. Over the years, others have insisted that procedural protections for small states are essential to the maintenance of a federal system. For some, the Senate's rules reduce the chance that a domineering president will become too powerful by placing a high obstacle to the enactment of the president's proposals. And yet others have argued that long debate gives the general public time to be educated on an issue and then to influence the behavior of their elected representatives in Congress. These are powerful arguments that are often made to attract the support of senators whose political position, doubts about the consequences of reform proposals, or unfamiliarity with Senate history leave them somewhat ambivalent about reform.

Arguments on behalf of the institutional welfare of the Senate, such as those made in the next section, are offered in favor of reforming Rule 22 as well. Over the decades, proponents of reform have insisted that important, desirable legislation has been blocked, diluted, or long delayed by filibustering senators. Some have argued that the indirect effects of filibusters—delaying or preventing action on other measures, crippling the Senate with holds, and so on—detract from the overall efficiency of the Senate and undermine the effectiveness of the American system of governance.

Merely finding interests behind these various principles about parliamentary procedure is no reason for denying the principles themselves. It would be convenient to believe that, as a general rule, senators decided procedural questions on the basis of their commitment to certain procedural principles about the collective needs of the Senate and the nation. But is the evolution of Senate limits on debate a product of senators' longstanding commitment to rules that serve the institution's general or collective interest and the interests of the larger nation the Senate represents? Do senators' procedural principles account for the emergence and lasting effects of a Senate tradition of weak limits on debate? Unfortunately, our answer is no. The Senate's rules are the by-product of an early procedural decision in 1806 and the subsequent evolution of senators' personal political interests. Indeed, few institutional choices have had as significant long-term consequences as the decision in 1806 to drop the rule allowing a majority to move the previous question and cut off debate. That decision locked into place a procedural arena that could be changed only with near-universal support of the Senate's members and only, it turns out, under somewhat extraordinary circumstances. Only when procedural reforms serve the interests of a bipartisan supermajority is institutional change likely in the Senate.

This is not to imply that policy preferences alone shape senators' positions on institutional reform. More explicitly political and electoral calculations are also likely to motivate senators' views about preferred rules of procedure. Senators whose policy views might dictate that they support strict limits on debate might for other reasons prefer to retain their personal privilege to debate freely. For example, the ability of a senator to take the floor whenever he or she chooses or to place a timely hold on a piece of legislation may contribute to his or her ability to capture a national audience, gain media attention, and, perhaps, attract campaign contributions. Plainly, the ability to filibuster, or to credibly threaten to filibuster, serves senatorial interests that extend well beyond the four walls of the Senate chamber and the enactment of legislation. Simply put, they enhance the importance of the senator in the larger polity. For that reason, a model that limits senators to policy-oriented goals is unlikely to fully explain the willingness of senators to preserve only weak limits on debate. Political interests—broadly defined—as well as policy goals shape senators' willingness to alter the rules of procedure.

This perspective does not lead to the conclusion that the nation's, or the institution's, interests play no role in shaping the rules of the Senate. All it means is that those larger concerns shape institutional choices only to the extent that they enter into senators' other calculations about the rules. They can do so in many ways. For example, public pressure may at times compel senators to adopt reforms that they would not otherwise endorse. Popular election of the Senate and the initial adoption of Rule 22 in 1917 seem to fit in that category. There may also be times when senators' pursuit of personal goals is undermined by the unpredictability of the Senate schedule or the disruption of action on matters other than those being filibustered. Floor leaders are delegated special privileges in order to minimize the harm done to individual senators. And sometimes new rules gain the support of most senators, as when the Senate has adopted rules to limit committee assignments in recent decades. In most cases, broader institutional concerns will influence procedural choices only to the extent that they are compatible with senators' political interests.

Nor does our perspective imply that senators have no principles. To the contrary, senators' principles about, or goals for, American society often provide a foundation for their policy positions, and these principles often dictate their views about the rules of the institution. To be sure, senators' commitments share some basic democratic values, but these values do not seem to be so elaborate as to determine their positions on the details of Rule 22. Rather, a redistributive view—of hardball politics fought over the evolving issues that have divided senators and fought under the rules inherited from the past—appears to be a better framework for understanding the slow and incremental changes in the Senate's practice of extended debate.

When might future changes in Rule 22 be expected? Change is unlikely to be the product of better arguments about the Senate's or the nation's interests. Rather, the current rule will change when more than a two-thirds majority of senators see reform in their interest. Reform is most likely when—for policy, political, or electoral motivations (or a combination thereof)—enough senators view procedural change as necessary to securing their most preferred legislative or political outcomes. Because inherited rules pose such a high threshold for change in the Senate, successful efforts to change the rules of debate should be expected on rare occasions. Here, history provides some guidance about the extraordinary conditions that might generate the supermajorities required to change the current rules.

First, a rules change can be expected when the general public is outraged by the ability of a Senate minority to block legislation that is widely recognized as desirable and important. Under those conditions, many senators would be expected to support procedural reforms if only to avoid blame for blocking salient policy change. The 1917 rule is such a case. The public, however, cannot be expected to be energized by a debate over parliamentary procedure. So, it is the unusual case—one in which the connection between a policy outcome and a Senate rule is particularly clear—that will stimulate the public to demand procedural reform. Presidential involvement, as in the 1917 case, may be an essential ingredient.

Second, a rules change can be expected when a majority of sufficient size is frustrated by minority obstructionism on an issue of substantial importance. The struggle to enact civil rights legislation produced a series of small procedural reforms, culminating in the 1975 change that reduced the threshold for cloture. Again, a clear link between a desired policy outcome and a Senate rule helping to obstruct its passage is essential to bolstering the proponents of reform. It is hard, of course, to imagine what the next such issue might be.

And third, a rules change can be expected when a sufficient number of senators find that achievement of their personal goals is being undermined by obstructionism for reasons that extend beyond senators' policy interests. A few senators, in pursuit of personal or constituency policy interests, may so abuse loopholes in the rules that their colleagues will be motivated to alter the rules to limit their own procedural options. The successful efforts to tighten post-cloture debate restrictions after 1975 fit in this category.

In each case, some special circumstance intensifies the consequences of obstructionism for enough senators so that they set aside their policy agenda for a few days or weeks in order to achieve the change. A sizable coalition, in short, finds existing rules costly to their political objectives and interests, and uses a temporary advantage over opponents to secure procedural reforms. But there also may be conditions that reduce the long-term value of Rule 22 for individual senators. Term limits, for example, may so shorten senators' time horizons that the long-term value associated with developing a national audience and attracting media attention will be so low that resistance to reform will weaken. Unfortunately, one can do no more than speculate about the conditions in the larger environment of the Senate that might change in a way that alters the value senators attach to Rule 22.

We doubt that the Senate is unique among political institutions in having the contending players argue about institutional arrangements primarily on the basis of collective interests and make choices about institutional arrangements primarily on the basis of redistributive considerations. And so, if we have seemed critical of U.S. senators, we do not intend to be. If we were senators, we would do the same thing. But as political scientists, it appears to us that the modern Senate cannot be explained on the basis of senators' arguments about procedural principles. Rather, we are compelled to account for their interests, interacting with the rules that they have inherited, in order to explain the politics that have produced the modern Senate.

Proposals for Reform

Conventional defenses of the filibuster provide little rationale for blocking passage of reforms intended to empower Senate majorities. Indeed, given the views of most party leaders in recent years that the chamber has become increasingly unmanageable, there are very strong reasons to revisit the issue of procedural reform in the Senate. Fundamental reform of the Senate is in order: reform that will simultaneously protect the Senate's comparative advantages over the House and ensure that majorities are able to secure final votes on measures they prefer.

Our goal in proposing reform of the Senate's Rule 22 is to secure a Senate in which lengthy deliberation is still possible, but so is final action by a determined majority. We are not the first to articulate this view. Henry Clay and Daniel Webster argued for a better balance between debate and action as well. The minority should still be able to raise issues perhaps too quickly considered by the House, address new issues that have arisen since House action, educate the public about the effects of bills, incorporate public feedback into the shape of Senate bills, and use the period of extended debate to its advantage in winning support for its positions. We do not, in other words, wish to tamper with the Senate's tolerance for extended debate. In fact, as we discuss below, in some cases we would like to see the minimum time guaranteed for debate increased—to ensure that minorities are not in fact trampled under foot by hasty majorities. Lengthy debate, after all, has served the Senate well—often making bills from the House more palatable to both a Senate majority and the president. The Senate's consideration of a measure to lessen the weight of unfunded mandates on state and local governments early in 1995, for example, shows well how the power of Senate minorities to recast issues during lengthy debate serves the cause of good public policy. Although the Republican majority first failed to gain cloture, after substantial revision of the bill on the floor a sizable majority favored limiting debate and voted in favor. Indeed, the unfunded mandates bill was one of the few legislative goals of the new Republican majorities in 1995 to be enacted into law.

Where we differ with defenders of extended debate is on the issue of final disposition of bills in the Senate. If lengthy, even exhaustive, debate is allowed to occur, we see little rationale for preventing the majority from eventually casting a final vote on pending bills. Indeed, lacking any constitutional, historical, or theoretical reason to require supermajority requirements to cut off debate on controversial legislation, defenders of the filibuster are on weak ground in arguing that supermajority requirements are essential to preserving the character of the Senate. Preventing a chamber majority from finally casting a vote on any legislation is unsustainable in a truly democratic and deliberative institution.

We focus on the six central aspects of the Senate's Rule 22: the threshold of votes required to invoke cloture, the advance notice requirement for filing a cloture petition, the number of hours of debate permitted after cloture is invoked, the subjects to which cloture can be applied, the types of motions on which cloture can be tried, and the time in the Senate's annual sessions when cloture can be invoked. Other proposals for reform are also discussed, most of which would not require changes in the Senate's Rule 22.

Number of Votes Required for Cloture

The heart of our proposal is to allow a simple majority of the Senate to eventually invoke cloture under the mechanics of Rule 22. One possible way to empower a Senate majority is to adopt a sliding scale of votes required to invoke cloture. Most recently, such a ratcheting down of the cloture threshold was proposed by Senators Tom Harkin and Joseph Lieberman, who advocated a sliding scale of sixty, then fifty-seven, then fifty-four, and finally fifty-one votes to end debate. Such a route to majority cloture would slow down the process of limiting debate while ensuring that final action could still be taken by a majority. Although the ratcheting-down proposal was most recently advocated by Senators Harkin and Lieberman at the start of 1995 (see chapter 6), many other senators have proposed schemes of majority cloture in the past—as early as the 1890s and repeatedly throughout the twentieth century.

Lowering the number of votes for cloture does not need much explanation. Indeed, such a move is consistent with the history of Rule 22—in which reform proposals have inevitably involved tinkering with the size of the coalition necessary to cut off debate. By making cloture contingent on a series of cloture votes, Senate majorities would not be able to control the floor as easily as majority coalitions do in the House. Moreover, retaining an initial sixty vote threshold would ensure that a sizable minority would still be able to draw attention to bills they believe require amendment or measures they wish to defeat. Progressive lowering of the threshold, however, ensured that a minority would no longer be able to control final outcomes in the Senate.

Advance Notice Requirements

Reducing the number of votes required to invoke cloture is only a viable solution to the Senate's dilemma if sufficient notice is given to participants in the debate. Lowering the required votes to fifty-one, but without guaranteeing adequate time for debate, would fail to achieve our central goal: ensuring that lengthy debate is still possible in the Senate. Advance notice requirements, in other words, are essential to reshaping Rule 22. Altering the number of days between the filing of a cloture petition and the casting of a cloture vote granted the minority ample time to raise issues that otherwise might be swept underfoot.

Under current rules, a cloture motion is ripe for a vote two days after it is filed in the Senate. Our general approach to revising Rule 22 would be to tie the length of advance notice required to the number of votes required for cloture. The fewer the votes, the longer the notice. In other words, in filing a petition at the sixty-vote threshold, the current two legislative days would be sufficient (or could be tightened to two calendar days). But if a majority leader wished to file a cloture petition under the fifty-one-vote requirement, a much longer interim period would be necessary. Senator Paul Douglas (Democrat of Illinois) in 1957, for example, proposed fifteen days' notice for majority cloture.[4] At least two weeks, in other words, would be guaranteed for the minority to raise issues, protected from the threat and pressure of a new cloture petition. Such a requirement—it might even be set at twenty-one days—would mean an even longer uninterrupted period for deliberation than senators currently enjoy. With such a broad expanse of time, the minority would gain another advantage in its ability to coordinate a much longer public campaign against the bill. Tinkering with advance notice requirements, in other words, would boost the very quality of extended debate that its defenders rightly cherish—the ability to reframe the debate in the Senate to ensure that the minority's perspective is given adequate airing before the public. For the cloture votes between the sixty- and fifty-one-vote thresholds, a proportionally extended advance notice requirement could also be set.

Post-Cloture Debate

Since reducing the cloture threshold from two-thirds to three-fifths in 1975, the Senate has experimented twice with the hours allotted for debate after cloture. In our view, the current thirty-hour limit serves the Senate well—allowing usually at least three long days of debate after cloture is invoked. It is rare that opponents of bills who have lost on cloture votes complain about the lack of time available post-cloture; if time for post-cloture debate is in short supply, it is usually because the opponents have loaded the docket with amendments to be considered after cloture is invoked. Indeed, Senate leaders continue to advocate further streamlining the post-cloture debate rules. Former Majority Leader George Mitchell, for example, proposed in 1993 to count the time consumed by quorum calls against the senator who originally suggested the absence of a quorum.[5] Currently, such procedural motions are counted against the overall thirty-hour cap, not the individual senator's allotted hour. Although we would not choose to tamper with the thirty-hour limit, time spent on procedural motions within the cap might be allocated along the lines of the Mitchell proposal in order to ensure that senators cannot exploit their right to call for quorums at the expense of other senators seeking floor time. Charging such time to individual senators might help eliminate any such gaming of the post-cloture rules.

Types of Measures Subject to Cloture

In proposing reforms to improve the Senate's capacity for legislative deliberation and subsequent action, we believe all issues should be brought under the rubric of a majority cloture procedure. Such a widespread application of majority cloture would mean of course that treaties and nominations, for example, could no longer be indefinitely filibustered. Nominations such as President Clinton's selection of Henry Foster as Surgeon General in 1995, for example, could no longer be denied an up-or-down vote on the Senate floor. Nor would rules changes be protected from the reach of majority cloture.

A more difficult issue is what to do about issues for which the Senate has already carved out exceptions to Rule 22. Statutory debate limits have already been put into place across a host of issues otherwise subject to cloture (see chapter 6). Most important, consideration of budget and trade matters is protected from a filibuster, with limited debate and guaranteed votes on both. Fast-track procedures for trade and other matters might reasonably be brought under the same majority cloture scheme. Such an arrangement would still ensure a final up-or-down vote (contingent on majority support for ending debate) and would still guarantee ample (and generally more than currently provided) time for floor consideration over the course of a few weeks, if necessary. Applying a majority cloture scheme to trade agreements would also protect the president's negotiating power on future trade agreements by prohibiting the Senate from essentially taking the fast-track procedure "hostage"; senators opposed to new trade agreements would no longer be able to obstruct consideration of future trade bills by the threat to oppose the extension of fast-track protection.[6]

Consideration of budget-related bills, however, raises an important question. Of all the restrictions on debate over parts of the budgetary process, the ten-hour debate limit for conference reports on reconciliation strikes us as unduly restrictive of the rights of the minority. Given the likelihood that a reconciliation bill can differ significantly when it emerges from a House–Senate conference and that it can include legislative (as well as budgetary) decisions, limiting debate to ten hours fails to give the minority a reasonable amount of time in which to raise flags about the majority-adopted decisions of the conference report. As much was suggested by Senator Byrd in 1995 during consideration of the Republicans' conference report on the fiscal year 1996 budget: "This reconciliation process . . . has become the antithesis of solid thorough legislating, and it makes a mockery of minority rights and the tradition of extended debate here in the Senate."[7] A potential solution would be to apply the majority cloture scheme to each stage of the reconciliation process. The minority—currently limited to twenty hours of debate on the reconciliation bill itself—would gain a considerable amount of time to challenge the majority's budget in the Senate, while a majority would preserve its guarantee of a final vote.

Motions Subject to Cloture

Six or more opportunities to filibuster a bill is simply too much. If the purpose of extended debate is to protect senators' right to raise objections against and possibly amend bills that unduly or unjustly affect interests they seek to protect, filibusters intended simply to keep legislation from moving forward through the legislative process are difficult to defend. First, it seems reasonable to prohibit filibusters on the motion to proceed to consideration of a bill. Numerous proposals to limit such debate have been offered in the past. Byrd, for example, advocated a strict thirty-minute debate limit in 1979.[8] Mitchell and others have proposed a two-hour debate limit. The two-hour limit seems reasonable to us, giving opponents an initial opportunity to signal their intentions on the upcoming bill. After September 1, near the end of most legislative sessions, limiting debate on the motion to proceed to thirty minutes might also be considered, on the ground that the press of business at the close of a session justifies procedures to speed up the calling of new business onto the floor. Second, the opportunity to filibuster the three procedural motions required to go officially to conference with the House seems ripe for obstructive tactics. Once the House and Senate are ready to go to conference, there is little rationale for allowing dilatory motions to prevent a conference from meeting. Thus, following the prescription of George Mitchell in 1993, we recommend a strict and short debate limit on the three procedural motions.

Eliminating the filibuster on procedural motions leaves extended debate possible on the bill itself, on any amendments raised during consideration of the bill, and on the conference report. Given that our majority cloture scheme would require at a minimum two or three weeks' advance notice before majority cloture could be tried on each of those three possible targets, we believe such a reform poses little threat to the right of individuals and minority coalitions to fully air their opposition to measures they deem controversial. Legislative strategies intended to prevent the Senate from casting a vote on pending bills would be impossible, but the quality deliberation supporters of the filibuster deem essential to preserving the Senate's role would be amply protected.

Time in Session

From time to time, reformers have suggested that some of the harmful effects of filibusters could be reduced by tightening limits on debate in the last month or so of each session of Congress, say, after September 1. This approach has the virtue of allowing current rules to apply for eight months of the year while allowing the Senate to get votes on priority measures during a period at the end of each year. We are sympathetic to such proposals and would favor them if the stronger measures suggested above were not adopted. We prefer to allow the Senate to conduct extended, although not unending, debate at any time an issue is ripe for floor action.

Other Proposals for Reform

Other proposals have on occasion been made for reforming the Senate. The first type of proposal calls for reinvigorated leadership, what might be called the "tough-guy solution." Some argue that what the Senate needs is not changes to Rule 22, but stronger leaders who are unwilling to tolerate their colleagues' obstructionism: "If they [the leaders] put senators' feet to the fire they would not have to worry about Rule 22. It [the filibuster] would work only when in fact it ought to work, never in all those ways that people have made it work as a threat. Let the leadership put people to the test and then watch them fold because they are being watched and look like fools to people in their own states."[9] Such tough-guy solutions entail leaders' calling the bluff of senators placing holds on bills and nominations and forcing senators to conduct full-fledged filibusters on the floor.

A second, closely related proposal calls for the elimination of tracking and instead creates two classes of filibusters.[10] A "Class I" filibuster would be the "classic" model, forcing senators to debate all day and night; a "Class II" filibuster would run along a second track, with a gradual ratcheting down of the number of votes required to invoke cloture. The assumption here is that the burdens of a Class I filibuster would persuade senators to reserve it only for the most important issues and would make it easier to invoke cloture: "Bring back the old-style filibuster for important issues. If it is important enough to delay, it is important enough to require senators to stay all night, and through weekends, with an extremely high personal discomfort level, to make their point. Cloture will come a lot easier if the alternative is another few nights on a narrow cot in the hallway."[11]

Such proposals would probably not effect much change in the Senate, however. Leaders are unlikely to be tougher with their colleagues if they still depend on gaining unanimous consent to conduct much Senate business. Individual senators simply have too much leverage under current rules to expect that more assertive leaders would solve the Senate's problems. We cannot imagine that majority leaders could be more assertive under existing rules than Byrd, Mitchell, or Robert Dole have been in recent years. Moreover, even when majority leaders force repeated votes on cloture—witness Senator Byrd's record number of cloture votes over campaign finance reform in 1987 and 1988—opponents to legislation rarely give up and allow the majority to proceed. When an issue lacks substantial visibility with the general public, as is typically the case with the modern filibuster, public opinion cannot discipline senators, and a persistent floor leader is not going to change that.

Returning the filibuster to its "classic model" also seems unlikely to succeed in reducing Senate obstructionism. Eliminating tracking or producing two classes of filibusters will only work if majority leaders are willing to delay other business in order to force senators to hold the floor during a filibuster. Party leaders—trying to cater to their members' frequent requests for a more predictable and family-friendly (let alone fund-raising friendly) schedule—are unlikely to want to enforce round-the-clock filibusters at the expense of creating a logjam of important legislative business. Nor are rank-and-file senators—most with legislative agendas they often wish to see advanced on the Senate floor—likely to tolerate such increased competition for already scarce floor time. This means that the pressure for leaders to track Class I filibusters will remain strong, giving senators little incentive to use the Class II route. Finally, the burden of round-the-clock filibustering actually falls more heavily on proponents than opponents of legislation, since proponents must repeatedly muster a quorum when called for by filibustering senators. In sum, devising reforms that take into account the Senate's ever increasing workload and senators' expanding legislative agendas is critical in crafting workable reforms to Rule 22.

Although we favor direct changes in cloture procedure, the Senate could pursue another approach to expedite Senate business without eliminating senators' ability to conduct extended debate (or to offer nongermane amendments). The Senate could allow a simple majority to limit debate temporarily (and bar nongermane amendments) for the limited purpose of considering amendments. The majority leader often gains unanimous consent to limit debate sharply on amendments that no one desires to debate at length, but this often comes after hours and sometimes days of unordered general debate and amending activity. If a simple majority were allowed to fix a period for limited debate on amendments, Senate floor action on large, complex bills could be expedited and the floor schedule would become a little more predictable. Senators seeking to obstruct Senate action could still do so before or after the period of limited debate on amendments. Although obstructionism would persist, a Senate majority would have the ability to lend more order to floor action on most measures without having to gain unanimous consent or invoke cloture.

Concluding Observations

Our public purpose has been to test the conventional wisdom about the filibuster so that future debates about Rule 22 can be conducted with a more accurate view of Senate tradition. Both proponents and opponents of reform have been guilty of selectively drawing on Senate history and defining Senate tradition in a self-serving manner. To clarify the record, we have turned to more general perspectives on institutions and rules, wherever possible developed more systematic evidence than has heretofore been brought to bear on bits of the conventional wisdom, and drawn inferences that appear most justified by the evidence. For the most part, the empirical arguments made by the defenders of unlimited debate have proven to be quite weak.

Our related scientific purpose has been to provide a fuller description and explanation of the procedural development of the Senate. Political interests, affected by a changing political environment and pursued under inherited rules, appear to drive the process of institutional change. As political scientists, we know far more about the remarkable two-century history of the Senate than we do about nearly any other political institution in the world. And yet we still lack critical pieces of evidence required for valid inferences about many of the important procedural developments in the history of the Senate. We hope that others will be stimulated to carry on where we leave off.

Finally, let us note that we would not have written this book if we did not value the Senate. The representation of the states in the federal government and the role of bicameralism in preserving liberty and stabilizing American government have been central to the success of the American union. Indeed, we do not believe our proposals for reform would fundamentally alter the role of the Senate. Our proposals, however, *would* change *who* influences policy outcomes in the chamber. No longer would the sixtieth senator—rather than the fifty-first—have decisive power to shape the Senate's agenda. The arguments for additional safeguards against precipitous governmental action that are made on behalf of Rule 22 simply do not have a strong grounding in the Constitution, the intentions of the framers, early Senate practice, or Senate tradition. Senate tradition, so frequently invoked on behalf of weak limits on debate, appears to be the by-product of hard-fought politics and not reasoned judgment. Even if we found arguments about Senate tradition convincing, we are inclined to conclude that changing political conditions have made dysfunctional Rule 22 and associated practices that may once have been well adapted to senators' individual purposes and the Senate's collective needs. Unfortunately, we find few reasons to be optimistic about the Senate's ability to change itself.

Notes

Chapter One

1. See Franklin L. Burdette, *Filibustering in the Senate* (Princeton University Press, 1940).

2. *Floor Deliberations and Scheduling,* Hearings before the Joint Committee on the Organization of Congress, 103 Cong. 1 sess. (Government Printing Office, May 25, 1993), S. Hrg. 103–119, p. 146.

3. *Congressional Record,* daily ed., January 4, 1995, p. S36.

4. Helms's obstruction in turn prompted a filibuster by Senator Jeff Bingaman (Democrat of New Mexico) against a constitutional flag protection amendment favored by Helms. See Helen Dewar, "Flag Amendment Blocked in Senate," *Washington Post,* December 7, 1995, p. A15.

5. The anecdote appears in Richard F. Fenno Jr., *The United States Senate: A Bicameral Perspective* (Washington, D.C.: American Enterprise Institute, 1982), p. 5.

6. As stated by James Madison in Max Farrand, ed., *The Records of the Federal Convention of 1787,* vol. 1 (Yale University Press, 1966), p. 151.

7. James Madison, Federalist no. 58, in Garry Wills, ed., *The Federalist Papers* (Bantam Books, 1982), p. 298. On supermajority requirements in the Continental Congress, see Calvin Jillson and Rick K. Wilson, *Congressional Dynamics: Structure, Coordination, and Choice in the First American Congress, 1774–1789* (Stanford University Press, 1994).

8. To be sure, as we note in chapter 2, senators showed themselves perfectly willing to manipulate the previous question motion for political advantage before it was dropped in 1806.

9. As cited in Jacqueline Calmes, "'Trivialized' Filibuster Is Still a Potent Tool," *Congressional Quarterly Weekly Report*, September 5, 1987, p. 2120.

10. Charles McC. Mathias, "Gridlock, Greedlock or Democracy?" *Washington Post*, June 27, 1994, p. A21.

11. Cited in Alan Ehrenhalt, "In the Senate of the 80s, Team Spirit Has Given Way to the Rule of Individuals," *Congressional Quarterly Weekly Report*, September 4, 1982, p. 2179.

12. The exception is on motions to proceed to a bill offered during the first two hours of a new legislative day (the period known as the "morning hour"). Such motions are nondebatable and have the effect of bringing any item on the Senate's calendar to the floor for debate. Rule VII, Senate Rules.

13. The three motions include disagreeing to House amendments or insisting on Senate amendments, requesting a conference or agreeing with the House to go to conference, and appointing Senate conferees.

14. Senator James B. Allen (Democrat of Alabama) is said to have been the first to exploit the post-cloture loophole. See Walter J. Oleszek, *Congressional Procedures and the Policy Process,* 4th ed. (Washington, D.C.: Congressional Quarterly Press, 1996), p. 257.

15. Establishing a reliable account of filibusters over time is exceedingly difficult (see Richard S. Beth, "What We Don't Know about Filibusters," paper prepared for the annual meeting of the Western Political Science Association, March 1995). Our count of filibusters is drawn from Burdette, *Filibustering in the Senate*; Richard S. Beth, "Filibusters in the Senate, 1789–1993," Memorandum, Congressional Research Service, February 18, 1994; and other secondary source accounts of Senate history. Where these sources conflict on the occurrence of a filibuster, we have sought wherever possible to locate evidence of the filibuster in the *Congressional Record* or its predecessor volumes.

16. See Richard S. Beth, "The Motion to Proceed to Consider a Measure in the Senate, 1979–1992," Congressional Research Service Report for Congress, 93-854 GOV, September 27, 1993, p. 17.

17. A majority, but not a supermajority, voted twice to go to conference: 57-43 and 52-46. See *Cloture Report of the Democratic Policy Committee*, 103 Cong. 2 sess. (October 11, 1994), p. 4.

18. On Metzenbaum and Senate holds, see Steven S. Smith, *Call to Order: Floor Politics in the House and Senate* (Brookings, 1989), p. 113.

19. On the connection between holds and unanimous consent agreements, see ibid., pp. 110–13. See also the discussion of holds in Toby J. McIntosh, "Senate 'Holds' System Developing as Sophisticated Tactic for Leverage, Delay," *Daily Report for Executives*, no. 165 (August 26, 1991): C-1.

20. Cited in Barbara Sinclair, *The Transformation of the U.S. Senate* (Johns Hopkins University Press, 1989), p. 130.

21. The Metzenbaum story appears in Ehrenhalt, "In the Senate of the 80s," p. 2179.

22. The episode is recounted in ibid., p. 2178.

23. Quoted in ibid.

24. Ibid.

25. See, for example, Smith, *Call to Order*; Sinclair, *Transformation of the U.S. Senate*; Fred R. Harris, *Deadlock or Decision: The U.S. Senate and the Rise of National Politics* (Oxford University Press, 1993); Lawrence J. DeNardis, "The New Senate Filibuster: An Analysis of Filibustering and Gridlock in the U.S. Senate, 1977–1986," Ph.D. dissertation, New York University, 1989; and Ehrenhalt, "In the Senate of the 80s."

26. On the connection between time and the incentive to filibuster, see Bruce I. Oppenheimer, "Changing Time Constraints on Congress: Historical Perspectives on the Use of Cloture," in Lawrence C. Dodd and Bruce I. Oppenheimer, eds., *Congress Reconsidered,* 3d ed. (Washington, D.C.: Congressional Quarterly Press, 1985), pp. 393–413.

27. On the origins and consequences of the tracking system, see Smith, *Call to Order.*

28. Party differences are calculated as the percentage of the majority party voting yea minus the percentage of the minority party voting yea, averaged over all roll-call votes for each Congress. For example, if on average across every vote in one Congress, 80 percent of the majority party voted yea and only 20 percent of the minority party voted yea, a party difference score of 60 percent would result. In contrast, if 80 percent of the majority and 60 percent of the minority voted yea, a difference of only 20 percent would result. Party difference scores calculated by the authors from ICPSR (Inter-university Consortium for Political and Social Research: United States Congressional Roll Call Voting Records, 1789–1991 [computer file]), Congressional Roll Call files (#00004), based on party identifications in Kenneth C. Martis, *Historical Atlas of Political Parties in the United States Congress, 1789–1989* (Macmillan, 1989).

29. See Stephen Gettinger, "New Filibuster Tactics Imperil Next Senate," *Congressional Quarterly Weekly Report,* November 5, 1994, p. 3198.

30. The connection between the expansion of the interest-group community in Washington and increased Senate activism is explored in detail in Sinclair, *Transformation of the U.S. Senate.*

31. The relationship between the nationalized political environment and Senate behavior is explored in detail in Harris, *Deadlock or Decision.* See also DeNardis, *The New Senate Filibuster.*

32. *Congressional Record,* daily ed., May 5, 1993, p. S5513.

33. Quoted in "Byrd Says Filibuster Is Here to Stay," *Congress Daily/A.M.,* November 10, 1993, p. 1.

34. The Quayle and Pearson-Ribicoff recommendations are summarized in "The Operation of the Senate," *Congressional Record,* daily ed., September 22, 1988, pp. S13052–13068. The Joint Committee's recommendations appear in *Organization of the Congress: Final Report of the Senate Members of the Joint Committee on the Organization of Congress,* S. Rept. 103-215, 103 Cong. 1 sess., vol. 1 (GPO, December 1993).

35. Cited in Ehrenhalt, "In the Senate of the 80s," p. 2182.

36. *Congressional Record,* daily ed., June 22, 1995, p. S8864.

37. The potential role of collective interests (often referred to as "social efficiency") and redistributive interests in shaping institutional choices is explored in

George Tsebelis, *Nested Games: Rational Choice in Comparative Politics* (University of California Press, 1990); and Jack Knight, *Institutions and Social Conflict* (Cambridge University Press, 1992).

38. The conditions leading distributive institutions to change shape over time are discussed in Knight, *Institutions and Social Conflict*, chap. 5.

39. "Cowing the Majority," *Washington Post*, October 26, 1993, p. A16.

Chapter Two

1. Quoted in "The Question of 'Cloture' in the United States Senate," *Congressional Digest*, vol. 32 (February 1953), p. 61.

2. Statement of Senator Robert C. Byrd (Democrat of West Virginia) in *Operations of the Congress*, Hearings before the Joint Committee on the Organization of Congress, 103 Cong. 1 sess. (GPO, February 2, 1993), S.Hrg. 103-26, p. 6.

3. See, for example, Lindsay Rogers, *The American Senate* (Alfred A. Knopf, 1926). Rogers states: "The devices that the framers of the Constitution so meticulously set up would be ineffective without the safeguard of senatorial minority action" (p. 164).

4. James Madison, in Max Farrand, ed., *The Records of the Federal Convention of 1787*, vol. 1 (Yale University Press, 1966), p. 151.

5. For an argument that the delegates intended to create an American version of the British House of Lords, see Elaine K. Swift, "The Making of an American House of Lords: The U.S. Senate in the Constitutional Convention of 1787," *Studies in American Political Development*, vol. 7 (Fall 1993), pp. 177–224.

6. Madison, Federalist no. 62, in Garry Wills, ed., *The Federalist Papers* (Bantam Books, 1982), p. 313.

7. Ibid., p. 315.

8. Madison, Federalist no. 63, p. 320.

9. Gordon S. Wood, *The Creation of the American Republic, 1776–1787* (W. W. Norton, 1969), p. 558.

10. Madison, Federalist no. 62, p. 314.

11. The importance to the framers of the Senate's state-based representation is seen most clearly in the Constitution's (Article 5) prohibition on constitutional amendments that would alter equal representation of the states. That prohibition stands in the way of reforming representation in the Senate, short of abolishing it altogether.

12. Madison, Federalist no. 62, p. 315.

13. See Farrand, *The Records of the Federal Convention of 1787*, vol. 2, p. 246.

14. The Morris and Madison amendments appear in ibid., pp. 254–55.

15. Madison, Federalist no. 58, p. 298.

16. On the politics of procedure in the Continental Congress, see Calvin Jillson and Rick K. Wilson, *Congressional Dynamics: Structure, Coordination, and Choice in the First American Congress, 1774–1789* (Stanford University Press, 1994), p. 140.

17. See Wills, *The Federalist Papers*, p. 107.

18. A previous question motion typically asks: "Shall the main question be now put?" In the modern House of Representatives, approval of the previous question

motion by a chamber majority brings the House to an immediate vote on the underlying question. Its defeat has the effect of prolonging debate. The previous question motion is the majority party's key tool for forcing votes on preferred alternatives. Without a previous question rule, the Senate has no means of forcing a vote at the will of a majority. House Rules, Rule 16. The use and effects of the previous question motion in the early Senate are discussed below.

19. "A History of the Committee on Rules: 1st to 97th Congress, 1789–1981," 97 Cong. 2 sess. (GPO 1983), p. 37.

20. See Roy Swanstrom, *The United States Senate 1787–1801: A Discussion on the First Fourteen Years of the Upper Legislative Body*, S. Doc. 100-31, 100 Cong. 1 sess. (GPO, 1988), pp. 189–91, 213.

21. Alternatively, the similarity in rules might be interpreted to mean that both the House and Senate started out by recognizing the importance of extended debate, but that the House soon thereafter developed rules empowering majorities. Although such an interpretation is plausible, it begs the question of why the House would have adopted such a lax set of debate rules. After all, arguments about the framers' intentions for the Senate explicitly make an argument about the House as well. Not only is it claimed that the Senate was intended to protect minority rights, but it is also claimed that the House was originally intended as the chamber in which majorities could work their will. Such claims imply that different sets of procedures should have been considered by the first House and Senate.

22. Senators, for example, tried to give themselves a pay increase over the salaries paid House members. See Richard Allan Baker, "The Senate of the United States: 'Supreme Executive Council of the Nation,' 1787–1800," in Joel H. Silbey, ed., *The Congress of the United States: Its Origins and Early Development*, vol. 1 (New York: Carlson Publishing, 1991), p. 143.

23. See, for example, Adams's comments in Charles F. Adams, ed., *Memoirs of John Quincy Adams: Comprising Portions of the Diary from 1795 to 1848*, vol. 1 (New York: Books for Libraries Press [1874–1877] 1969), pp. 323–24.

24. Ibid., p. 325. Giles, Adams points out, had petitioned the governor of New Jersey to grant a stay of prosecution for Burr, who had been indicted for murder by a grand jury.

25. The partisan conditions surrounding the change in the previous question rule are explored in Sarah A. Binder, "Partisanship and Procedural Choice: Institutional Change in the Early Congress, 1789–1823," *Journal of Politics*, vol. 57, no. 4 (November 1995), pp. 1093–1118.

26. See Joseph Cooper, *The Previous Question: Its Standing as a Precedent for Cloture in the Senate of the United States*, S. Doc. 87-104, 87 Cong. 2 sess. (GPO, 1962), p. 15.

27. The following account of the early Senate's use of the previous question motion is drawn largely from Cooper, *The Previous Question*.

28. *Jefferson's Manual*, sec. XXXIV, in *Constitution, Jefferson's Manual, and Rules and Practice, House of Representatives, 101st Congress*, H.Doc. 100-248, 100 Cong. 2 sess. (GPO, 1988), pp. 225–26.

29. See *Jefferson's Manual*, secs. XXXIII, XXXIV, pp. 211–26.

30. *Defeating* the previous question motion—in effect saying, "the main question shall *not* be put"—made it possible to push the main question off the agenda, at

least for the day. Of course, *approval* of the previous question meant that a vote on the main question might then follow. Still, unlike today's previous question motion, there was no prohibition against intervening debate; the previous question motion might pass, but debate might still continue. Cooper, *The Previous Question*.

31. *Jefferson's Manual*, sec. XXXIV, p. 226.

32. The full account appears in Cooper, *The Previous Question*, p. 18.

33. Roll-call vote appears in Inter-university Consortium for Political and Social Research (ICPSR), United States Congressional Roll-Call Voting Records 1789–1991, File #00004 (Ann Arbor, 1991), 5 Sen. 2 sess., variable 89.

34. ICPSR variable 90.

35. Pearson's R = .92, test of independence between the Hunter and Lloyd motions rejected.

36. See William S. White, *Citadel: The Story of the U.S. Senate* (Harper & Brothers, 1957), p. 60.

37. Adams, *Memoirs of John Quincy Adams*, vol. 1, p. 365.

38. But note: Burr suggests that the defeat of the previous question motion in fact brought a *permanent*, rather than *temporary*, suppression of the main question.

39. Adams, *Memoirs of John Quincy Adams*, p. 366. Burr's speech was apparently so moving that a later House speaker, John White of Kentucky, plagiarized it in a speech of his own. Shortly thereafter, his source exposed and himself humiliated, White committed suicide. See Alvin M. Josephy Jr., *On the Hill: A History of the American Congress* (Simon and Schuster, 1979), p. 127.

40. References to committee meetings appear in Adams, *Memoirs of John Quincy Adams*, vol. 1, pp. 386, 419.

41. See Robert C. Byrd, "The United States Senate: The Senate Rules—An Overview, 1789–1981," in *Congressional Record*, February 16, 1981, pp. 2191–92.

42. See Sarah A. Binder, *Minority Rights, Majority Rule: Partisanship and the Development of Congress* (Cambridge University Press, forthcoming).

43. Kenneth R. Bowling and Helen E. Veit, eds., "The Diary of William Maclay and Other Notes on Senate Debates," in *Documentary History of the First Federal Congress, 1789–1791*, vol. 9 (Johns Hopkins University Press, 1988), p. 157. On early Senate debate, see Franklin L. Burdette, *Filibustering in the Senate* (Princeton University Press, 1940), chap. 2, "An Instrument of Policy Development"; and Swanstrom, *The United States Senate, 1787–1801*.

44. See Barbara Sinclair, *The Transformation of the U.S. Senate* (Johns Hopkins University Press, 1989); Steven S. Smith, "The Senate Needs to Be Fixed," *Roll Call*, April 22, 1993, pp. 22–26; and Fred R. Harris, *Deadlock or Decision: The U.S. Senate and the Rise of National Politics* (Oxford University Press, 1993).

45. On the Senate's status as a reactive body to the more prominent House, see Swanstrom, *The United States Senate, 1787–1801*, chap. 8; and Elaine K. Swift, "Reconstitutive Change in the U.S. Congress: The Early Senate, 1789–1841," *Legislative Studies Quarterly*, vol. 14, no. 2 (May 1989), pp. 178–79.

46. Adams, *Memoirs of John Quincy Adams*, vol. 1, p. 269.

47. Ben Perley Poore, *Perley's Reminiscences of Sixty Years in the National Metropolis* (Philadelphia, Pa.: Hubbard Brothers, 1886), vol. 1, p. 63.

48. Indexes to the House *Journal* tally all bills considered by the House chamber

in any given session of Congress. Bills passed by the House are distinguished in the indexes by their legislative (House or Senate) origin.

49. The difference, however, is not statistically significant.

50. The House cast on average 173 votes per Congress in that period, while the Senate averaged only 128 (the difference is statistically significant at $p < .1$, one-tailed t-test).

51. Days in session are counted from the Senate *Journal* for every fifth Congress (plus the 32d Congress).

52. See Swift, "Reconstitutive Change in the U.S. Congress," pp. 178–79; George H. Haynes, *The Senate of the United States: Its History and Practice* (New York: Russell & Russell, 1960), vol. 1; Swanstrom, *The United States Senate, 1787–1801*; Baker, "The Senate of the United States"; and Charles Stewart III, "Responsiveness in the Upper Chamber: The Constitution and the Institutional Development of the Senate," in Peter F. Nardulli, ed., *The Constitution and American Political Development: An Institutional Perspective* (University of Illinois Press, 1992).

53. See Elizabeth G. McPherson, "The Southern States and the Reporting of Senate Debates, 1789–1802," in *Journal of Southern History*, vol. 12, no. 2 (May 1946), pp. 223–46.

54. Although McPherson considers the opening of the galleries and reporting of debates a response to pressures from southern states and their senators, the partisan—not simply regional—dimension to the vote is striking (ICPSR variable no. 36, 7 Cong.).

55. Swift, "Reconstitutive Change in the U.S. Congress," p. 179.

56. Ibid., pp. 183, 198. Swift's sample was drawn from 11 Cong. 3 sess., 14 Cong. 2. sess., 17 Cong. 2 sess., and 20 Cong. 2 sess.

57. Comparison of the original House and Senate chambers in Washington appears in United States Senate Commission on Art and Antiquities, *The Senate Chamber 1810–1859* (GPO, 1978), p. 1.

58. *Congress A to Z* (Congressional Quarterly, 1988), p. 498.

59. Swanstrom, *The United States Senate, 1787-1801,* chap. 12, p. 204.

60. Ibid., p. 203.

61. The forced constitutional adjournment of the Senate on March 3 of odd-numbered years imposed a strict deadline on Senate business; in even-numbered years, Congress's tendency to appoint a joint committee to recommend an adjournment date created arbitrary deadlines at the close of the first session as well (ibid., p. 204).

62. One of the earliest—if not the first—use of a unanimous consent agreement to set a time certain for a vote on final passage occurred in 1846 during consideration of an Oregon territory bill. See Robert Keith, "The Use of Unanimous Consent in the Senate," in *Committees and Senate Procedures: A Compilation of Papers Prepared for the Commission on the Operation of the Senate,* 94 Cong. 2 sess. (GPO, 1977), p. 148. Keith attributes the 1846 date to a memo on Senate floor practices by the Congressional Research Service. Discussion of the agreement appears in *Congressional Globe*, April 13, 1846, p. 659.

63. *Congressional Globe*, June 24, 1852, p. 1606.

64. We attribute a dilatory intent to any motion to adjourn that failed to garner

a simple majority. In such cases, it is likely that the mover of the motion only intended to consume the time of the Senate in rounding up a quorum and taking a vote. Successful motions to adjourn, in contrast, more likely reflect a moderate consensus among senators that a break is due, rather than an attempt to obstruct the Senate. All data concerning dilatory motions are drawn from codebooks for ICPSR roll-call records (File #00004).

65. See, for example, the repeated offering of failed dilatory motions during consideration of an import duties bill in 1833 (Gale & Seaton's *Register of Debates in Congress*, vol. 9, 22 Cong. 2 sess., February 7 and 12, 1833, pp. 403, 482) and during consideration of an Oregon territory bill in 1848 (*Congressional Globe*, July 26, 1848, p. 1001).

66. Cooper, *The Previous Question,* p. 9, n. 34.

Chapter Three

1. Vice President John Breckinridge, *Congressional Globe*, 35 Cong. 2 sess., January 4, 1859, p. 203.

2. See, for example, "The Golden Age: 1829–1861," in *Origins and Development of Congress*, 2d ed. (Washington, D.C.: Congressional Quarterly, 1982), chap. 20, p. 214; Robert C. Byrd, *The Senate 1789–1989: Addresses on the History of the United States Senate,* vol. 2 (GPO, 1988–91), p. 161; and Merrill D. Peterson, *The Great Triumvirate: Webster, Clay, and Calhoun* (Oxford University Press, 1987), pp. 234–35.

3. "We must not forget," admonished Senator Robert C. Byrd, "that the right of extended, and even unlimited debate is the main cornerstone of the Senate's uniqueness. . . . Without the right of unlimited debate, of course, there would be no filibusters, but there would also be no Senate, as we know it." *Congressional Record*, daily ed., January 4, 1995, p. S44.

4. "The debates in the Senate," noted Senator John Parker Hale (Free Soil of New Hampshire) in 1852, "have heretofore been conducted upon the assumption that the Senate had discretion and judgment and wisdom enough to conduct its deliberations without so many restrictive rules as have been found necessary in the more popular branch of the National Legislature" (*Congressional Globe*, June 24, 1852, p. 1605).

5. Lindsay Rogers, *The American Senate* (Alfred A. Knopf, 1926), p. 6.

6. *Congressional Globe*, Appendix, March 3, 1851, p. 368.

7. *Congressional Globe*, July 15, 1841, p. 204.

8. See, for example, arguments by Josiah Quincy (Federalist of Massachusetts) and Timothy Pitkin (Federalist of Connecticut) in 1811 when the Republican majority in the House revamped the previous question motion to limit House floor debate (*Annals of Congress*, 12 Cong. 1 sess., December 23, 1811, pp. 572–78).

9. *Congressional Globe*, July 12, 1841, p. 184.

10. John C. Calhoun, "A Disquisition on Government," in Ross M. Lence, ed., *Union and Liberty: The Political Philosophy of John C. Calhoun* (Indianapolis: Liberty Fund, 1992), p. 21.

11. Ibid., p. 31.

12. Ibid., p. 28.

13. See, especially, Calhoun's last speech in the Senate, "Speech on the Admission of California—and the General State of the Union," in Lence, *Union and Liberty*, esp. pp. 600–01. See also Eric Foner, *Politics and Ideology in the Age of the Civil War* (Oxford University Press, 1980), chap. 3.

14. Richard Hofstadter, *The American Political Tradition and the Men Who Made It* (Vintage Books, 1973), p. 116.

15. *Congressional Globe*, July 15, 1841, p. 204.

16. *Congressional Record*, January 22, 1891, p. 1697.

17. The debate appears in *Congressional Globe*, August 28, 1850, pp. 1687–90.

18. *Congressional Record*, March 19, 1873, p. 114.

19. William S. White, *Citadel: The Story of the U.S. Senate* (Harper and Brothers, 1957), p. 12.

20. Ibid., chap. 1.

21. Success rates are based on our reading of filibuster accounts in Franklin L. Burdette, *Filibustering in the Senate* (Princeton University Press, 1940). In designating a filibuster as "successful" in killing a measure, we consider only the fate of the measure in the Senate; the data do not account for the preferences of either the House or the president. The outcome of the filibuster was either ambiguous or not noted by Burdette in one of the thirteen filibusters in the first period and in three of the thirty filibusters in the second.

22. Burdette, *Filibustering in the Senate*, p. 79.

23. *Congressional Globe*, February 27, 1865, p. 1127.

24. See Burdette, *Filibustering in the Senate*, pp. 34–35.

25. *Congressional Globe*, Appendix, July 2, 1856, p. 761.

26. Timing of filibusters is drawn from Burdette, *Filibustering in the Senate*. A filibuster is counted as "end of session" for those filibusters that according to Burdette began within a few days of a scheduled adjournment.

27. In his visit to the United States in the 1830s, for example, Alexis de Tocqueville observed that "when one enters the House of Representatives at Washington, one is struck by the vulgar demeanor of that great assembly. One can often look in vain for a single famous man. . . . A couple of paces away is the entrance to the Senate, whose narrow precincts contain a large proportion of the famous men of America. . . . Every word uttered in this assembly would add luster to the greatest parliamentary debates in Europe." *Democracy in America*, J. P. Mayer, ed. (Anchor Books, 1969), pp. 200–01. Even Thomas Hamilton, a visitor to the United States in the 1830s who had little good to say about either house of Congress, preferred the debates of the Senate: "There is the same loose, desultory, and inconclusive mode of discussion in both; but in the Senate there is less talking for the mere purpose of display, and less of that tawdry emptiness and vehement imbecility which prevails in the Representatives. . . . [T]here is . . . more statesmanlike argument . . . considerably less outcry, and a great deal more wool." *Men and Manners in America* (New York: Augustus M. Kelley, 1968 [1833]), pp. 286–87.

28. From our sampling of every fifth Congress (dropping the outlying First Congress and adding the Thirty-Second Congress), the Senate averaged 217 days in session between 1789 and 1859; between 1869 and 1919, an average Congress lasted 270 days (the increase statistically significant at $p < .01$, one-tailed test). But note, even by the 1850s, senators still appear to have spent relatively few hours in

session each day. Senator William Seward claimed in 1856, for example, that the typical Senate session lasted about three to four hours. *Congressional Globe*, Appendix, July 22, 1856, p. 788.

29. Bills introduced are counted from the indexes to the Senate *Journal*. Bills passed are also counted from the indexes to the Senate *Journal*, and reflect Senate passage of bills originating in either the House or Senate.

30. When the Twenty-Seventh Congress (1841–43) is excluded (822 votes), mean votes per congress are still significantly higher in the latter period.

31. *Congressional Globe*, 38 Cong. 2 sess., February 27, 1865, p. 1127.

32. The heating and ventilating systems of the new Senate wing were said to be "the largest in the world—those of the English House of Parliament not excepted. . . . The air is graduated according to the atmospheric temperature without, and the political excitement within—during a sectional debate never to exceed 90, and on ordinary occasions to range between 70 degrees and 73 degrees" ("The New Hall," *New York Herald*, January 5, 1859, p. 5).

33. Gale & Seaton's *Register of Debates in Congress*, 22 Cong. 2 sess., February 21, 1833, p. 689. Conditions were particularly uncomfortable between 1828 and 1835 when one of the visitors' galleries had been taken down; it was reportedly too hot in the gallery for visitors to weather the hours-long Senate debates. Instead, visitors simply flooded the Senate floor during the debates. During the famous Webster–Hayne debate in 1830, for example, there were said to be some three hundred women on the Senate floor, as senators (including Senator Hayne) were "obliged to relinquish their chairs of State to the fair auditors who literally sat in the Senate" (diary account of Margaret Bayard Smith, as cited in United States Senate Commission on Art and Antiquities, *The Senate Chamber 1810–1859* [GPO, 1978], p. 5).

34. James Henry Hammond, as cited in Drew Gilpin Faust, *James Henry Hammond and the Old South* (Louisiana State University Press, 1982) p. 348.

35. *Congressional Globe*, January 21, 1859, p. 507. For an overview of the mechanical defects of the new Senate chamber, see Glenn Brown, *History of the United States Capitol* (Da Capo Press, 1970), chap. 14.

36. Benjamin Harrison to M. Peltz, May 12, 1881, as cited in David J. Rothman, *Politics and Power: The United States Senate 1869–1901* (Atheneum, 1969), p. 143.

37. Rothman, *Politics and Power*, p. 143.

38. The introduction of modern air conditioning in the 1930s is considered to have had significant effects as well. "The installation of air conditioning in the 1930s did more, I believe, than cool the Capitol: it prolonged the sessions. . . . The southerners especially had no place else to go that was half as comfortable," noted Joseph Martin, who served as Speaker of the House when the Republicans twice controlled the chamber in the 1950s. Martin's comment appears in Nelson W. Polsby, "The Washington Community, 1960–1980," in Thomas E. Mann and Norman J. Ornstein, eds., *The New Congress* (American Enterprise Institute, 1981), p. 30. Some claim that the introduction of air conditioning also helped to reduce a higher than average death toll among members of the House and Senate in the first half of the twentieth century. See Forrest Maltzman, Lee Sigelman, and Sarah Binder, "Leaving Office Feet First: Death in Congress," *P.S.: Political Science and Politics* (December 1996).

39. *Origins and Development of Congress*, p. 220. See also Alvin M. Josephy Jr., *On the Hill: A History of the American Congress* (Simon and Schuster, 1979), p. 198.

40. Elaine K. Swift, "Reconstitutive Change in the U.S. Congress: The Early Senate, 1789–1841," *Legislative Studies Quarterly*, vol. 14, no. 2 (May 1989), p. 185.

41. Ibid.

42. This discussion of the Senate canvass is drawn from William H. Riker, "The Senate and American Federalism," in *American Political Science Review*, vol. 49, no. 2 (June 1955), pp. 452–69, esp. pp. 463–67.

43. Ibid., p. 467.

44. Ibid., p. 463.

45. Party differences are calculated as the percentage of the majority party voting yea minus the percentage of the minority party voting yea on each roll-call vote, averaged over all roll-call votes for each congress.

46. A list of proposed reforms appears in *Congressional Record*, February 13, 1915, pp. 3721–23.

47. Ibid., p. 3717.

48. Consider, for example, the discussion of minority party strategy by Thomas Hart Benton (Democrat of Missouri) in 1841: "He [Clay] was impatient to pass his bills, annoyed at the resistance they met, and dreadfully harassed by the species of warfare to which they were subjected; and for which he had no turn. The democratic senators acted upon a system, and with a thorough organization, and a perfect understanding. Being a minority, and able to do nothing, they became assailants, and attacked incessantly." Thomas Hart Benton, *Thirty Years' View: A History of the Working of the American Government for Thirty Years from 1820 to 1850*, vol. 2 (D. Appleton and Co., 1897), p. 249.

49. Burdette, *Filibustering in the Senate*, p. 79.

50. See Steven S. Smith, "The Senate in the Postreform Era," in Roger H. Davidson, ed., *The Postreform Congress* (St. Martin's Press, 1992), pp. 169–92; and Sarah A. Binder and Steven S. Smith, "Acquired Procedural Tendencies and Congressional Reform," in James A. Thurber and Roger H. Davidson, eds., *Remaking Congress: Change and Stability in the 1990s* (Congressional Quarterly Press, 1995), pp. 53–72.

51. Lauros G. McConachie, *Congressional Committees: A Study of the Origins and Development of Our National and Local Legislative Methods* (New York: Burt Franklin Reprints, 1978), p. 339. McConachie's selections were King, Mangum, Sevier, Cass, Douglas, Bright, Clay, Trumbull, Anthony, Edmunds, Sherman, Gorman, and Allison.

52. John F. Kennedy, during a dedication ceremony in 1959, as cited in Fred R. Harris, *Deadlock or Decision: The United States Senate and the Rise of National Politics* (Oxford University Press, 1993), p. 27. The Kennedy committee named Webster, Clay, and Calhoun—as well as twentieth-century senators LaFollette and Taft—as their five outstanding senators.

53. See Harris, *Deadlock or Decision*, p. 277, n. 28. The historians' list included the following nineteenth-century senators: Clay, Calhoun, Webster, Douglas, and Sumner.

54. See Josephy, *On the Hill*; and Rogers, *The American Senate*.

55. "Sessions of Congress," *Congressional Directory*, 103d Congress, pp. 581–

83. The seven senators are King, Mangum, Bright, Cass, Anthony, Edmunds, and Sherman.

56. *Congressional Globe*, July 15, 1841, p. 203.

57. *Congressional Globe*, June 24, 1852, p. 1606.

58. *Congressional Globe*, August 14, 1848, p. 1084.

59. Admittedly, these findings are driven at least in part by the preponderance of Republican senators on the list. Gorman, the only Democrat who made the various lists of notable senators, was clearly opposed to allowing a majority to impose cloture on debate—a position he stated when successfully filibustering a federal elections bill in 1891. *Congressional Record*, January 22, 1891, p. 1667.

60. *Congressional Record*, September 21, 1893, pp. 1635–39.

61. *Congressional Globe*, August 28, 1850, pp. 1687–90.

62. Peterson, *The Great Triumvirate*, p. 304.

63. Benton, *Thirty Years' View*, vol. 2, p. 253.

64. Ibid., p. 257.

65. *Congressional Record*, January 22, 1891, p. 1667.

66. On the merger of the two filibusters, see Rogers, *The American Senate*, p. 168.

67. See Robert Keith, "The Use of Unanimous Consent in the Senate," in *Committees and Senate Procedures: A Compilation of Papers Prepared for the Commission on the Operation of the Senate*, 94 Cong. 2 sess. (GPO, 1977), p. 148.

68. *Congressional Globe*, April 13, 1846, p. 659.

69. See comments by John Crittenden (Whig of Kentucky) in *Congressional Globe*, April 16, 1846, p. 682.

70. *Congressional Globe*, April 19, 1870, p. 2822.

71. *Congressional Record*, February 18, 1902, p. 1850.

72. A rule change in 1914 converted the agreements into formal orders of the Senate. See Keith, "The Use of Unanimous Consent in the Senate," p. 149. It is difficult to be more precise about the degree to which senators came to rely on UCAs in the late 1800s to structure floor debate, since indexes to both the *Congressional Record* and the Senate *Journal* only sporadically include entries indicating the Senate's use of UCAs. To judge by the compilation of Senate precedents covering Senate procedure from 1883 to 1981, the first (although just a handful) of precedents concerning UCAs were set in the first decade of the 1900s. This suggests that only after 1900 were UCAs considered regular features of the Senate and thus liable to be a subject of decisions made by the presiding officer. See Floyd M. Riddick, *Senate Procedure: Precedents and Practices* (GPO, 1981), pp. 1064–1102.

73. *Congressional Record*, January 11, 1913, p. 1393.

74. *Congressional Globe*, June 25, 1870, pp. 4841–42.

75. Ibid.

76. H. Von Holst, "Shall the Senate Rule the Republic?" *Forum*, vol. 16 (November 1893) pp. 18–19.

77. On adoption of Rule 22, see Burdette, *Filibustering in the Senate*, chap. 5, p. 127; George H. Haynes, *The Senate of the United States: Its History and Practice*, vol. 1 (Russell & Russell, 1960), chap. 8, pp. 403–04, "A Study of Congressional-Presidential Authority"; and Thomas W. Ryley, *A Little Group of Willful Men* (Port Washington, N.Y.: Kennikat Press, 1975).

78. See *Congressional Record*, March 10, 1949, p. 2145; "Gregory Asked for Opinion," *New York Times*, March 6, 1917, p. 2; "Change Is Opposed by Few," *New York Times*, March 8, 1917, p. 1.

79. Burdette, *Filibustering in the Senate*, p. 128.

80. *Congressional Globe*, June 24, 1852, p. 1606.

Chapter Four

1. George Will, "Our Government Reflects Our Confusion," *Washington Post*, December 23, 1982, p. A17.

2. *Congressional Record*, November 23, 1985, p. S33453.

3. "The Last Word: Thomas F. Eagleton, Democrat of Missouri," *Washington Post*, October 31, 1986, p. A25.

4. *Congressional Record*, daily ed., May 7, 1993, p. S5718.

5. John B. Gilmour, "Senate Democrats Should Curb the Filibuster," *Public Affairs Report*, Institute of Governmental Affairs, March 1994, p. 10.

6. The figure is based on our count of filibusters as discussed in chapter 1, note 15.

7. On the changes in the targets of filibusters, see Samuel C. Patterson, Gregory A. Caldeira, and Eric N. Waltenburg, "Cloture Voting in the United States Senate, 1919–1989," paper presented at the annual meeting of the Southern Political Science Association, Savannah, Georgia, November 3–6, 1993.

8. Franklin L. Burdette, *Filibustering in the Senate* (Princeton University Press, 1940), pp. 103–15.

9. Ibid., pp. 134–35.

10. Ibid., p. 43.

11. See John F. Manley, "The Conservative Coalition in Congress," in Lawrence C. Dodd and Bruce I. Oppenheimer, eds., *Congress Reconsidered* (Praeger, 1977), pp. 75–95; James T. Patterson, *Congressional Conservatism and the New Deal: The Growth of the Conservative Coalition in Congress, 1933–1939* (University of Kentucky Press, 1967); Nicol C. Rae, *Southern Democrats* (Oxford University Press, 1994); and Mack C. Shelley II, *The Permanent Majority: The Conservative Coalition in the United States Congress* (University of Alabama Press, 1983). On the Democratic coalition early in the New Deal, see Richard Franklin Bensel, *Sectionalism and American Political Development 1880–1980* (University of Wisconsin Press, 1984), pp. 147–255.

12. The shifting alignments are nicely demonstrated in Keith T. Poole and Howard Rosenthal, *Congress: A Political-Economic History of Roll Call Voting*, Typescript, 1995, chap. 4.

13. Patterson, *Congressional Conservatism and the New Deal*, p. 132.

14. Poole and Rosenthal, *Congress: A Political-Economic History of Roll Call Voting*.

15. Roger H. Davidson, "The Emergence of the Postreform Congress," in Roger H. Davidson, ed., *The Postreform Congress* (St. Martin's Press, 1992), pp. 10–11; Joseph S. Clark and others, *The Senate Establishment* (Hill and Wang, 1963); Paul H. Douglas, *In the Fullness of Time: The Memoirs of Paul H. Douglas* (Harcourt Brace Jovanovich, 1972), pp. 206–11; William S. White, *Citadel: The Story of the U.S. Senate* (Harper and Brothers, 1957).

16. On norms in the Senate, see Barbara Sinclair, *The Transformation of the U.S. Senate* (Johns Hopkins University Press, 1989), pp. 14–22; and Steven S. Smith, *Call to Order: Floor Politics in the House and Senate* (Brookings, 1989), pp. 130–67.

17. To argue otherwise would require an explanation for the lack of compliant behavior at the turn of the century. Perhaps the norms had not yet emerged by that time, or perhaps norms wax and wane in response to some external force. The wax-and-wane thesis is argued by political scientist Eric M. Uslaner, in *The Decline of Comity in Congress* (University of Michigan Press, 1993), pp. 103–25. Uslaner argues that norms of comity change in response to the ebb and flow of tranquility and turbulence in the society at large. Unfortunately, evidence for the character of Senate norms is weak for nearly all of Senate history except recent decades, and the correlation to specific forms of senatorial behavior, such as the filibuster, is largely unexamined.

18. *Congressional Record*, daily ed., October 12, 1995, p. S15082.

19. Burdette, *Filibustering in the Senate*, p. 43.

20. See, for example, David J. Rothman, *Politics and Power: The United States Senate 1869–1901* (Atheneum, 1969). No doubt the coincidence of sectional and partisan divisions heightened the intensity of partisanship. See David Brady, Richard Brody, and David Epstein, "Heterogeneous Parties and Political Organization: The U.S. Senate, 1880–1920," *Legislative Studies Quarterly*, vol. 14, no. 2 (May 1989), pp. 205–23.

21. Sliced another way, 286 senators cast cloture votes with respect to at least ten measures, with only seven of them always voting against cloture and only two always voting for cloture, leaving the other 97 percent with less than uniform cloture voting records. Senate roll-call votes (ICPSR File #00004).

22. For a measure or amendment subject to more than one cloture vote, we selected the vote with the most "yea" votes to capture all senators who expressed a willingness to limit further debate on the issue.

23. *Congressional Record*, daily ed., January 5, 1995, pp. S434–35.

24. It should be noted that the mathematical extremes have not been realized. At no time since 1917, when the cloture rule was adopted, has a cloture vote pitted small-state senators against larger-state senators. In fact, a prominent defender of the filibuster, political scientist Lindsay Rogers, noted in 1926 that Senate history "has completely falsified the confident anticipations of the framers of the American Constitution: few if any issues have arisen to make the small states require protection against the more populous states." Lindsay Rogers, *The American Senate* (Alfred A. Knopf, 1926), pp. 3–4. Nevertheless, large states do appear to have more influence over policy in the House than in the Senate. This influence is manifested occasionally, for example, on grant-in-aid formulas.

25. Most small states had more House seats in earlier Congresses, but we use their most recent size, reflected in the number of House seats they have, to define the category throughout this analysis. Other cutoff points were tried but none showed as much distinctive behavior for small-state senators as this one does. Thus, our measure maximizes the chances of finding significant differences between small-state and large-state senators.

26. *Congressional Record*, daily ed., February 26, 1986, p. S1663.

27. Ibid., p. S1664.

28. Ibid.

29. Henry Cabot Lodge, "The Struggle in the Senate," *North American Review* vol. 157 (November 1893), p. 527.

30. *Congressional Record*, February 15, 1915, p. 3786.

31. Seniority is coded by the number of the Congress in which the senator first served, so that the lower the value the higher the seniority.

32. The Pearson r correlation between seniority and percentage support for cloture is −.08 for the entire period between 1919 and 1994. That is, more senior members are only very marginally less likely to support cloture. In the 1955–68 period, the correlation is −.39.

33. We thank Professors Keith Poole and Howard Rosenthal for access to their data. The statistical technique is explained in their "Patterns of Congressional Voting," *American Journal of Political Science*, vol. 35, no. 1 (February 1991), pp. 228–78. Also see their forthcoming book, *Congress: A Political-Economic History of Roll Call Voting*. Scale scores run from −1.0 to 1.0, with higher scores on the first dimension associated with more conservative (right) positions. Higher scores on the second dimension indicate pro–civil rights positions.

34. Note that the factors identified do a better job of predicting cloture voting in the last two decades of the twentieth century than in earlier periods. Two explanations for this seem viable, although we cannot evaluate them directly. The first is that the civil rights dimension does not measure the underlying policy positions as well as the left-right dimension does. One reason for this is the scarcity of civil rights votes during the early and mid–twentieth century, which makes it difficult to accurately gauge differences among senators on the underlying issues. Another reason is more technical. The statistical technique for calculating the Democrat NOMINATE scores forces the second (civil rights) dimension to be orthogonal (uncorrelated) with the first (left-right) dimension. If civil rights positions are correlated with liberal-conservative views, as they surely are, then the second dimension may not accurately capture the underlying distribution of senators' policy positions. This would cause the observed correlation between the civil rights dimension and cloture voting to be lower than it really is and reduce the goodness of fit for the equations in those periods in which cloture voting is driven by civil rights attitudes. The same considerations apply to the analysis of support and opposition to cloture reform that follows.

35. The correlation between party and the left-right alignment is .95 for senators in the Fifty-First Congress. Senate roll-call votes (ICPSR File #00004).

36. The table is calculated on the basis of measures rather than votes. That is, it reflects the percentage of measures on which each senator voted at least once for cloture. Thus multiple cloture votes on the same measure, which occur far more frequently in the 1960s and 1970s than earlier, do not affect the count.

37. See chapter 5 for more discussion of the history of civil rights legislation and filibusters.

38. The relative strength of the effects of the two policy dimensions on cloture reform voting can be seen by transforming the coefficients to make them directly comparable. Standardizing the unit of analysis but not normalizing the variance for the independent variables, we calculate the following values for voting on reform in the 1969 model (table 4-6): −13.5 for the left-right policy dimension, 19.5 for

the civil rights policy dimension, and 5.8 or less for all other coefficients. On this technique, see Christopher H. Achen, *Interpreting and Using Regression* (Beverly Hills: Sage Publications, 1982), p. 77.

39. The 1995 vote to table a reform proposal is discussed in chapter 6. Majority party Republicans favored tabling the proposal to avoid a drawn-out debate that might delay action on other legislation.

40. John B. Gilmour, "The Contest for Senate Cloture Reform, 1949–1975," paper prepared for the 1995 annual meeting of the American Political Science Association, p. 9.

41. More detail on the 1975 reform is provided in chapter 6.

42. Lawrence J. De Nardis, "The New Senate Filibuster: An Analysis of Filibustering and Gridlock in the U.S. Senate, 1977–1986," Ph.D. dissertation, New York University, 1989, pp. 154, 179.

43. As cited in Ross K. Baker, *Friend and Foe in the U.S. Senate* (Free Press, 1980), p. 215.

44. The story appears in Jonathan Fuerbringer, "In the Senate, Once More unto the Breach," *New York Times*, July 22, 1987, p. A24; also in Sinclair, *Transformation of the U.S. Senate*, p. 205.

45. Fuerbringer, "In the Senate," p. A24.

46. In 1977, southern Democrats, led by James Allen—credited with originating the post-cloture filibuster in the 1970s—actually supported Senator Robert Byrd's proposed cloture reforms in 1977, at least in part out of fear that the Democratic leadership would propose more radical reform of Rule 22. Ann Cooper, "The Senate and the Filibuster: War of Nerves—and Hardball," *Congressional Quarterly Weekly Report*, September 2, 1978, p. 2310.

47. Donald R. Matthews, *U.S. Senators and Their World* (University of North Carolina Press, 1960), p. 101.

48. Uslaner, *Decline of Comity*.

49. On Senate norms, see David W. Rohde, Norman J. Ornstein, and Robert L. Peabody, "Political Change and Legislative Norms in the U.S. Senate, 1957–1974," in Glenn R. Parker, ed., *Studies of Congress* (Congressional Quarterly Press, 1985), pp. 147–88.

50. On the connection between members' power goal and the power of their institution, see Lawrence C. Dodd, "Congress and the Quest for Power," in Dodd and Oppenheimer, eds., *Congress Reconsidered*, pp. 269–307.

51. A second alternative explanation is that the Senate of the late twentieth century became nearly saturated with filibusters. Perhaps the Senate could not have had many more filibusters than it has had. With so many manifest filibusters, even the threat of a filibuster might have become a more effective tool for keeping a measure off the floor, thereby reducing the need to actually filibuster and capping the total number of filibusters at some level below the theoretical capacity of the Senate for filibusters. We view this as a variant of the explanation based on senators' self-interest.

Chapter Five

1. In 1926 political scientist Lindsay Rogers insisted that "even if the filibustering minorities kill some meritorious legislation and treaties, the price will be a small

one to pay for retaining some measure of legislative control of the executive." For Rogers, placing a higher obstacle to the enactment of the president's program was a positive good. See Rogers, *The American Senate* (Alfred A. Knopf, 1926), p. 6.

2. Ibid., p. 169. In 1971 political scientist Raymond Wolfinger asserted that the filibuster is "a veto that is seldom exercised by a minority against a majority." See Raymond E. Wolfinger, "Filibusters: Majority Rule, Presidential Leadership, and Senate Norms," in Raymond E. Wolfinger, ed., *Readings on Congress* (Prentice Hall, 1971), p. 301.

3. Also see the minority views to the committee report on the 1949 cloture reform proposal found in *Limitation on Debate in the Senate,* Hearings before the Senate Committee on Rules and Administration, 82 Cong. 1 sess. (GPO, 1951), pp. 292–99. The minority views were signed by Democratic Senators John Stennis, Russell Long, and Lester Hunt and stand, in our view, as the most coherent defense of a high cloture threshold.

4. Ibid., pp. 294–95.

5. Bill Frenzel, "Defending the Dinosaur: The Case for Not Fixing the Filibuster," *Brookings Review* (Summer 1995), p. 48.

6. Robert C. Byrd, *The Senate 1789–1989: Addresses on the History of the United States Senate*, vol. 2 (GPO, 1988–91), p. 162.

7. *Congressional Record*, daily ed., January 13, 1995, p. S933.

8. On several bills that died at the end of the Fifty-Seventh Congress in 1903, see Franklin L. Burdette, *Filibustering in the Senate* (Princeton University Press, 1940), pp. 75–76.

9. Paul Starobin, "Backers Win Procedural Vote: Senate Product Liability Bill Killed after Brief Filibuster," *Congressional Quarterly Weekly Report*, September 27, 1986, p. 2316. The House did not take action on this product liability legislation, so it is not listed in table 5-1.

10. "Aldrich Currency Bill Cannot Pass," *New York Times*, March 3, 1903, p. 1.

11. See, for example, Congressional Research Service, *Senate Cloture Rule: Limitation of Debate in the Congress of the United States and Legislative History of Paragraph 2 of Rule XXII of the Standing Rules of the United States Senate Cloture Rule*, S. Prt. 99-95, 99 Cong. 1 sess. (GPO 1985), p. 74.

12. Jon Healey, "Product Liability: Filibuster Halts Liability Bill; Supporters Look to 1995," *Congressional Quarterly Weekly Report*, July 2, 1994, pp. 1781–82.

13. "Move to Displace Anti-Lynching Bill," *New York Times*, January 22, 1938, p. 5.

14. Errors of inference might also occur if the House passes a bill knowing that some senators intend to filibuster when the bill reaches their chamber. Members of the House, that is, might vote for bills they might otherwise have tried to defeat, knowing that the bill would likely be killed or delayed in the Senate.

15. However, an element of the Republican effort was the filibuster against Wilson's proposal to arm merchant ships. The filibuster backfired on the Republicans and precipitated the creation of Rule 22. See Burdette, *Filibustering in the Senate,* pp. 115–23.

16. Ibid., pp. 147–49.

17. *Congressional Quarterly Almanac, 1962*, vol. 18 (Washington: Congressional Quarterly Service, 1962), pp. 404–05.

18. We exclude filibusters that were clearly targeted at amendments other than committee amendments.

19. Burdette, *Filibustering in the Senate,* pp. 118–28.

20. *Congressional Record*, March 9, 1949, pp. 2042–49. The speech is discussed in John A. Goldsmith, *Colleagues: Richard B. Russell and His Apprentice, Lyndon B. Johnson* (Washington: Seven Locks Press, 1993), pp. 15–17.

21. Edward G. Carmines and James A. Stimson, *Issue Evolution: Race and the Transformation of American Politics* (Princeton University Press, 1989).

22. "Limitation of Debate in the Senate," p. 295.

23. Ibid., p. 296.

24. Particularly noteworthy was the racial attitude of Senator Richard Russell (Democrat of Georgia), the informal leader of the southern Democrats in the Senate from the 1940s to the early 1960s. See Gilbert C. Fite, *Richard B. Russell Jr., Senator from Georgia* (University of North Carolina Press, 1991), pp. 224–42.

25. On the 1890 bill, see Richard Welch Jr., "The Federal Elections Bill of 1890: Postscripts and Prelude," *Journal of American History*, vol. 52, no. 3 (December 1965), pp. 511–26.

26. Eugene Gressman, "The Unhappy History of Civil Rights Legislation," *Michigan Law Review*, vol. 50, no. 8 (June 1952), pp. 1323–58.

27. H. Wayne Morgan, "The Republican Party 1876–1893," in Arthur M. Schlesinger Jr., ed., *History of U.S. Political Parties*, vol. 11: *1860–1910, The Gilded Age of Politics*, pp. 1411–48 (Chelsea House, 1973).

28. Patricia A. Hurley and Rick K. Wilson, "Partisan Voting Patterns in the U.S. Senate, 1877–1986," *Legislative Studies Quarterly,* vol. 14, no. 2 (May 1989), pp. 225–50.

29. Ibid.

30. National Association for the Advancement of Colored People, *Thirty Years of Lynching in the United States, 1889–1918* (New York: Negro Universities Press, reprint, 1969).

31. Michal R. Belknap, *Federal Law and Southern Order: Racial Violence and Constitutional Conflict in the Post-*Brown *South* (University of Georgia Press, 1987); John Dollard, *Caste and Class in a Southern Town*, 3d ed. (University of Wisconsin Press, 1988); Arthur F. Raper, *Mass Violence in America: The Tragedy of Lynching* (Arno Press and the New York Times, 1969); and Walter White, *A Man Called White: The Autobiography of Walter White* (Viking Press, 1948).

32. See Robert L. Zangrando, *The NAACP Crusade against Lynching, 1909–1950* (Temple University Press, 1980), pp. 69, 128, 149–53; and Congressional Research Service, *Senate Cloture Rule*, pp. 38–39.

33. Frederick R. Barkley, "Senate Filibuster Near End," *New York Times*, November 22, 1942, p. IV-8.

34. Frederick R. Barkley, "Poll Tax Upheld as Senate Defeats Closure, 41 to 37," *New York Times*, November 24, 1942, pp. 1, 17.

35. See "History, Techniques of Senate Filibuster," *Congressional Quarterly Weekly Report*, April 27, 1962, pp. 660–62; and "Failure to Break Filibuster Shelves Literacy Test Bill," *Congressional Quarterly Weekly Report*, May 18, 1962, p. 835.

36. Quoted in "Breaking a Filibuster," *Congressional Quarterly Weekly Report*, May 11, 1962, p. 791.

37. ICPSR (File #00004).

38. "Senate Votes on Open-Housing, Antiriot Amendments," *Congressional Quarterly Weekly Report*, March 8, 1968, p. 447.

39. So, for example, the list excludes significant concessions that were made by Democratic leaders to attract Republican moderates to their health care reform plan in 1994.

40. In placing items in table 5-2, we did not take into account whether the provisions in a measure that were affected by a filibuster or threatened filibuster survived the full legislative process and were enacted into law. Nevertheless, the table includes only measures or conference reports that were approved by the Senate after the noted action occurred.

41. John Felton, "Tough South African Sanctions Backed by Senate Committee," *Congressional Quarterly Weekly Report*, August 2, 1986, pp. 1732–34.

42. Rogers, *American Senate*, p. 183.

43. "Strife Marks Closing Hours of Congress," *New York Times*, March 4, 1903, p. 1.

44. Burdette, *Filibustering in the Senate*, p. 227; Rogers, *American Senate,* pp. 173–74.

45. Helen Dewar, "Congressional Agenda Falls under '88 Spell: Legislative Stalemates Dominate Senate," *Washington Post*, May 26, 1987, p. A4.

46. "'Obstructionist' GOP Faces Counterattack: Byrd Threatens to Delay Senate Recess," *Washington Post*, June 15, 1987, pp. A1, A10.

47. Quoted in Helen Dewar, "House Wraps Up, Senate Grapples with Gridlock in Congress's Last Gasp," *Washington Post*, October 8, 1994, pp. A1, A12.

48. David S. Broder, "What Went Down," *Washington Post,* October 12, 1994, p. A23.

49. We should add that the slowdown strategy is sometimes employed on individual bills. In 1992, for example, it was widely believed that the Republicans, with the tacit support of the Bush White House, dragged out negotiations and eventually stalled an anticrime bill so that the majority party Democrats could not take credit for the measure as they headed home for campaigns in the fall of that year. See Guy Gugliotta, "Crime Bill a Hostage of Politics: Traditional Election-Year Package Tied Up in Symbolism," *Washington Post*, August 5, 1992, p. A1.

50. On the effects of party reputation on elections, see Gary W. Cox and Mathew D. McCubbins, *Legislative Leviathan: Party Government in the House* (University of California Press, 1993), pp. 109–17. For another example of party reputation influencing strategy, see David Maraniss and Michael Weisskopf, "Speaker and His Directors Make the Cash Flow Right," *Washington Post*, November 27, 1995, pp. A1, A8–A9.

51. *Congressional Record*, daily ed., January 5, 1995, p. S434.

52. See Burdette, *Filibustering in the Senate,* p. 74.

53. Senator Joseph Biden (Democrat of Delaware), then in the majority party, spelled out the cynical logic of this strategy on the floor of the Senate. See *Congressional Record*, daily ed., October 7, 1994, p. S14627.

54. George H. Haynes, *The Senate of the United States: Its History and Practice* (Houghton Mifflin, 1938), p. 400.

55. Gugliotta, "Crime Bill a Hostage of Politics," p. A1; and *Congressional Quarterly Almanac, 1992*, vol. 48 (Congressional Quarterly, 1992), p. 9.

56. See Arthur Krock, "In the Nation: The Political Problem of the South," *New York Times*, January 14, 1938, p. 22, and "In the Nation: Unusual Aspects of Anti-Lynching Bill Fight," *New York Times*, January 28, 1938, p. 20. Also see "Move to Displace Anti-Lynching Bill," p. 5.

57. On unanimous consent agreements and holds in the modern Senate, see Steven S. Smith, *Call to Order: Floor Politics in the House and Senate* (Brookings, 1989), pp. 99–119.

58. For a broad discussion of holds and many examples, see Lawrence J. De Nardis, "The New Senate Filibuster: An Analysis of Filibustering and Gridlock in the U.S. Senate, 1977–1986," Ph.D. dissertation, New York University, 1989, pp. 232–94.

59. Quoted in Sarah A. Binder and Thomas E. Mann, "Slaying the Dinosaur: The Case for Reforming the Senate Filibuster," *Brookings Review* (Summer 1995), p. 44.

60. Ann Cooper, "Mood of Militancy: The Senate and the Filibuster: War of Nerves—and Hardball," *Congressional Quarterly Weekly Report*, September 2, 1978, pp. 2307–10.

61. De Nardis, *New Senate Filibuster*, p. 240.

62. Smith, *Call to Order*, pp. 111–13.

63. A recent expression of this argument is found in Frenzel, "Defending the Dinosaur," pp. 48–9.

64. Quoted in Alan Ehrenhalt, "Dusting Off the Filibuster," *Congressional Quarterly Weekly Report*, August 5, 1978, p. 2023.

65. We must add that many bills involve more than one distinct issue or dimension. In that case, a majority of senators can be created any number of ways, as can a majority of the electorate. This possibility makes claims about matching the preferences of a Senate majority and a popular majority especially dubious.

Chapter Six

1. Raymond E. Wolfinger, "Filibusters: Majority Rule, Presidential Leadership, and Senate Norms," in Raymond E. Wolfinger, ed., *Readings on Congress* (Prentice Hall, 1971), p. 293.

2. The proposal provided for cloture by a three-fifths majority of senators present and voting. Congressional Research Service, *Senate Cloture Rule: Limitation of Debate in the Congress of the United States and Legislative History of Paragraph 2 of Rule XXII of the Standing Rules of the United States Senate Cloture Rule*, 99 Cong. 1 sess., S. Prt. 99-95 (GPO, 1985), p. 29.

3. ICPSR (File #00004).

4. As a continuing body, the Senate's rules remain in place from one Congress to the next. In contrast, the House must vote to adopt a set of rules at the start of each new Congress.

5. In 1851 the Senate rejected on a 22-27 vote a proposal to make the motion to proceed nondebatable. We do not count this as a vote directly on the issue of

majority cloture or a previous question because it was restricted to the motion to proceed. *Congressional Globe*, January 22, 1851, p. 296.

6. *Congressional Record*, March 19, 1873, p. 114.

7. Ibid.

8. Ibid.

9. Ibid., p. 115. Another Republican rose in support of referring the matter to committee but noted that he opposed limiting debate in the Senate. Ibid., p. 117. Only one other Republican spoke on Wright's motion and he endorsed the proposal.

10. ICPSR (File #00004).

11. *Congressional Record*, March 21, 1873, p. 135.

12. Ibid., p. 136.

13. Wright, appearing to realize his predicament but holding on to a thread of hope, preempted that motion to table by offering to bring the matter up at the next session of Congress.

14. *Congressional Record*, June 3, 1918, p. 7279.

15. For the debate on the resolution, see the *Congressional Record*, June 3, 1918, to June 13, 1918, pp. 7279–7728.

16. *Congressional Record*, June 13, 1918, p. 7704.

17. Ibid., p. 7713.

18. Ibid., p. 7707.

19. Ibid., pp. 7726–27, 7728.

20. Congressional Research Service, *Senate Cloture Rule*, p. 20.

21. Quoted in Robert C. Albright, "Vote to Halt Filibuster Fails, 46–41," *Washington Post*, March 12, 1949, p. 9.

22. Marshall Andrews, "Majority Vote Gag on Senate Debate Fails," *Washington Post*, March 6, 1949, p. 8M.

23. Robert C. Albright, "Lucas Gives Up Hope on Civil Rights," *Washington Post*, March 17, 1949, pp. 1, 8.

24. Andrews, "Majority Vote Gag on Senate Debate Fails," p. 1M.

25. Robert C. Albright, "Split Party Decision May Settle Future of Filibuster," *Washington Post*, March 2, 1949, pp. 1, 4.

26. Robert C. Albright, "GOP-Dixie Coalition Takes Over Control of Senate, Ends 16-Day Rules Filibuster," *Washington Post*, March 16, 1949, pp. 1, 17.

27. Congressional Research Service, *Senate Cloture Rule*, p. 24.

28. "Will the Senate Change Rule 22?" *Congressional Quarterly Weekly Report*, January 2, 1959, pp. 13–20.

29. This argument was made in the brief submitted to the vice president by the proponents of reform in 1967. The brief was reprinted in the *Congressional Record*, January 18, 1967, pp. 910–18.

30. Congressional Research Service, *Senate Cloture Rule, pp. 77, 85.*

31. The brief, debate, and vote on the McGovern motion can be found in *Congressional Record*, January 18, 1967, pp. 910–33.

32. Humphrey ruled that the McGovern motion could be divided into two parts: to limit debate on the motion to proceed by majority vote and to limit debate to two hours. Ibid., p. 918–20.

33. Ibid., p. 921.

34. Ibid., p. 921.

35. Not only might the cloture rule be subject to wrangling at the start of each new Congress, but all rules—committee jurisdictions, the order of business, and so on—might be subject to a free-for-all every two years. Even with a lower threshold for cloture, reconsideration of the many proposals for reform of the rules at the start of each new Congress could greatly delay Senate action on substantive legislation. While most senators were plainly concerned about getting reform of Rule 22, Senator Mansfield seemed to be hinting at these other likely consequences as well.

36. For the Senate debate in 1969, see the *Congressional Record*, January 14 and 16, 1969, pp. 585, 592–607, 982–984, 989–95, 1053–54.

37. *Congressional Record,* January 14, 1969, pp. 593–94.

38. *Congressional Record,* January 16, 1969, pp. 994–95.

39. *Congressional Record*, January 18, 1967, p. 921.

40. *Congressional Quarterly Almanac*, 1969 (Washington: Congressional Quarterly, 1969), p. 30.

41. Congressional Research Service, *Senate Cloture Rule,* p. 120.

42. "Reformers Lose Chance to Modify Filibuster," *Congressional Quarterly Weekly Report*, February, 22, 1975, p. 412.

43. "Reformers Consider Filibuster Compromise," *Congressional Quarterly Weekly Report*, March 1, 1975, pp. 448–52, 460–61.

44. "Senate Close to Accord on Filibuster Change," *Congressional Quarterly Weekly Report*, March 8, 1975, pp. 502–04.

45. *Congressional Record,* daily ed., January 4, 1995, p. S423.

46. Ibid., p. S37.

47. The House parliamentarians maintain in the *House Manual* a list of current laws that include provisions that are considered to have the effect of House rules. Most of these laws apply to the Senate as well.

48. Burdette, *Filibustering in the Senate,* pp. 228–29.

49. *Congressional Record*, March 20, 1939, p. 2954.

50. *Congressional Record*, March 16, 1939, pp. 2810–11.

51. Ibid., p. 2810.

52. Ibid., p. 2807. Note that the Senate Rule 22 would apply to any resolution providing for a change in the procedure provided in the reorganization act.

53. Ibid., p. 2808.

54. The Senate voted down the amendment, 46–43. *Congressional Record*, March 21, 1939, p. 3050.

55. *Congressional Record*, March 16, 1939, p. 2814.

56. For background on the origin of fast-track procedures for trade agreements, see I. M. Destler, *American Trade Politics: System under Stress* (Washington: Institute for International Economics and New York: Twentieth Century Fund, 1986), pp. 62–69; and *Making Foreign Economic Policy* (Brookings, 1980), pp. 176–79.

57. *Congressional Quarterly Almanac, 1974* (Congressional Quarterly, 1974), p. 558.

58. *Congressional Record*, daily ed., June 30, 1993, p. S8327.

59. See, for example, the comments of Senator Fritz Hollings (Democrat of South Carolina), and Strom Thurmond (Republican of South Carolina) and others

in the *Congressional Record*, daily ed., June 30, 1993, pp. S8312, S8321, S8322, S8324.

60. Ibid., p. S8346.

61. Allen Schick, *The Federal Budget: Politics, Policy, Process* (Brookings, 1995), pp. 79, 85.

62. The language is: "The Congress enacts the provisions of this part—(1) as an exercise of the rule-making power of the Senate and the House of Representatives, respectively, and as such these provisions shall be considered as part of the rules of each House, respectively, or of that House to which they specifically apply, and such rules shall supersede other rules only to the extent that they are inconsistent therewith; and (2) with full recognition of the constitutional right of either House to change such rules (so far as relating to such House) at any time, in the same manner, and to the same extent as in the case of any other rule of such House." *Omnibus Budget Reconciliation Act of 1993*, H.R. 2264, sec. 14004, 103 Cong.

63. *Congressional Record*, March 20, 1974, p. 7483.

64. *Congressional Record*, March 19, 1974, p. 7148.

65. *Congressional Record*, daily ed., November 3, 1995, p. S 16691.

66. Alissa J. Rubin, "Senate's Last-Minute Changes Kept Floor Action Lively," *Congressional Quarterly Weekly Report*, November 4, 1995, pp. 3358–60.

67. *Congressional Record*, daily ed., May 21, 1996, S5418.

68. Ibid., p. S5415.

69. The vote was 53–47, and the ruling of the chair was upheld. See *Congressional Quarterly Weekly Report*, May 25, 1996, p. 1494.

70. John Felton, "Conflicts of Prerogative: Over War Powers and a Required Report on Visas to Soviets," *Congressional Quarterly Weekly Report*, December 12, 1987, p. 3060.

71. The regulatory reform bill died under filibuster. Bob Benenson, "Procedural Overhaul Fails after Three Tough Votes: Senate Rejects Attempt to Lessen Burden on Businesses, Bill Could Be Reborn," *Congressional Quarterly Weekly Report*, July 22, 1993, pp. 2159–62. Also in 1996 Congress passed a line-item veto bill that would give the president "enhanced rescission" power, allowing him to cancel items in spending bills unless blocked by two-thirds of Congress. A disapproval bill of the rescission would be considered under expedited procedures in the Senate, after approval of a nondebatable motion to proceed, allowing only a specified number of amendments, and with no more than ten hours of debate on the bill. Andrew Taylor, "Line Item Veto Act," *Congressional Quarterly Weekly Report*, April 13, 1996, pp. 1007–08.

Chapter Seven

1. *Congressional Record*, daily ed., January 5, 1995, p. S436.

2. *Congressional Record*, daily ed., January 4, 1995, p. S37.

3. Merrill D. Peterson, *The Great Triumvirate: Webster, Clay, and Calhoun* (Oxford University Press, 1987), pp. 234–35.

4. Congressional Research Service, *Senate Cloture Rule: Limitation of Debate in*

the Congress of the United States and Legislative History of Paragraph 2 of Rule XXII of the Standing Rules of the United States Senate Cloture Rule, S. Prt. 99-95 (1985), p. 24.

5. "Statement of Majority Leader George J. Mitchell before the Joint Ccmmittee on the Organization of Congress," Press Release, Office of the Majority Leader, January 26, 1993.

6. See, for example, Majority Leader Robert Dole's floor speech in 1995 in which he argued that it would be a mistake to extend fast-track authority (*Congressional Record*, daily ed., November 3, 1995, p. S16695).

7. *Congressional Record*, daily ed., November 3, 1995, p. S16695.

8. "Filibuster Rules Change," *Congressional Quarterly Almanac, 1979* (Congressional Quarterly, 1979), p. 594.

9. Former senator Warren Rudman, as quoted in James L. Sundquist, ed., *Beyond Gridlock? Prospects for Governance in the Clinton Years—and After* (Brookings, 1993), p. 52.

10. See Norman Ornstein, "Rule XXII (Cont'd.): Everybody Missed the Point," *Washington Post*, May 11, 1993, p. A19.

11. Ibid.

Index